Christian Congregational Music
Performance, Identity and Experience

Edited by

MONIQUE INGALLS
University of Cambridge, UK

CAROLYN LANDAU
King's College London, UK

TOM WAGNER
Royal Holloway University of London, UK

Routledge
Taylor & Francis Group

LONDON AND NEW YORK

First published 2013 by Ashgate Publishing

Published 2016 by Routledge
2 Park Square, Milton Park, Abingdon, Oxfordshire OX14 4RN
711 Third Avenue, New York, NY 10017, USA

First issued in paperback 2016

Routledge is an imprint of the Taylor & Francis Group, an informa business

British Library Cataloguing in Publication Data
A catalogue record for this book is available from the British Library

The Library of Congress has cataloged the printed edition as follows:
Christian congregational music : performance, identity, and experience / edited by Monique
Ingalls, Carolyn Landau and Thomas Wagner.
    pages cm
 Includes bibliographical references and index.
 ISBN 978-1-4094-6602-4 (hardcover : alk. paper)
 1. Music in churches. 2. Church music. I. Ingalls,
Monique Marie. II. Landau, Carolyn, 1978– III. Wagner, Thomas, 1980–
 ML3001.C512 2013
 264'.2—dc23
                                                                2013002716

ISBN 13: 978-1-138-27018-3 (pbk)
ISBN 13: 978-1-4094-6602-4 (hbk)

Contents

List of Figures and Tables

ch 8. repertoire & global army forces of music production

Notes on Contributors

Gordon Adnams teaches at Redeemer University College in Ancaster, Ontario, coordinates worship at his church and leads workshops to encourage and enrich churches in their congregational singing. He has held positions as Associate Professor and co-chair of the Music Department at Taylor University College in Edmonton and taught in the area of worship and congregational singing at Taylor Seminary. He has also served Baptist churches in Canada as full-time Minister of Music. Gordon earned both MusBac and MusM degrees from the University of Toronto and a PhD from the University of Alberta. His dissertation is entitled 'The Experience of Congregational Singing'.

Will Boone is a PhD candidate at the University of North Carolina at Chapel Hill. His dissertation, entitled 'Hearing Faith: Experience, Belief, and Popular Music in the Lives of African American Spirit-Filled Christians', is an ethnographic exploration of sound and dance in contemporary black pentecostal worship. His entries on African American religious music and hip hop appear in the *Grove Dictionary of American Music*. His work also appears in *Pneuma: The Journal for the Society of Pentecostal Studies* and in an edited collection entitled *The Spirit of Praise: Music and Worship in Pentecostal-Charismatic Christianity* (Penn State University Press, forthcoming).

June Boyce-Tillman is Professor of Applied Music at the University of Winchester, where she runs the Research Centre for the Arts as Well-being. She is also an ordained Anglican priest and an honorary chaplain to Winchester Cathedral. Awarded an MBE for her services in music education, she has taught in many schools in the London area and has published widely in the area of education, most recently on spirituality, liminality and music education. She is a composer active in community music making, exploring the possibilities of intercultural/interfaith sharing in events like *Space for Peace* in Winchester Cathedral. Her collection of hymns and liturgical music, *A Rainbow to Heaven*, is used internationally.

Jonathan Dueck is a Fellow in the Thompson Writing Program of Duke University; he has also taught at the University of Maryland as well as the University of Alberta. Currently, his research interests centre on tying social theory to ethnographic study and understanding music's circulation in world Christianities; ethnomusicological models of conflict; choral art-music and theories of the musical art object; and shape note singing, nostalgia and media. He is also interested in fostering a relationship between teaching and theorizing.

Sarah Eyerly is Assistant Professor of Musicology at Butler University. She holds a PhD in musicology and criticism from the University of California, Davis, and a MM in historical performance practices from the Mannes College of Music. As a Fulbright Fellow to the Netherlands, she studied at the Royal Conservatory, The Hague. She has taught at UCLA and the University of Southern California. She is currently working on a book manuscript, *Utopia Improvised: the Heavenly Lotteries of the Moravian Church*, and is a member of the Council of the American Musicological Society and the Board of Directors of the Society for Eighteenth-Century Music.

Gesa Hartje-Döll is a PhD candidate at the Leuphana Universität Lüneburg, where she previously studied Applied Cultural Sciences (Musicology and Communication Studies). Her doctoral thesis is about the development of Praise and Worship Music in the United States, with an emphasis on recent changes of the perception of the music within the industry. In the course of her research she spent fourteen months in Chicago as a research scholar at the University of Chicago (on a DAAD scholarship) as well as the Lutheran School of Theology at Chicago.

Monique Ingalls is a Postdoctoral Fellow and Affiliated Lecturer in Popular Music & Culture at the University of Cambridge. She received her PhD in Ethnomusicology from the University of Pennsylvania. Monique has published articles in the journals *Ethnomusicology* and *Culture and Religion* exploring the intersections of music, religion and popular culture in North America and the UK. She is currently co-editing a book on music in global Pentecostal-charismatic Christianity with Amos Yong and is co-founder and co-organizer of the *Christian Congregational Music: Local and Global Perspectives* conference.

Carolyn Landau is Leverhulme Early Career Fellow in the Department of Music at Kings College London, her current research focusing on the role of music for diverse Muslim communities in London. She received her PhD in Ethnomusicology from City University, London in 2010. She recently co-guest edited a special issue of *Ethnomusicology Forum* on archives and communities, and has chapters in the edited volumes *Migrating Music* (Toynbee and Dueck, Routledge, 2011) and *Arab Youth* (Khalaf and Khalaf, Saqi, 2011). She is also a member of the Music and Religion Working Group on the Mellon Initiative, *Religion Across the Disciplines*, at the University of Notre Dame.

Anna Nekola is a Visiting Assistant Professor at Denison University. She received her PhD in Musicology at the University of Wisconsin-Madison. Her research interests include music in American religious practice and disputes over the moral and cultural value of music. She recently authored a chapter on worship music for the anthology *Mediating Faiths: Religion and Socio-Cultural Change in the Twenty-First Century*. In addition to her work on Christian worship music, Anna is currently researching a project on 1950s-era African American jazz musicians and their embrace of Amadiyyah Islam. She also maintains an active career as a professional oboist.

Martyn Percy is Principal of Ripon College at Cuddesdon, Oxford. He is also a Professor of Theological Education at King's College London, a Professorial Research Fellow at Heythrop College London and an Honorary Canon of Salisbury Cathedral. He has served as a Director of the Advertising Standards Authority, and the Portman Group as an Independent Adjudicator. He is currently a Commissioner for the Direct Marketing Authority, and an Advisor to the British Board of Film Classification. Some of his recent books include *Clergy: The Origin of Species* (2006), and a trilogy on ecclesiology with Ashgate Publishing.

Deborah Smith Pollard, PhD, is Professor of English Literature and Humanities at the University of Michigan-Dearborn. She is also host/producer of 'Strong Inspirations', a gospel music programme, heard on Detroit's hip hop and R&B station FM 98 WJLB. Dr. Pollard has lectured internationally on gospel music. Her book, *When the Church Becomes Your Party: Contemporary Gospel Music* (Wayne State University Press, 2008), was named a Library of Michigan 'Notable Book'. Her research has been featured in journals and in the anthologies *More than the Blues* (University of Illinois Press, 2007) and *Rhythms of the Afro-Atlantic World* (University of Michigan Press, 2010).

Mark Porter is currently pursuing a doctorate in Ethnomusicology at City University, London, having previously studied Music at University College, Oxford and King's College, London. He has served in a number of roles within church music; as a parish organist, worship band member, worship leader, musical director, V.J. and choir trainer. An active musician, he regularly plays flute in amateur orchestras around Oxford.

Kinga Povedák is an assistant research fellow and PhD candidate at the University of Szeged, Hungary, where she previously studied Ethnology, Cultural Anthropology and American Studies. Her PhD thesis is on the hotly-debated contemporary Christian music among Catholics, focusing on and analysing the peculiarities of vernacular religiosity during the socialist times through the study of the origins of the movement in Hungary. Her main fields of interest include popular religiosity of postmodern times, vernacular religion, modernism and Catholicism, and religion and youth.

Martin D. Stringer is Professor of Liturgical and Congregational Studies at Birmingham University. Trained as an anthropologist, he has published material on contemporary perception of worship, sociological approaches to the history of Christian worship, the origins of the Eucharist and the place of religion within urban contexts.

Tom Wagner is a PhD candidate in Ethnomusicology at Royal Holloway, University of London. His dissertation explores the relationship between worship music, marketing and transcendence in consumer cultures. His work on this subject has recently appeared as an article in the *Australian Journal of Communication* co-authored with Tanya Riches, and as a chapter in the forthcoming Ashgate volume, *Religion as Brands: New Perspectives on the Marketization of Religion and Spirituality.*

Acknowledgements

This book is based on some of the papers and keynote presentations that were given at the first meeting of the *Christian Congregational Music: Local and Global Perspectives* conference, held in the autumn of 2011 at Ripon College Cuddesdon, Oxford. This stimulating, productive and enjoyable occasion was initially intended to be, simply, an afternoon cup of tea and informal chat on the theme of Christian congregational music between the principal of Ripon College Cuddesdon, Martyn Percy, and the editors of this volume. Thanks to the generous support and encouragement of Martyn, a cup of tea quickly evolved into a three-day international and interdisciplinary conference. Many outstanding papers and keynote presentations were delivered and an important and long-awaited conversation was begun. Following the conference, it was Martyn's continued encouragement, guidance and wisdom – for which we are exceptionally grateful – that led to the conception and development of this book. In particular, then, we would like to thank Martyn Percy for his time, energy and vision. In addition, we would like to thank Sarah Lloyd at Ashgate for her assistance throughout the editing process. Finally, we extend our thanks to everyone who contributed to the first meeting of the *Christian Congregational Music: Local and Global Perspectives* conference. As we look forward to its second meeting in August 2013, we hope that our readers will find this edited volume of selected essays a valuable resource as they join, or continue, in this conversation – perhaps over an afternoon cup of tea.

Prelude
Performing Theology, Forming Identity and Shaping Experience: Christian Congregational Music in Europe and North America

Monique Ingalls, Carolyn Landau and Tom Wagner

Congregational music-making has long been a vital and vibrant practice within Christian communities worldwide. Congregational music comes into being in public and private acts of worship, shaping participant identities and enabling powerful, transformational experiences. It reflects, informs and articulates religious belief even as it creates sonic space for differences in interpretation. Performing shared repertoires of music can unify communities of faith across geographical and cultural boundaries; conversely, it can re-inscribe or challenge particular regional, class or denominational identities. While Christian congregational music-making and the varying songs, styles and performance practices it encompasses are found the world over, the experiences it engenders are indelibly stamped with the particular.

Christian Congregational Music: Performance, Identity and Experience is an edited volume whose chapters explore the many roles that congregational music plays within Christian communities, focusing primarily on present-day Europe and North America. Many of the chapters of this book originated as papers or keynote presentations at the first meeting of the international and interdisciplinary conference *Christian Congregational Music: Local and Global Perspectives*, held in the autumn of 2011 at Ripon College Cuddesdon, Oxford. The book draws on perspectives from across academic disciplines in order to illuminate the ways in which music-making in and by congregations reflects and shapes the performance of theology, the interplay of identities and religious experience. The co-editors of this volume – as ethnomusicologists whose work encompasses religion – have chosen this set of inter-related themes because they are key issues within our scholarly community and, we believe, crucial for understanding the diverse practices of Christian music-making. By contributing to these timely discourses and contending that church music scholars must broaden their theoretical and methodological horizons, this book endeavors to point a way forward for future congregational music study.

In exploring these themes, contributors provide ethnographic and historical case studies, analytical perspectives and theological ruminations on congregational music in Christian communities, both historically and in the contemporary moment. The plurality of approaches represented in this volume, we hope, represents the future of congregational music scholarship: one situated in particular disciplines and perspectives but in open dialogue with scholars of other Christian musical forms working across geographical and cultural space.

In this brief introduction, we will first explore the nuances of the category 'Christian congregational music', explaining why we believe this to be a helpful catch-all term for Christian music-making. We then situate each chapter within the three subtopics of the volume – *Performing Theology*, *Interplay of Identities*, and *Experience and Embodiment* – in terms of the broader interdisciplinary concerns of recent musical and religious studies scholarship.

Defining 'Christian Congregational Music'

Finding a category in which to place the various forms, styles and repertoires integral to the musical life of Christian congregations is not a straightforward task; a number of terms, including 'hymnody', 'sacred music', 'worship music' and 'congregational song' have been used as overarching categories to describe this vast repertoire. For this volume we have chosen the term 'Christian congregational music', by which we mean any and all music performed in or as worship by a gathered community that considers itself to be Christian. The tem 'congregation' is used broadly as well, for often the same music sung within the bounds of a church service spills over into private devotion or civic ceremony. What unites the disparate musics under this umbrella are their potential for use in formative corporate acts of worship.

'Christian hymnody' is a closely related term frequently employed for the same or similar purposes. In much academic usage, and in the more generic sense of the term, 'hymnody' refers to a song repertoire used in corporate worship of a deity. This general and academic definition would indeed apply to many of the musical styles and repertoires discussed in this volume; however, within many contemporary Christian contexts, particularly within contemporary Europe and North America, 'hymnody' has taken on a much more partial meaning. Academic commentators, conservators of musical 'tradition' and congregation members alike often contrast 'hymns', by which they refer to a wide range of musical styles defined or perceived to be 'traditional', to newly composed 'contemporary' songs, often set to popular music styles, whose names range from 'praise choruses' to 'worship songs'. The binary of 'traditional' and 'contemporary' is frequently invoked when describing music in congregational worship; however, these terms often obscure more than they illumine, as they can refer to vastly differing styles and repertoires depending on the context.[1] Because Christian

---

[1]   For further discussion of the relationship between hymns and contemporary worship songs and the traditional-contemporary discourse, see Birgitta J. Johnson, "'Oh, For a

music-making frequently incorporates expressions both old and new, we wish to side-step the entrenched associations—in particular, the evocation of the traditional/contemporary binary—that the term 'hymnody' brings with it. Though some chapters in this volume elect to use 'hymns' and 'hymnody' to frame their topics, we have elected to use the broader umbrella term 'congregational music' to broaden the scope of this volume's musical exploration and to avoid needless confusion as to our subject matter.

We have chosen the category 'congregational music' rather than 'congregational *song*' for two related reasons: to highlight the important role of instruments within many Christian traditions, and to acknowledge improvisatory traditions in which music-making does not necessarily draw from or result in a fixed musical 'text'. Song has long been the privileged musical expression in Christian worship, for a variety of practical and ideological reasons related to the association of 'presence' with the human voice.[2] We chose 'music' in recognition that instruments, while often subservient to the voice, are evocative and necessary components of many Christian worship traditions, sometimes stepping out of their accompanying role and driving powerful spiritual experiences. Further, the broader term 'music' also emphasizes the ephemerality of sonic performances in which there is not a clear script, creating space for the many Christian traditions around the world in which musical improvisation occurs within or among pre-composed pieces.

Thousand Tongues to Sing": Music and Worship in Black Megachurches of Los Angeles, California' (PhD diss., University of California, Los Angeles 2008) and 'Back to the Heart of Worship: Praise and Worship Music in a Los Angeles African American Megachurch', *Black Music Research Journal* 31/1 (2011), pp. 105–29; Monique M. Ingalls, 'Awesome in This Place: Sound, Space and Identity in Contemporary North American Evangelical Worship' (PhD diss., University of Pennsylvania 2008); Anna E. Nekola, 'Between This World and the Next: The Musical "Worship Wars" and Evangelical Ideology in the United States 1960–2005' (PhD diss., University of Wisconsin-Madison, 2009); Deborah Smith Pollard, *When the Church Becomes Your Party: Contemporary Gospel Music* (Wayne State University Press, 2008); Jonathan Dueck, 'Binding and Loosing in Song: Conflict, Identity, and Canadian Mennonite Music', *Ethnomusicology*, 55/2 (27 May 2011): pp. 229–54.

[2] The human voice has long been understood within both Western philosophy and Christian theology as an unmediated representation of being; instruments, by contrast, have often been seen as artificial technologies because they involve a degree of separation from the body. Amanda Weidman calls attention to and problematizes the presumed 'naturalness' of the human voice, showing instead the ways the voice is discursively constructed, both materially and metaphorically. For an overview of how the human voice has been conceived within a variety of academic and musical practitioner perspectives, see Weidman, *Singing the Classical, Voicing the Modern: The Post-Colonial Politics of Music in South India* (Duke University Press, 2006), pp. 1–24. For parallel explorations of why the use of musical instruments is contested within Islam and Judaism, respectively, see L.I. Al Faruqi, 'Music, Musicians and Muslim Law', *Asian Music*, 17/1 (1985): pp. 3–36; and J.A. Levine, 'Judaism and Music', in Guy L. Beck (ed.), *Sacred Sound: Experiencing Music in World Religions* (Wilfred Laurier University Press, 2006), pp. 29–59.

Performing Theology

Sometimes, scholars have treated Christian congregational music as an autonomous 'text' – an object with a fixed form that is believed to carry inherent meaning for the scholar to 'decode' regardless of the varying contexts of its performance. Recent musicological work has shown this model to be reductionist, arguing that musical meaning is constructed in and through performance and moving toward the model that explores 'musicking' as a social practice, activity or performance.[3] An examination of how belief is performed through 'musicking' intersects in interesting ways with recent formulations of 'lived religion'.[4] Contrasting to 'official' forms of religion promoted by institutions, 'lived religion' is not 'fixed, unitary, or even particularly coherent',[5] and instead is often ambivalent and subject to a variety of meanings. Congregational music often operates at the nexus between official and 'lived' Christian theologies, acting variously and unevenly as a source of indoctrination or challenge, complicity or contest.

Each chapter in the *Performing Theology* section shows that congregational music-making is an important way in which theological and other meanings are performed through the interplay of the musical creators' intentions, performance contexts, previous associations inhering to music style and various situated meanings of song texts. Will Boone's chapter speaks to the role of musical performance as a temporal event that brings together past, present and future for African American Christians. At Faith Assembly Christian Center in Durham, North Carolina, worship enables participants to bring together through performance both collective and personal memories of traumas past with hope for the future in an experiential present.

Deborah Smith Pollard's exploration of the rise of 'Praise and Worship' in Detroit-area churches also shows how the performance of worship in contemporary Black American churches expresses a common past of both subjugation and triumph. Smith Pollard demonstrates the wide range of historical and geographical influences – from the post-emancipation lining out tradition to the reclamation of Old Testament Hebrew terms for worship – through which these worshippers understand worship and interpret their musical performances. Both Boone's and Smith Pollard's chapters show how the concepts of 'new' are invariably rooted in the 'old': even in creating the future, participants imagine the past through

---

[3]   See especially Christopher Small, *Musicking: The Meanings of Performing and Listening* (Wesleyan University Press, 1998); John Blacking, *How Musical is Man?* (University of Washington Press, 1973); and Nicholas Cook, 'We're All Ethnomusicologists Now' in Henry Stobart (ed.), *The New (Ethno)Musicologies* (Scarecrow, 2008), pp. 48–70.

[4]   See Nancy T. Ammerman (ed.), *Everyday Religion: Observing Modern Religious Lives* (University Press, 2006); David D. Hall (ed.), *Lived Religion in America: Toward a History of Practice* (Princeton University Press, 1997); and Meredith B. McGuire, *Lived Religion: Faith and Practice in Everyday Life* (Oxford University Press, 2008).

[5]   McGuire, *Lived Religion*, p. 185.

their performance. In musical performance, then, multiple histories are brought together in a meaningful experience of times, people and places.

Boone's and Smith Pollard's studies of performed musical theologies are followed by theological reflections on musical performance from two Anglican theologians. Because congregational music is one of the most important factors in shaping religious experience, June Boyce-Tillman calls on the practitioners of church music – particularly the people who choose and lead the music – to be more aware of the various components that make up the holistic experience of music-making. Boyce-Tillman also calls scholars to a greater interdisciplinary awareness; for her, various musicological disciplines, including ethnomusicology, historical musicology and music psychology, each offer important insights into the musical experience. Her chapter suggests that it is only by bringing these strands together that churches can provide space for a meaningful musical experience.

As several other chapters in this section attest, to understand how many Christian groups perform theology, it is important to pay attention to congregational music that is improvised, or 'created in the course of performance'.[6] In his reflection on the character of worship in the Church of England, Anglican theologian Martyn Percy suggests that Anglicanism can be compared to jazz – particularly Brazilian *bossa nova* – in terms of its incomplete character subtly evolving in the act of performance. While recognizing the diversity of ways to perform theology, both Percy and Boyce-Tillman argue that Christian liturgy must include not only pre-scripted performance, but also improvisational elements in order to reflect the complexity of human experience and the in-breaking activity of God.

Interplay of Identities

Music-making is an important means of individual and group identity formation: people use music to identify with or against certain groups, to create new identities and to maintain or challenging existing identities.[7] Identity is performative; that is, it is not a static or essential category, but rather is (re-) produced through repeated actions, including music-making as a part of public ritual performances,[8] as well

---

[6] Bruno Nettl, 'Introduction: An Art Neglected in Scholarship', in Bruno Nettl and Melinda Russell (eds), *In the Course of Performance: Studies in the World of Musical Improvisation* (University of Chicago Press, 1998), p. 1.

[7] Simon Frith, 'Music and Identity', in Stuart Hall and Paul du Gay (eds), *Questions of Cultural Identity* (Sage, 1996), pp. 108–27.

[8] For approaches to the interface of music and religious ritual within musical scholarship, see Steven Friedson, *Remains of Ritual: Northern Gods in a Southern Land* (University of Chicago Press, 2009); Carol Muller, *Rituals of Fertility and the Sacrifice of Desire: Nazarite Women's Performance in South Africa* (University of Chicago Press, 1999); and Deborah Wong, *Sounding the Center: History and Aesthetics in Thai Buddhist Performance* (University of Chicago Press, 2001).

as more personal 'performances' of daily life.[9] Music often serves a central role in processes of identification within religious communities because collective music-making allows for the negotiation of religious identities in dialogue with those of race/ethnicity,[10] national and regional affiliations,[11] generational difference[12] and denominational or parachurch affiliations.[13]

The *Interplay of Identities* section emphasizes the dynamic relationships between the varieties of identifications available to Christian congregations; many of the chapters foreground the increasingly important role of musical media in negotiating these relationships. Each chapter in this section demonstrates that congregational singing always embeds an understanding of Christian religious identity within senses of regional, national, ethnic, generational or (trans)denominational belonging, and that the relationship between these modes of identification is always in the process of negotiation.

Jonathan Dueck's chapter foregrounds the interplay between ethnic, denominational and diasporic identities in exploring a musical 'artefact' from the Mennonite diaspora in North America. Pushing against reified notions of 'culture'

---

[9]   For approaches to music in everyday life, see Tia DeNora, *Music in Everyday Life* (Cambridge University Press, 2000); and Simon Frith, 'Music and Everyday Life', *Critical Quarterly*, 44/ 1 (April 2002), pp. 35–48.

[10] See Melvin Butler, 'The Weapons of Our Warfare: Music, Positionality, and Transcendence Among Haitian Pentecostals', *Caribbean Studies*, 36/2 (2008): pp. 23–64; Judah Cohen, 'Hip-Hop Judaica: The Politics of Representin' Heebster Heritage', *Popular Music*, 28/1 (2009): pp. 1–18; Deborah A. Kapchan, 'Singing Community/Remembering in Common: Sufi Liturgy and North African Identity in Southern France', *International Journal of Community Music*, 2/1 (2009): pp. 9–23; and Gerardo Marti, *Worship Across the Racial Divide: Religious Music and the Multiracial Congregation* (Oxford University Press, 2012).

[11] See Melvin Butler, '"*Nou Kwe nan Sentespri*"/"We Believe in the Holy Spirit": Music, Ecstasy, and Identity in Haitian Pentecostal Worship', *Black Music Research Journal*, 22/1 (Spring 2002): pp. 85–125; and Timothy Rommen, 'Protestant Vibrations? Reggae, Rastafari, and Conscious Evangelicals', *Popular Music*, 25/2 (2006): pp. 235–63.

[12] See Carolyn Landau, 'Music Consumption and the Navigation of Identities: Transnational Moroccan Youth in Britain', in Khalaf and Khalaf (eds), *Arab Youth: Social Mobilization in Times of Risk* (Saqi Books, 2011), pp. 337–58; Daniel B. Reed, '"The Ge Is in the Church" and "Our Parents Are Playing Muslim": Performance, Identity, and Resistance among the Dan in Postcolonial Côte d'Ivoire', *Ethnomusicology*, 49/3 (Fall 2005): pp. 347–67; Smith Pollard, *When the Church Becomes Your Party*.

[13] Jonathan Dueck, 'Binding and Loosing in Song: Conflict, Identity, and Canadian Mennonite Music', *Ethnomusicology*, 55/2 (27 May 2011): pp. 229–54; Monique M. Ingalls, 'Singing Praise in the Streets: Performing Canadian Christianity through Public Worship in Toronto's Jesus in the City Parade', *Culture and Religion*, 13/3 (2012): pp. 349–71; Jeffrey A. Summit, *'The Lord's Song in a Strange Land': Music and Identity in Contemporary Jewish Worship* (Oxford University Press, 2000); Johnson, '"Oh, For a Thousand Tongues to Sing"'.

and 'identity', Dueck shows instead how the feelingful and experiential power of music-making, conjured by artefacts of performance, is an important means by which complex musical and religious subjects are formed. In her chapter, Kinga Povedák highlights a similarly multifaceted set of negotiations within Catholic congregational music-making in socialist and post-socialist-era Hungary. As Povedák's chapter shows, a complex combination of aesthetic, religious and political factors have shaped the reception and use of transnational vernacular styles within Hungarian Catholic congregations. In the wake of the Second Vatican Council's imperative to localize music and liturgy, musical style has become a source of contention through which worshippers construct – then identify with or against – the 'traditional' and the 'modern'.

Both Dueck's and Povedák's chapters point to ways in which church networks and transnational media industries have influenced local congregational music-making. The two remaining chapters in this section each address the role of media more directly, highlighting the ways in which mass-mediated sounds and images enable listeners to take on new 'local' and 'global' affiliations, whether as 'worshippers' or members of a global religious imaginary.[14] In an era in which mass media and migration are ever increasing the speed at which cultural elements move within and across social groups,[15] congregations and individual worshippers around the world have unprecedented access to mass media. As a result, new congregational styles and songs are spread through commercial and social media more quickly than ever before. Congregations use mass-mediated music styles in processes of identity negotiation in a variety of ways: some reject and define themselves against certain styles, others perform transnational congregational song genres to claim a place within larger Christian movements or publics, and still others adopt nonlocal musical styles in an attempt to transcend the problems of their local contexts.

Anna Nekola's analysis of the changing marketing of US Christian worship music highlights well the role of media in bringing together 'the technological sublime and the religious sublime', enabling consumers to be transported into a place of divine encounter. Nekola demonstrates how advertisements in the US Christian media industry propagate certain ideas of how to worship, arguing that the circulation of these images has reflected and contributed to the privatization of religious experience. It is likely that many of the worshippers Nekola describes would be listening to the musical subjects of Gesa Hartje's chapter: the Australian modern worship band Hillsong United. Anthropologist Birgit Meyer, in her work

---

[14] For further discussion of the interface between religion and globalization, see Simon Coleman, *The Globalisation of Charismatic Christianity* (Cambridge University Press, 2000); Thomas J. Csordas (ed.), *Transnational Transcendence: Essays on Religion and Globalization* (University of California Press, 2009).

[15] Arjun Appadurai, *Modernity at Large: The Cultural Dimensions of Globalization* (Minneapolis: University of Minnesota Press, 1996); Ulf Hannerz, Transnational Connections: Culture, People, Places (Routledge, 1996).

with Pentecostal media, has noted ways in which religious identity is embodied and mediated through what she terms 'aesthetic formations'.[16] In order to 'have religious messages experienced as true ... and experienced as real', Meyer writes, translocal religious imagined communities 'must become tangible by materializing in spaces and objects, and by being embodied in subjects'.[17] Gesa Hartje's chapter addresses this process, showing how Hillsong's mediated and live performances of worship, and the shared experience of concert attendees and listeners, creates an 'imagined community'[18] of fan-worshippers united by a common musical language. Both Hartje's and Nekola's chapters demonstrate how the use of mass media technologies in public and private settings has influenced the ways in which personal and collective Christian identities are formed and mediated; further, these technologies have enabled the images of worship circulating through global media to become embodied in new contexts.

Experience and Embodiment

Discussions of mediation and embodiment within the *Interplay of Identities* section set the stage for the book's third and final thematic focus: *Experience and Embodiment*. Religious experience is comprised of moments that are both extraordinary and mundane; it encompasses both singular rituals and the practices of everyday life. Exploring congregational music as a locus of Christian experience can provide insight into the human religious impulse conceived more broadly: in particular, the ways that individual and collective performances shape belief and create identity at the site of these powerful musical experiences. In any conversation about Christian religious experience, music is particularly crucial to consider because it is frequently central to worship across a wide spectrum of liturgical forms.

Rather than remaining separate from or subordinate to belief, experience – and the powerful emotions it involves – is integral to embodying it. In his work on gospel music in African American congregations, ethnographer Glenn Hinson notes the interlocking of experience, knowledge and belief within what he calls the circle of faith, in which 'experience grants knowledge, knowledge informs belief; belief invites further experience'.[19] Hinson's circle is clearly at work in Sarah

---

[16]   Birgit Meyer, 'Introduction: From Imagined Communities to Aesthetic Formations: Religious Mediations, Sensational Forms and Styles of Bonding', in Birgit Meyer (ed.), *Aesthetic Formations: Media, Religion, and the Senses* (Palgrave Macmillan, 2009), pp. 1–30.

[17]   Ibid., p. 6.

[18]   Benedict Anderson, *Imagined Communities: Reflections on the Origin and Spread of Nationalism*, Revised ed., (Verso Books, 1983/2006).

[19]   Glenn Hinson, *Fire in My Bones: Transcendence and the Holy Spirit in African American Gospel* (University of Pennsylvania Press, 2000), p. 11.

Eyerly's chapter on eighteenth-century Moravian ritual and experience. According to Eyerly, 'For the Moravians, sensual experience of Christ's suffering was a necessary component of theological learning. And music, with its ability to elicit emotion, was particularly useful in guiding comprehension of theology "through the heart"'. For Moravians, as in many traditions around the world, participation in congregational music-making is one of the central collective activities that enables the creation and mediation of powerful religious experiences and the embodiment of belief.[20]

While some Christian traditions maintain and cultivate powerful 'sensual experiences', for others the emphasis on experience has receded. Liturgical scholar Martin Stringer suggests that in some contexts, Christian congregational music has become 'muzak': music in the background that is 'safe', innocuous and unobtrusive. Combining philosophical reflection with his personal experience in various English churches, Stringer's chapter engenders an important theological critique: he suggests what may be missing in many 'comfortable' contemporary contexts is a sense of danger, which he argues is necessary for religious practice to reflect the varying experiences of life.

Yet while music as part of ritual is an important part of the sensual experience of embodying worship, it is only effective when the 'work' is done by the worshipper. Expectation and enculturation are integral parts of experience, and worshippers must be socialized into particular traditions in order to experience transcendence.[21] Yet, just as musical and religious experience often eludes description, so does the question of 'how to get there'. This is the central quandary faced by Gordon Adnams' respondents in his contribution. Adnams' phenomenological study provides a richly-textured account of Canadian Protestant participants' experiences of worship during corporate singing in their churches. Adnams uses the term 'being-in-song' to describe the experiential state his consultants characterize as 'really worshipping', showing that the embodied transcendent experience is one in which the singer is involved in 'multi-layered interactions with and around music and word, content and context, attention and intent'.

One of the central paradoxes of musico-religious experience is that it is at once social and personal; further, these forms of experience often interweave elements considered 'sacred' and 'secular' together in complex and contradictory ways. Participants from differing backgrounds and perspectives may experience

---

[20]   Judith Becker, *Deep Listeners: Music, Emotion, and Trancing* (Indiana University Press, 2004); Melvin Butler, 'Songs of Pentecost: Experiencing Music, Transcendence, and Identity in Jamaica and Haiti' (PhD diss., New York University, 2005); Steven M. Friedson, *Dancing Prophets: Musical Experience in Tumbuka Healing* (University of Chicago Press, 1996). Benjamin D. Koen, *Beyond the Roof of the World: Music, Prayer, and Healing in the Pamir Mountains* (Oxford University Press, 2008).

[21]   Becker, *Deep Listeners*; Mandi M. Miller and Kenneth T. Strongman, 'The Emotional Effects of Music on Religious Experience: A Study of the Pentecostal-Charismatic Style of Music and Worship', *Psychology of Music*, 30/1 (2002): pp. 8–27.

the same event very differently; the same is true of scholars of congregational
music-making. Mark Porter's chapter, similar in approach to Adnams', focuses
on the experience of musicians at a charismatic Anglican church in Oxford, UK.
In describing their experience of music and worship, these musicians' accounts
often defy any clear separation of 'sacred' and 'secular', even as their remarks
sometimes re-inscribe these categories. Porter shows how each worshipper, while
attending the same church, employs idiosyncratic strategies to smooth over the
dissonances between the various musical worlds he or she inhabits both inside
and outside of the church. Porter's account productively questions to what extent
simultaneous experience may or may not equate to *shared* experience.

Conclusion: The Promise of Plural Approaches to Christian Congregational Musical Scholarship

In highlighting the overlapping themes of performance, identity and experience,
this volume presents congregational music-making as a *gestalt* in which mind,
body, emotions and spirit are inextricably linked – part of the larger experience
of being human. We, the editors, hope that this volume is able to serve as an
example of the promise of plural perspectives in Christian congregational music
scholarship. Envisioned as a polyphonic collection – with moments of consonance
and dissonance – *Christian Congregational Music* seeks to model what we believe
to be a crucial aspect missing from much scholarship on Christian congregational
music: a multi-voiced dialogue between methodological approaches, disciplinary
perspectives and the positioning of scholars in relationship to the communities
they represent.

The volume's focus on fluid, dynamic aspects of music in and as performance
calls for scholars and practitioners to use a range of analytical methods that extend
beyond textual analysis of music and lyrics. Participant-observation, analysis of
visual media texts, interviews with musical creators and performers and insights
gleaned from performance are some of the many methods from which contributors
draw to explore how congregational music-making performs theology, forms
identity and shapes experience.

Similarly, the scholars contributing to this volume approach their topics from
a variety of disciplinary backgrounds, including phenomenology, sociology,
psychology, theology, (ethno)musicology, media studies and cultural studies.
This rich variety of cross-disciplinary approaches results, we believe, in a wider
perspective on many issues pertinent to scholars of Christian congregational
music, as well as bringing useful insights to particular scholarly communities.

As well as bringing together numerous methodological and disciplinary
perspectives, this volume includes scholarly voices from a variety of geographical
and cultural perspectives within North America, Western and Eastern Europe. By
juxtaposing these accounts, the similarities and differences between how people
in different contexts experience and perform congregational music come into

fuller relief. The kinds of conversations that characterize the first section of this volume can be seen as a microcosm of the entire volume: in this sense, it can be understood as a conversation between scholars and practitioners. In reading each account, however, it becomes difficult to find a clear delineation between who is a 'participant', 'observer' or 'practitioner': like their ethnographic consultants, each author in this section, and indeed the volume, negotiate multiple identities, performing them in part through the act of writing itself.[22]

Though there is much more work to be done, it is our hope that, through modelling collaboration across methods, disciplines and backgrounds, this volume points the way forward for congregational music studies. In this way, scholarship is like Christian congregational music itself: it takes a plurality of voices to perform knowledge, shape understanding and bring identity into being. We therefore hope that you, the reader, will find perusing the pages of this volume a thought-provoking, enjoyable and ultimately inspirational experience.

References

Al Faruqi, L.I., 'Music, Musicians and Muslim Law', *Asian Music,* 17/1 (1985): 3–36.

Ammerman, Nancy T. (ed.), *Everyday Religion: Observing Modern Religious Lives* (New York and London: Oxford University Press, 2006).

Anderson, Benedict, *Imagined Communities: Reflections on the Origin and Spread of Nationalism*, Revised ed. (London: Verso Books, 1983/2006).

Appadurai, Arjun, *Modernity at Large: The Cultural Dimensions of Globalization* (Minneapolis: University of Minnesota Press, 1996).

Becker, Judith, *Deep Listeners: Music, Emotion, and Trancing* (Bloomington: Indiana University Press, 2004).

Blacking, John, *How Musical is Man?* (Seattle: University of Washington Press, 1973).

Butler, Melvin, '"Nou Kwe nan Sentespri"/"We Believe in the Holy Spirit": Music, Ecstasy, and Identity in Haitian Pentecostal Worship', *Black Music Research Journal*, 22/1 (Spring 2002): 85–125.

Butler, Melvin, 'Songs of Pentecost: Experiencing Music, Transcendence, and Identity in Jamaica and Haiti' (PhD diss., New York University, 2005).

Butler, Melvin, 'The Weapons of Our Warfare: Music, Positionality, and Transcendence Among Haitian Pentecostals', *Caribbean Studies, Special Issue: Interrogating Caribbean Music: Power, Dialogue, and Transcendence*, 36/2 (2008): 23–64.

---

[22] James Clifford, 'Introduction: Partial Truths', in James Clifford and George E. Marcus, *Writing Culture: The Poetics and Politics of Ethnography* (University of California Press, 1989), pp. 1–26.

Clifford, James, 'Introduction: Partial Truths', in James Clifford and George E. Marcus (eds), *Writing Culture: The Poetics and Politics of Ethnography* (University of California Press, 1989).

Cohen, Judah, 'Hip-Hop Judaica: The Politics of Representin' Heebster Heritage', *Popular Music*, 28/1 (2009): 1–18.

Coleman, Simon, *The Globalisation of Charismatic Christianity* (Cambridge: Cambridge University Press, 2000).

Cook, Nicholas, 'We're All Ethnomusicologists Now' in Henry Stobart (ed.), *The New (Ethno)Musicologies* (London: Scarecrow, 2008).

Csordas, Thomas J. (ed.), *Transnational Transcendence: Essays on Religion and Globalization* (Berkeley: University of California Press, 2009).

DeNora, Tia, *Music in Everyday Life* (Cambridge: Cambridge University Press, 2000).

Dueck, Jonathan, 'Binding and Loosing in Song: Conflict, Identity, and Canadian Mennonite Music', *Ethnomusicology*, 55/2 (27 May 2011): 229–54.

Friedson, Steven M., *Dancing Prophets: Musical Experience in Tumbuka Healing* (Chicago and London: University of Chicago Press, 1996).

Friedson, Steven M., *Remains of Ritual: Northern Gods in a Southern Land* (Chicago and London: University of Chicago Press, 2009).

Frith, Simon, 'Music and Identity', in Stuart Hall and Paul du Gay (eds), *Questions of Cultural Identity* (London: Sage, 1996).

Frith, Simon, 'Music and Everyday Life', *Critical Quarterly*, 44/1 (April 2002): 35–48.

Hall, David D. (ed.), *Lived Religion in America: Toward a History of Practice* (Princeton: Princeton University Press, 1997).

Hannerz, Ulf, *Transnational Connections: Culture, People, Places* (London: Routledge, 1996).

Hinson, Glenn, *Fire in My Bones: Transcendence and the Holy Spirit in African American Gospel* (Philadelphia: University of Pennsylvania Press, 2000).

Ingalls, Monique M., 'Awesome in This Place: Sound, Space and Identity in Contemporary North American Evangelical Worship' (PhD diss., University of Pennsylvania, 2008).

Ingalls, Monique M., 'Singing Praise in the Streets: Performing Canadian Christianity through Public Worship in Toronto's Jesus in the City Parade', *Culture and Religion*, 13/3 (2012): 349–71.

Johnson, Birgitta J., '"Oh, For a Thousand Tongues to Sing": Music and Worship in Black Megachurches of Los Angeles, California' (PhD diss., University of California, Los Angeles, 2008).

Johnson, Birgitta J., 'Back to the Heart of Worship: Praise and Worship Music in a Los Angeles African American Megachurch', *Black Music Research Journal*, 31/1 (2011): 105–29.

Kapchan, Deborah A., 'Singing Community/Remembering in Common: Sufi Liturgy and North African Identity in Southern France', *International Journal of Community Music*, 2/1 (2009): 9–23.

Kapchan, Deborah A., *Traveling Spirit Masters: Moroccan Gnawa Trance and Music in the Global Marketplace* (Middletown, CT: Wesleyan University Press, 2007).

Koen, Benjamin D., *Beyond the Roof of the World: Music, Prayer, and Healing in the Pamir Mountains* (New York and Oxford: Oxford University Press, 2008).

Landau, Carolyn, 'Music Consumption and the Navigation of Identities: Transnational Moroccan Youth in Britain', in Khalaf and Khalaf (eds), *Arab Youth: Social Mobilization in Times of Risk* (London: Saqi Books, 2011).

Levine, J.A., 'Judaism and Music', in Guy L. Beck (ed.), *Sacred Sound: Experiencing Music in World Religions* (Waterloo, Ontario: Wilfred Laurier University Press, 2006).

Marti, Gerardo, *Worship Across the Racial Divide: Religious Music and the Multiracial Congregation* (Oxford and New York: Oxford University Press, 2012).

McGuire, Meredith B., *Lived Religion: Faith and Practice in Everyday Life* (New York: Oxford University Press, 2008).

Meyer, Birgit, 'Introduction: From Imagined Communities to Aesthetic Formations: Religious Mediations, Sensational Forms and Styles of Bonding', in Birgit Meyer (ed.), *Aesthetic Formations: Media, Religion, and the Senses* (New York: Palgrave Macmillan, 2009).

Miller, Mandi M. and Kenneth T. Strongman, 'The Emotional Effects of Music on Religious Experience: A Study of the Pentecostal-Charismatic Style of Music and Worship', *Psychology of Music*, 30/1 (2002): 8–27.

Muller, Carol, *Rituals of Fertility and the Sacrifice of Desire: Nazarite Women's Performance in South Africa* (Chicago and London: University of Chicago Press, 1999).

Nekola, Anna E., 'Between This World and the Next: The Musical "Worship Wars" and Evangelical Ideology in the United States 1960-2005' (PhD diss., University of Wisconsin-Madison, 2009).

Nettl, Bruno, 'Introduction: An Art Neglected in Scholarship', in Bruno Nettl and Melinda Russell (eds), *In the Course of Performance: Studies in the World of Musical Improvisation* (University of Chicago Press, 1998).

Reed, Daniel B., '"The Ge Is in the Church" and "Our Parents Are Playing Muslim": Performance, Identity, and Resistance among the Dan in Postcolonial Côte d'Ivoire', *Ethnomusicology*, 49/3 (Fall 2005): 347–67.

Robbins, Joel, 'Is the Trans in Trans-local the Trans- in Transcendent? On Alterity and the Sacred in the Age of Globalization', in Thomas J. Csordas (ed.), *Transnational Transcendence: Essays on Religion and Globalization* (Berkeley: University of California Press, 2009).

Rommen, Timothy, *'Mek Some Noise': Gospel Music and the Ethics of Style in Trinidad* (Berkeley: University of California Press, 2007).

Rommen, Timothy, 'Protestant Vibrations? Reggae, Rastafari, and Conscious Evangelicals', *Popular Music*, 25/2 (2006): 235–63.

Small, Christopher, *Musicking: The Meanings of Performing and Listening* (Middletown, CT: Wesleyan University Press, 1998).

Summit, Jeffrey A., *'The Lord's Song in a Strange Land': Music and Identity in Contemporary Jewish Worship* (New York: Oxford University Press, 2000).

Smith Pollard, Deborah, *When the Church Becomes Your Party: Contemporary Gospel Music* (Detroit: Wayne State University Press, 2008).

Weidman, Amanda, *Singing the Classical, Voicing the Modern: The Post-Colonial Politics of Music in South India* (Durham [USA] and London: Duke University Press, 2006).

Wong, Deborah, *Sounding the Center: History and Aesthetics in Thai Buddhist Performance* (Chicago and London: University of Chicago Press, 2001).

PART I
Performing Theology

Chapter 1

On One Accord: Resounding the Past in the Present at One African American Church

Will Boone

Now we are looking at Acts and talking about Pentecost,
But I'm trying to let you know how much it's going-to-cost.
Because it ain't just about Pentecost, it's about you.
I'm translating this to you.
You're the ones that need it during the week.
You need to know how He comes.
So when He comes you won't be shocked.

> – Bishop Leroy McKenzie, Faith Assembly Christian Center,
> Durham, North Carolina, 9 October 2011

The experience of time significantly shapes the religious beliefs and practices of the African American pentecostal[1] believers at Faith Assembly Christian Center in Durham, North Carolina. Worshippers declare with equal triumph that 'old things have passed away' and that they will be exalted 'in due time'.[2] Their memory of the past is filled with the harsh facts of generational poverty, oppression and racism – a legacy of actual and symbolic bondage. They imagine a future bright with potential. The present, they affirm, holds the key to negating the old and embracing the new. Believers gather together each week in worship so that their present might be empowered with the transformational presence of the Holy Spirit.

---

[1] I borrow the usage of the term 'pentecostal' with a 'small-P' from James K.A. Smith who follows Douglas Jacobsen and others in his employment of the term. Small-p 'pentecostal' is not meant to connote a particular denominational affiliation but to instead refer to 'the diversity of pentecostal/charismatic theolog*ies* while at the same time recognizing important family resemblances and shared sensibilities'. James K.A. Smith, *Thinking in Tongues*: *Pentecostal Contributions to Christian Philosophy* (Eerdmans, 2010), p. xvii.

[2] 2 Corinthians 5:17 – 'Therefore if any man be in Christ, he is a new creature: old things have passed away; behold, all things are become new.' 1 Peter 5 – 'Humble yourselves therefore under the mighty hand of God, that He may exalt you in due time.' These and all following scriptural citations will come from the King James Version as this is the preferred translation at Faith Assembly.

In this chapter I suggest that, for believers at Faith Assembly, a present empowered with presence is often inextricably interwoven with knowledge of the past. Importantly, however, this knowledge is enacted and embodied as much as it is 'known' in the intellectualist sense. Such an interpretation of knowledge is consistent with the epistemological position that the church's founders, Bishop Leroy and Pastor Mary McKenzie, hold in regard to the Word of God. They claim that effective Christian discipleship requires that a believer seek not only to understand and apply the Word, but also to 'eat the Word', and to 'sow your body into God'.[3]

Musical practice is one of the most powerful ways in which such holistic knowledge comes into being. Faith Assembly's musical repertoire is composed almost entirely of songs released as commercial recordings in the last ten or fifteen years. Paradoxically, however, when the congregation uses music to collectively move into experiential spaces where they believe that the Holy Spirit makes 'all things new', they frequently abandon this repertoire and create more improvisatory sounds that resonate with established cultural traditions and biblical narratives. This chapter will offer an analysis of an approximately 20-minute segment of a single worship service in which an improvised musical journey led from a contemporary gospel recording, through several musical moments that drew on longstanding African American church traditions, to something like an impromptu reenactment of the scene which begins the second chapter of Acts, where on the day of Pentecost some 120 people suddenly began praying and crying out to God in strange new languages 'as the Spirit gave them utterance'.[4] Sonically-driven moments like this one offer a means through which believers can embody a holistic knowledge of cultural tradition and biblical narrative that adds a layer of complexity to the content of preached messages at Faith Assembly; messages that often forcefully exalt the future and renounce the past.

This work builds on that of recent scholars of contemporary African American worship and musical practice who have shown how particular churches consciously adopt practices that preserve tradition even as they foster innovation.[5] While these authors have written about how the dialectic between tradition and innovation shapes repertoire selection, liturgical structure and congregational identity, I focus instead on how this dialectic – between tradition and innovation, past and future – plays out in the experiential present.

My involvement at Faith Assembly dates back to 2002 when a classmate in an undergraduate music class asked me to join the church band. Despite being white

[3]   Bishop Leroy McKenzie, Faith Assembly Christian Center, 18 March 2012.

[4]   Acts 2:4, 'And they were all filled with the Holy Ghost, and began to speak with other tongues, as the Spirit gave them utterance.'

[5]   See especially, Birgitta Johnson, '"Oh, For a Thousand Tongues to Sing": Music and Worship in African American Megachurches of Los Angeles, California' (PhD diss., UCLA, 2008); and Deborah Smith Pollard, *When the Church Becomes Your Party: Contemporary Gospel Music* (Wayne State University Press, 2008).

and having at the time very little interest in religion in general and no experience with African American pentecostal music, I agreed. Although initially I was very much an outsider at Faith Assembly, by the time I started my dissertation research in 2010 I was thoroughly ensconced in the community. Thus, the descriptions and analyses that follow inevitably reflect the fact that my roles as researcher and participant at Faith Assembly are inextricably intertwined.[6]

Past versus Future at Faith Assembly

The extent to which members of Faith Assembly value newness is reflected in their very decision to join a church that is less than 20 years old and has no denominational affiliation. Faith Assembly has no hymnals, no written out liturgy and no illustrious denominational pioneers anchoring them to an historical legacy with stone gazes from beyond the grave. Their church building is a renovated former nightclub furbished to suggest stylish contemporaneity. Traditional Christian iconography can't be found. A large mural stretching across the side wall just below the ceiling shows clouds and dark-skinned angels in misty pastels. Its stylized spray-painted title, 'City of Faith', looks like the work of a Christian graffiti artist, and seems to suggest that even Heaven might have a modern black urban flavour.

Church members' desires for the new are bound up with a desire to move away the socioeconomic instability that many of them have experienced in the past and toward a stability that may be coalescing on the horizon. Most of the church's members reside in what Jonathan Walton, a religious studies scholar who has written extensively about contemporary African American Christianity, has called the 'nebulous category between the working and middle class'.[7] Some are first generation college graduates and some are the first in their families to own homes. Among the members there are a number of professionals including nurses, teachers, small business owners and various kinds of government employees. Nevertheless, very few are strangers to poverty; its spectre lingers in their neighbourhoods, their families and their own pasts. They live with a day to day knowledge of the facts reported in a recent study by the Institute of Assets and Social Policy at Brandeis University – that 'only 26 per cent of African American middle-class families have

---

[6]   In recent decades many anthropologists and ethnomusicologists have problematized the insider/outsider binary that traditionally informed assumptions about the nature and goals of fieldwork. For a rich synthesis of this scholarship see Chapter 1, 'Fielding Questions: Positionality and Reflexivity in Contemporary Ethnomusicology', in Melvin Butler's dissertation 'Songs of Pentecost: Experiencing Music, Transcendence, and Identity in Jamaica and Haiti' (PhD diss., New York University, 2005), pp. 26–52.

[7]   Jonathan Walton quoted in Laurie Goodstein, 'Believers Invest in the Gospel of Getting Rich', *New York Times* (15 August 2009), http://www.nytimes.com/2009/08/16/us/16gospel.html?_r=0.

the combination of assets, education, sufficient income, and health insurance to ensure middle-class financial security', and that 'one in three (33 per cent) are at high risk of falling out of the middle class'.[8] Believers frequently express belief that the future holds the key to greater well-being and stability, particularly as they echo the rhetoric of prominent African American mega-pastors and televangelists such as T.D. Jakes, and proclaim faith in the imminence of prosperity, 'new levels' and 'financial breakthroughs'.

But the desire to leave the past behind is not only a matter of economics. Bishop Leroy McKenzie's idea to found the church was a direct result of the murder of his 17-year-old nephew, a victim of street violence. Durham, North Carolina's rate of violent crime consistently ranks well above national and state averages, and African Americans are prosecuted for such crimes far disproportionately to whites.[9] Everyone at Faith Assembly has family members, friends or acquaintances that are, or have been, incarcerated. One of the stalwarts of the church community is the mother of a son serving a lifetime prison sentence.

Church members look to the future with the hope of leaving behind this grim legacy of crime and imprisonment. Bishop McKenzie encourages believers to base their faith on 'where [they] are going and not where [they] have been'.[10] And nearly every aspect of worship at Faith Assembly is imbued with a sense of forward focus; even their songs. 'The Best is yet to Come', they sing, 'It's A New Season'. We're 'Moving Forward'.[11]

Musical Practice at Faith Assembly

Music and Newness

Each Sunday morning worship service at Faith Assembly opens with Praise and Worship where songs are brought forth in a concert-like manner from a small group of singers (the Praise Team) who perform from a stage. Participation is

---

[8]   Tatjana Meschede, Thomas M. Shapiro, Laura Sullivan and Jennifer Wheary, *Economic (In)Security: The Experience of the African-American and Latino Middle Classes'*, Institute on Assets and Social Policy (Brandeis University, 2008), p. 1.

[9]   North Carolina Department of Corrections' Annual Statistical Reports can be accessed through the North Carolina Office of Research and Planning website, http://www. doc.state.nc.us/rap/index.htm.

[10]   This quotation comes from a sermon McKenzie preached on 23 October 2011, but he expresses similar sentiments frequently.

[11]   These are the titles of popular songs performed frequently at Faith Assembly. 'New Season', Israel and New Breed, *New Season* (Integrity Media, 2001); 'The Best is Yet to Come', Donald Lawrence and The Tri-City Singers, *Go Get Your Life Back* (EMI/Chordant, 2002); and 'Moving Forward', Hezekiah Walker and The Love Fellowship Crusade Choir, *Souled Out* (Verity, 2008).

encouraged, but the Praise Team uses microphones and the sound of their amplified voices coupled with the accompanying electric instruments greatly overpowers the sound of the congregation. The songs that they sing are almost exclusively versions of popular recordings released in the last fifteen years. They regularly add new songs to their repertoire, often singing in church the same songs that are current gospel radio hits.

There is a hipness factor that figures into the allure of musical newness for Faith Assembly. This is paralleled by many members' tastes for the latest fashions in hairstyles, apparel and automobiles. But they hope that musical newness and its corollary hipness also serve evangelistic ends. Bishop McKenzie explicitly encourages an embrace of musical newness because he believes it makes the church more welcoming to potential members, young people in particular. In one meeting with the Praise Team and musicians he explicitly urged us to play more of what was 'hot', more of the 'stuff that's on the radio'. Not only would this help 'bring new people in', but it was biblical. The Psalms, he reminded us, exhort believers to 'sing unto the Lord a new song'.[12]

As Bishop McKenzie's reminder suggests, there are also theological factors in the embrace of musical newness at Faith Assembly. God's abundance is a central theme for them – partially a reflection of the influence of the prosperity-inflected theology that has inundated African American pentecostalism in recent decades.[13] God's blessings, believers at Faith Assembly say, do not operate on a scarcity model. He is a God of 'more than enough'; one who does 'exceeding abundantly above all that we ask or think'.[14] It follows that God did not gift all of His best songs at some point in the past. To rely exclusively on a hymn book or to sing only the songs sung by one's parents and grandparents is to enact a lack of faith in God's continuing abundance. If God desires a 'new song', as it suggests in the Psalms, then He must be continually providing such songs. And these new songs often bring, in the words of believers at Faith Assembly, a 'fresh anointing', a 'right-now Word', or inspire a 'right-now praise'. Songs that lack this 'freshness' and 'right-nowness' are considered to be far less effective in helping people deal with their current 'situations and circumstances'. Furthermore, believers suggest, churches that sing only old songs risk being disobedient to God and being poor stewards of the new gifts that He is giving.

For many at Faith Assembly a focus on musical newness is also about separation from the past. Music has a propensity to become inextricably interwoven with particular circumstances and events in a person's life. In one rehearsal at Faith

---

[12]   See, for example: Psalms 33:3, 40:3, 96:1, 98:1 and 144:9.

[13]   See Milmon Harrison, *Righteous Riches: The Word of Faith Movement in Contemporary African American Religion* (Oxford University Press, 2005).

[14]   The first quotation is an often repeated phrase at Faith Assembly and also the title of a song that was at one time a favourite for the church's Praise Team: 'More Than Enough', Gary Oliver, *More Than Enough* (Integrity/Epic, 2000). The second quotation comes from Ephesians 3:20, a very commonly cited scripture at Faith Assembly.

Assembly the drummer began playing the kind of BOOM-chick, BOOM-chick pattern that is associated for many African American Christians with traditional quartet-style gospel music. The lead singer of the Praise Team wrinkled her nose. 'You better get out of here with that Baptist music', she scolded playfully. 'Nobody here wants to hear that. We left that behind.'[15] The sound of certain 'old' songs or performance styles is, for some members of Faith Assembly, the sound of a place that they hoped to resign to the past. That 'place' might be a life of poverty, or it might be the Baptist church that they grew up in. In any case, to sing new songs – often songs that didn't even exist during those past circumstances – is a statement of separation. 'By singing this music', one implicitly says, 'I am not that; I am not what I used to be.'

Music and 'The Programme'

Preaching one Sunday about the faith of the disciples who dropped everything to follow Jesus, Bishop Leroy McKenzie said,

> You got to be careful when you tell Jesus you're going to follow him,
> Because you don't know where he's going to go.
> Most of the time church folks want to know everything about where they're going.
> 'When's the next hymn going to come?
> 'What's the next part of the programme?'
> And they want to *look* at a programme.
> But I found out Jesus is the only programme I know;
> He *is* the programme![16]

There are no written programmes at Faith Assembly – a reflection of an African American pentecostal ethos in which the unplanned and the mysterious must be welcomed if worshippers are to encounter the magnitude of the Spirit's power. The lack of a programme means that services at Faith Assembly are not beholden to a predetermined plan, and that there is always flexibility, as participants say, to 'follow the move of the Spirit'.

But while there is always a measure of unpredictability in Faith Assembly's services Table 1.1 shows that they do, in fact, follow the same basic outline week after week.

Table 1.1 shows that songs sung by the Praise Team and choreographed dances are the only 'programmed' music at Faith Assembly. But there are a number 'unprogrammed' musical practices that figure prominently in the act of worship. Believers at Faith Assembly expect these to emerge as necessary during the course of the service. As this music's placement in the service is not predetermined, there

---

[15] Rehearsal at Faith Assembly Christian Center, 21 June 2012.

[16] Bishop Leroy McKenzie, Faith Assembly Christian Center, 11 December 2011.

Table 1.1   Standard Order of Events for Worship Services at Faith Assembly

Segment	Leader/Activity	Approximate Length
Intercessory Prayer		5–15 minutes
Praise and Worship	Praise Team, 2 or 3 songs	15–25 minutes
	Master of Ceremonies (MC), exhortation and welcome	5 minutes
	Choreographed Dance	5–10 minutes
	MC, exhortation and recognition of birthdays, anniversaries, and visitors	10 minutes
	Praise Team, 1 or 2 songs	10–15 minutes
The Word (Sermon)	Bishop or Pastor McKenzie	60–90 minutes
Altar Call		10–30 minutes
Announcements	Pastor McKenzie	5 minutes
Offering	Church Deacons	5 minutes
Closing Prayer / Benediction	Bishop or Pastor McKenzie	2 minutes

is an implied demand that these kinds of music be spiritually inspired – that they be part of Jesus' 'programme' rather than the programme of 'church folks'.

Being prescheduled, songs from the Praise Team and choreographed dances will occur even if believers do not perceive immediate spiritual inspiration. There is an expectation at Faith Assembly that these practices should be 'anointed' – that is, that the bodies and voices of those dancing or singing should be mediums for the Holy Spirit – but members are quick to point out that 'the anointing is not always flowing'. Perhaps a dancer has not repented for particular sins, or a singer sings with egotistical or impure motives; for whatever reason, congregants sometimes simply do not feel the Spirit move during these scheduled segments of the service.

But sometimes they do feel the Spirit move powerfully during a choreographed dance or a Praise Team performance. Often, when this happens, temporal space opens as Faith Assembly uses more improvisational musical practices to journey away from the preset schedule of events – away from what Pastor Garry Mitchell terms 'protocol' – and into a state of being with a fluidity and unpredictability that only increases its spiritual potential. When believers at Faith Assembly talk about such moments of musical and experiential transformation, they often speak of collapsing boundaries – the boundaries between individuals as well as boundaries between human and divine. In the ethnographic description that follows I'll explore this phenomenon of boundary collapse, paying special attention to the collapse of the boundaries between present and past.

Sunday Morning, 9 January 2011, approximately 10:20 AM

Following 'protocol' closely, Pastor Garry Mitchell, the Master of Ceremonies (MC), introduces a group of five women to dance a choreographed dance to a recording of 'Expect the Great' by Jonathan Nelson.[17] Enacting the lyrics of the up-tempo song with enthusiastic synchronized movements, the dancers stir the congregation, bringing most of them to their feet. As the recording fades out and the dance concludes, the band begins to reprise the vamp from the end of the song and Pastor Garry takes the stage. He leads the congregation in singing the lyrics from the vamp – repetitions of 'The blessing is on you'. The congregation's voices fill the sanctuary and Pastor Garry interjects with exhortations and words of praise. Even after the MC concludes the song, the musicians sonically linger with sustained notes and shimmering cymbals. Congregants continue moving their bodies, many of them crying out 'hallelujah!' or 'thank you, Jesus!' The musicians' swelling sounds soon transform into the distinctive double-time rhythms of African American pentecostal 'shout music'. Congregants begin dancing ecstatically as they experience an infilling of the Holy Spirit. After several minutes of shouting, Pastor Garry motions to the musicians to 'break' the music, bringing the 100-plus decibels pounding from the church's sound system to a dramatic halt. Immediately, the soundscape is saturated with the voices of congregants speaking in tongues, praying and giving thanks. Beneath these voices, the piano player begins to improvise softly, gradually establishing a pattern over which Pastor Garry improvises lyrics. In song, he acknowledges that the church is entering into the manifest presence of God. 'We come into Your presence, right now, to worship You', he sings repeatedly.

After a few improvised verses and many more repetitions of this refrain, Pastor Garry leaves the constraints of language behind and begins to simply hum the melody. Humming, he leads the song, measure by measure, toward silence. He speaks softly as the music gradually dies away. Then he shushes into the microphone, 'ssshhhhhhh', 'ssshhhhhhhh', 'sssshhhhhhh', and instructs the congregation to 'be still'. There is a moment of almost total silence and then ripples of murmuring prayer and tongues speech fill the congregation. Twenty minutes have passed since the conclusion of the women's dance.[18]

The moment of collective prayer and tongues speech I have just described felt like a moment of arrival – the telos of a 20 minute journey away from protocol. Moving from a contemporary gospel recording through various kinds of improvised music, Faith Assembly reached back into the biblical past to create a soundscape that resonated with the description of the spiritual takeover in the second chapter of Acts. In order to have such a resonance, the moment had to

---

[17]   'Expect the Great', Jonathan Nelson, *Better Days* (Integrity Media, 2010).
[18]   This description is derived from a combination of field notes and reference to the audio recording that I made of the 9 January 2011 service.

be unplanned.[19] Christian philosopher James K.A. Smith reminds us that the 'inbreaking of the Spirit' experienced by the Apostles in the book of Acts 'was not something that was anticipated or predelineated'.[20] Thus, the moment of arrival had to be achieved rather than scripted.[21] In what follows, I'll discuss how, in the process of this achieving, Faith Assembly's believers enacted and embodied key elements of their theology including the significance of the deep congregational unity known as 'one accord', the interplay of faith and work and the idea of 'radical openness' to the 'continuing operations of the Spirit'.[22] While these concepts may instruct what happens inside of the preset order of events, they come to be known by worshippers on a deeper level as they emerge in the temporal spaces outside the bounds of protocol.

The segment began with a choreographed dance performed to the 2010 recording 'Expect the Great'. This dance was pre-planned. But when the recording was reprised by the church's musicians and Pastor Garry led the congregation in repetitions of the last refrain, the church collectively made a commitment to move away from the familiarity of protocol. By itself, this initial commitment was not particularly remarkable. Similar things happen in most services. Most pentecostals consider a service that does not go some way towards venturing outside of a predetermined structure to be 'dry' and ineffective.[23] But in this instance the service did not return to protocol after a few minutes away as it commonly does. Instead the church continued to go deeper 'in'.

'Going in' – meaning 'in' to the Holy Spirit's presence – is how Pastor Garry describes what happens in intensified moments of worship. The phrase is not Pastor Garry's own but a commonly invoked description of experience among African American pentecostals. This evocative concept provides a window into the pentecostal experience of Spirit-filled worship. The idea of 'going in' implies some volition on the part of the goer – to some extent one must choose to go in and choose to come out. But this creates a possible conflict in terms of agency. In moments of experiential intensity Pastor Garry often affirms that 'there has been

---

[19] Even though it was unplanned, this moment was not necessarily unexpected. In fact, there is much evidence to suggest that culturally-scripted expectations play a key role in musically-facilitated ecstatic experience. See, for example, Judith Becker's *Deep Listeners: Music, Emotion, and Trancing* (Indiana University Press, 2004). See also footnote 23 below.

[20] Smith, *Thinking in Tongues*, p. 33.

[21] Glenn Hinson writes of 'one accord': 'Such deep devotion never "just happens". Rather it must be actively *achieved*'. Glenn Hinson, *Fire in My Bones: Transcendence and the Holy Spirit in African American Gospel* (University of Pennsylvania Press, 2000), p. 89 (emphasis in the original).

[22] Smith, *Thinking in Tongues*, p. 12.

[23] James K.A. Smith writes, 'One of the reasons pentecostal spirituality is so often linked to spontaneity is that pentecostal worship makes room for the unexpected. Indeed, we might say that, for pentecostals, the unexpected is expected. The surprising comes as no surprise'. Smith, *Thinking in Tongues*, p. 33.

a shift', or that 'the Holy Ghost is in charge of the programme'. On the surface it seems that these claims would imply that human volition is irrelevant. But Pastor Garry's simultaneous emphasis on 'going in' makes the situation more complex. His often stern exhortations that congregants participate physically imply that human will is a crucial factor in the process of entering into a holy presence. For example, in one service Pastor Garry chanted emphatically,

> Sometimes God comes in and He shifts things, but you've got to be ready for the shift.
> Lift up those hands and look unto Him from which cometh your help.
> God is trying to get something to *you* ...
> God is about to make some stuff happen in your life ...
> But you got to come out of yourself, and begin to lift up holy hands, and let go and let God in this place.
> Lift up those hands, lift up those hands, Come on!
> Lift up those hands all over the building! Come on!
> And just *cry out* to Him! ...
> Lift them up!
> Begin to just wave them!
> Everybody on one accord, come on! ...
> Manifestation is taking place.
> Healing is taking place.
> Deliverance is taking place.
> If you want something from God,
> *You* stretch out on Him right now! Come on!
> *You* stretch out on Him! ...
> Somebody that loves God give Him some real praise in this place.
> Oh, come on, give Him some real praise, don't pattycake Him.[24]

To go into the Holy Spirit's presence, then, takes work. Even if the Spirit moves powerfully during a service, the congregation still must collectively 'press in [His] presence' as one popular song puts it.[25] Individually, worshippers must be willing to offer a 'sacrifice of praise'; to 'present [their] bodies' to God and to praise Him with the 'fruit of [their] lips' even at the risk of looking silly or losing control of their 'natural' selves.[26] This is all part of a process of creating an intense state of congregational unity or 'one accord'. In his masterful ethnographic account of 'transcendence and the Holy Spirit in African American gospel', Glenn Hinson writes that 'one accord' is 'something far deeper than a simple state of harmony.

---

[24]   Pastor Garry Mitchell, Faith Assembly Christian Center, 20 February 2011.

[25]   'Press in Your Presence', Shana Wilson, *The Nations are Waiting* (self-released, 2008).

[26]   Faith Assembly's scriptural basis for the idea of a 'sacrifice of praise' comes from Jeremiah 17:26, Romans 12:1 and Hebrews 13:15, which is also the scripture from which the terminology 'fruit of our lips' comes.

When the saints speak of 'coming to accord', they mean recreating in spirit and mood the focused reverence that prevailed among the apostles on the day of Pentecost'.[27]

As believers work to establish 'one accord' among the individuals that make up the congregation – a prerequisite to entering into the depths of God's presence – they are simultaneously working to connect themselves to the biblical past. Following Hinson, we can understand 'one accord' not simply as a state of unity among a group of worshippers in the present, but also a state of unity with the past; with the 'radical' believers of the early Christian church.

According to Faith Assembly's believers, the extent to which 'one accord' is established correlates to how deep 'in' the congregation can go. Believers liken the Holy Spirit's presence to an immersive substance – something like the ocean. The deeper the congregation goes, the more they encounter wonders that cannot exist at the surface. At the same time, going deeper takes preparation and work, and it requires that they be able to withstand increasing pressure. Many times Faith Assembly ventures away from protocol only momentarily, wading in the shallows of spiritual presence. If we zoom in on the transition to shout music I described briefly above, we see that this kind of wading is what appeared to be happening on 9 January 2011. But the insistence of the organist and the moving bodies of the congregation eventually spurred the service further toward the deep.

After the musicians reprised 'Expect the Great' and Pastor Garry led the congregation in collective repetitions of the song's refrain for about two minutes, he signalled for a cadence and the music temporarily ceased. Pastor Garry continued with heightened exhortations while the congregation clapped and cheered, but after about a minute of this, he began speaking as if he were returning to protocol and even asked for the lights to be turned on. (Faith Assembly uses theatre-style lighting during Praise Team singing and choreographed dances, and overhead fluorescent lighting for most other parts of the service. The switch from one to the other visually emphasizes the demarcation of different segments of the service.) Many congregants remained standing, moving their bodies, seeming to feel aftershocks from the wave of congregational accord they had just experienced while singing together. Brother Wade, the Hammond organist, began a series of repetitive licks that sonically suggested shout music and disregarded Pastor Garry's rhetorical moves toward protocol. Following this lead, Pastor Garry started moving his body with subtle Holy Dance-like gestures,[28] and Brother Sylvester, the drummer, entered with a high-hat crescendo starting with the cymbals closed tightly and gradually increasing in volume while allowing the cymbals to separate, creating a swell of white noise. Pastor Garry screamed 'Somebody's going to catch on fire in a minute!' Taking this as his cue, Brother Vince entered with chromatic

---

[27] Hinson, *Fire in My Bones*, p. 89.

[28] African American pentecostals frequently refer to the rhythmic movements of Spirit-filled believers as the Holy Dance. Although each individual's dance is unique, in general, the Holy Dance consists of intricate footwork and rapid vigorous movements.

eighth notes on the bass and I followed with choppy dominant ninth chords on the guitar. Brother Sylvester brought in the characteristic kick/snare alternation. With the shout music in full bloom, Pastor Garry danced front and centre in the church and yelled into the microphone, 'Somebody better help me praise Him!' All across the congregation people were dancing with their own 'shouts'. The music continued for about five minutes morphing through five or six variations on the basic pattern with Pastor Garry periodically voicing loud encouragements into the microphone.

As the church shouted, church members' cultural and religious pasts became much more present in the service. Most African American pentecostals who grew up in church recognize shouting as a fundamentally traditional activity. Many contemporary believers remember seeing their mother, grandmother and perhaps even great-grandmother dancing the Holy Dance in church. And the sound of shout music brings years of accrued personal and cultural memory to the surface. Much has been written about the extent to which sound is deeply interwoven with memory.[29] A few bars of a popular recording that one once listened to with a first lover can trigger waves of emotion and rekindle the very feelings experienced 'way back when'. For African American pentecostals the sound of shout music runs through generations of shared ecstatic and transcendent experience. Although new variations and new harmonic and melodic patterns are continually mixed with more traditional sounds, shout music retains a core rhythmic identity that some believe traces back to the ring shout practised by slaves; a practice likely brought over from West Africa.[30] In the shouting moment, then, the spiritual ecstasy of going 'deeper in' is densely interwoven with tradition and cultural memory.

On 9 January 2011 shouting was not the end of Faith Assembly's extended venture away from protocol. In a particularly potent moment Pastor Garry signalled for the musicians to 'break' the shout music (that is, to stop abruptly). This is a common tactic among leaders of African American pentecostal worship, used in part to test the intensity of the anointing and the zeal of the praisers.[31] Will the congregation continue dancing, clapping and crying out to God even without the foundation and cover of music? Will they allow themselves to be exposed,

---

[29]   For examples of scholarly works for which memory is a central concern see Earle Waugh, *Memory, Music, and Religion: Morocco's Mystical Chanters* (University of South Carolina Press, 2005); or the essays in Karin Bijsterveld and Jose van Dijck (eds), *Sound Souvenirs: Audio Technologies, Memory and Cultural Practices* (Amsterdam University Press, 2009).

[30]   Scholars such as Samuel Floyd have placed great emphasis on the practice of the ring shout and its generative power not only in the creation of religious music, but *all* African American music. See Floyd, *The Power of Black Music: Interpreting its History from Africa to the United States* (Oxford University Press, 1995).

[31]   For a detailed discussion of this practice in an African American Holiness church see William Dargan, 'Congregation Gospel Songs in a Black Holiness Church: A Musical and Textual Analysis' (PhD diss., Wesleyan University, 1983).

with attention now directed to their own voices and movements rather than the overwhelming volume coming from the speakers? Very often this is a short test, maybe lasting a few seconds. If the congregation's praise continues in the absence of music, then the musicians will reenter and go on with the shout music. In this particular instance, however, shout music did not return. The break in the music revealed a soundscape in which congregants were not merely clapping and praising, but fervently crying out, weeping and speaking in tongues. One woman's voice rang out above the others, 'I thank you, Lord. For every breath that I breathe! For every breath that I breathe! You didn't have to do it, but you did. You didn't have to do it, but you did!' For close to a minute the musicians laid out. And rather than returning with shout music, the keyboardist began softly playing a progression in a minor mode. With gravitas, Pastor Garry spoke into the microphone, 'We've done tapped into some worship.'

This declaration is a powerful one for believers at Faith Assembly. They commonly pit 'praise' against 'worship', declaring the latter to be a deeper state of devotion. A praise and worship handbook written by Dr Leonard Scott, the founder of black gospel record label Tyscot, draws on the language of Psalm 100 to characterize a three-tiered progression – moving from thanksgiving, to praise, to worship – that leads deeper into the presence of God.

> Coming through the first barrier to His presence, the gates, is to be accompanied with thanksgiving. We leave the gates and proceed into His courts with praise. Then we go into His very presence with worship as we bless His name.[32]

Pastor Garry's words 'we've done tapped into some worship' thus announced that Faith Assembly had entered 'His very presence', what believers sometimes call the 'Holy of holies'.[33] For about seven minutes Pastor Garry improvised a song, returning again and again to the refrain, 'We come into Your presence, right now, to worship You.' At times, members of the Praise Team accompanied him in harmony. The congregation 'caught' the refrain, and for a few repetitions he held the microphone toward them, focusing attention on the collectivity of the singing. Between repetitions of the refrain Pastor Garry interspersed a number of improvised verses, one of which was an adaptation of the lyrics of the hymn 'Father, I Stretch My Hand to Thee':

---

[32] Leonard Scott, *Be Lifted Up! A Call to Lift Up the Mighty Name of Jesus in Praise and Worship* (Evergreen Press, 2008), p. 4.

[33] In the Hebrew Scriptures this term is used to denote the inner sanctuary of the Tabernacle where the Ark of the Covenant was stored. Contemporary African American pentecostals have adopted it to refer to an overwhelming experiential state. This usage became especially common following Deitrick Haddon's 1999 recording 'We Worship You' (*Chain Breaker*, Tyscot Records), a song that has become a standard in many African American pentecostal churches and includes the lyrics, 'Into the holy of holies / That's where I want to be'.

I stretch my hands to you,
No other help I know,
If you withdraw your hand from me, God,
I got nowhere; I don't know where to go.[34]

The hymn's lyrics, written by Charles Wesley in 1741, have long been sung in many African American congregations. Thus, even as Pastor Garry created something very new – a 'spontaneously composed' song – he grounded it in religious and cultural history by interpolating the lyrics of this hymn.

But even beyond this borrowing from an old hymn text, the very act of creating a new religious song in the moment resonates with accounts of the creation of spirituals long forwarded by many composers and scholars of African American religious music. In an introduction that accompanied the publication of some of his arranged spirituals during the years around 1920, composer HT Burleigh wrote that spirituals 'were never "composed", but sprang into life, ready made, from the white heat of religious fervor …'[35] More recently Jon Michael Spencer has postulated that some spirituals likely emerged when 'extemporaneous sermonizing' 'crescendoed' into 'intoned utterance' and was joined by a 'tonal response from the congregation' that 'resulted in the burgeoning of song'.[36] Though without recorded evidence it is impossible to know how spirituals actually came into being, this lineage of thought about their origins makes it easy to imagine that the process which resulted in extemporized song at Faith Assembly on 9 January 2011 was something like the process that gave birth to many musical utterances in the African American religious past.

After about six minutes of singing Pastor Garry dispensed with lyrics altogether and began to simply hum, leading the church in a long decrescendo. He then spoke quietly into the microphone, 'Begin to worship, begin to worship, begin to worship, begin to worship', and followed with, 'Now. Just worship.' The musical texture reduced to only synthesized strings and high hat and Pastor Garry spoke softly. He mixed tongues-speech with declarations of thanksgiving and words of encouragement. This led to many quiet repetitions of 'Thank you, God.'

Immediately following this last whispered 'Thank you, God', Pastor Garry shushed into the microphone. The musicians, already near silent, stopped playing completely. The shushing sound was a signal to listen. It was also the sound of breath, of the everlasting give and take of inspiration and expiration on which life depends. For believers it was a sound that potentially brought to the surface an

---

[34]   See hymn #127 in the *African American Heritage Hymnal* (GIA Publications, 2001), where the lyrics are printed as, 'Father, I stretch my hands to Thee; / No other help I know. / If Thou withdraw Thyself from me, / O! whither shall I go?'

[35]   See, for example, HT Burleigh, *The Celebrated Negro Spirituals* (Ricordi, 1917–24).

[36]   Jon Michael Spencer, 'African American Religious Music from a Theomusicological Perspective', in Philip Bohlman, Edith Blumhofer and Maria Chow (eds), *Music in American Religious Experience* (Oxford University Press, 2006), pp. 43–4.

awareness of their own primordial core in the sense that 'God formed man of the dust of the ground, and breathed into his nostrils the breath of life; and man became a living soul.'[37] Pastor Garry expelled three long 'shhhhhhhhhhhhs', emptying his lungs of air entirely each time. A long moment passed and then he whispered 'be still ... be still ... be still ... be still ... be still ... be still ... be still ... be still'.

There was a feeling of arrival. A long journey deeper and deeper 'in', through praise and through worship, was completed. For several minutes the only sounds in the atmosphere were the murmuring of tongues speech and prayers. Faith Assembly had reached its 'Acts two moment'. An ancient narrative – one of the foundational stories for all pentecostal believers – was reanimated in the present. Members at Faith Assembly say that encounters such as this one work to transform their immediate circumstances. They receive relief from, and revelation about, the cares and weights and issues that they brought with them into the service, even as they viscerally experience connection to the distant past. For them, the moment is a display of the power of the Holy Ghost, and a direct experiencing of the timelessness of that power.

In the epigraph that began this article, taken from one of Bishop McKenzie's sermons about the Acts chapter two narrative, the pastor told his congregation that '... it ain't just about Pentecost, it's about you'. This is a common rhetorical move for African American pentecostal pastors – to claim that what happened in the Bible is relevant to how believers live today. What is especially significant about the events at Faith Assembly on 9 January 2011, however, is that they take this sentiment beyond the realm of idea. Worshipping together, believers felt and heard events narrated in the Bible, embodying a relationship with those events that transcended intellectual understanding. It was the type of holistic experience on which they claim that faith is built; the kind of experience that strengthens their certainty in the transformative power of the Holy Spirit. Moving from contemporary gospel song, through historically and culturally affirmative improvised practices, to a music-less moment of collective Spirit-led speech, Faith Assembly journeyed beyond simple 'knowing' to a place of 'knowing that they know that they know'.[38]

In the course of my work I am often led back to the most basic questions: 'Why do Faith Assembly's members go to church? Why is it that they return week after week and invest considerable amounts of time, energy, and money?' Of course there are no answers to these questions that apply equally to each churchgoer.

---

[37] Genesis 2:7. My interpretation draws on a comment made by Bishop McKenzie during an altar call on 24 June 2012. Although the altar call at Faith Assembly is usually accompanied by music, on this Sunday as the band began to play McKenzie said sternly, 'No. Stop the music. We ain't going with no music today. See I'm convinced that sometimes we just need to listen to the breath of life that's on the inside [of us].'

[38] 'I know that I know that I know' is a common pentecostal phrase. James K.A. Smith claims that the phrase encapsulates a 'pentecostal epistemology' that is a '... critique of the rationalism (or cognitivism or "intellectualism") that characterizes modern accounts of knowledge'. Smith, *Thinking in Tongues*, p. 52.

Broadly, Faith Assembly (like any religious institution) plays the role of affirming belief, culture and a sense of local community. Even as it performs these roles, however, it does something else. It provides a space for the transformation of time. Churchgoers come to church from an imperfect past and when they leave they head toward an uncertain future. But at church they embrace the idea that their pasts can be erased and their futures can be more prosperous than they ever imagined. Singing songs that glitter with the fragile tinsel of newness, they proclaim the gospel of forward momentum. But they also come to church to be assured that there is something deeper; something that transcends time. And in the fullness of its presence there is no past and no future. Presence emerges only in the present. Making music, sounding and resounding as a congregation, believers at Faith Assembly journey to places where they can be on one accord, present together.

References

African American Heritage Hymnal: 575 Hymns, Spirituals, and Gospel Songs (Chicago: GIA Publications, 2000).

Becker, Judith, *Deep Listeners: Music, Emotion, and Trancing* (Bloomington, IN: Indiana University Press, 2004).

Burleigh, H.T., *The Celebrated Negro Spirituals* (New York: Ricordi, 1917–24).

Dargan, William T., 'Congregational Gospel Songs in a Black Holiness Church: A Musical and Textual Analysis' (PhD diss., Wesleyan University, 1983).

Floyd, Samuel A., *The Power of Black Music: Interpreting Its History from Africa to the United States* (New York: Oxford University Press, 1995).

Hinson, Glenn, *Fire in My Bones: Transcendence and the Holy Spirit in African American Gospel* (Philadelphia: University of Pennsylvania Press, 2000).

Johnson, Birgitta, '"Oh, For A Thousand Tongues to Sing": Music and Worship in African American Megachurches of Los Angeles, California' (PhD diss., UCLA, 2008).

Meschede, Tatjana, Shapiro, Thomas M., Sullivan, Laura and Wheary, Jennifer, *Economic (In)Security: The Experience of the African-American and Latino Middle Classes*, Institute on Assets and Social Policy (Brandeis University, 2008).

Pollard, Deborah Smith, *When The Church Becomes Your Party: Contemporary Gospel Music* (Detroit: Wayne State University Press, 2008).

Scott, Leonard, *Be Lifted Up! A Call to Lift Up the Mighty Name of Jesus in Praise and Worship* (Mobile, AL: Evergreen Press, 2008).

Smith, James K.A., *Thinking in Tongues: Pentecostal Contributions to Christian Philosophy* (Grand Rapids: William B. Eerdmans Publishing, 2010).

Spencer, Jon Michael, 'African American Religious Music from a Theomusicological Perspective', in Edith Blumhofer, Philip Bohlman and Maria Chow (eds), *Music in American Religious Experience* (New York: Oxford University Press, 2006).

Chapter 2

'Praise Is What We Do': The Rise of Praise and Worship Music in the Black Church in the US

Deborah Smith Pollard

If the young people were allowed to ... take over the church, we would lose Devotion. They think Devotion is a waste of time.

Sister Rosie Sims[1]

Judith Christie McAllister is great ... because she is tied to her past. If you listen to what she does, incorporated in her new stuff, you can hear the sound of old gospel.

Pastor Marvin L. Winans[2]

While the words *praise and worship* individually and collectively have come to have a range of meanings around the world, this chapter focuses on how the phrase is most often utilized within the Black Church[3] and among gospel music singers and fans in the United States. Currently the label 'praise and worship' is used by these groups in reference to a particular musical repertoire and mode of performance that emerged during the last decades of the twentieth century. Generally, praise and worship music is used during the opening period of a church worship service, gospel musical or concert; however, its rising popularity has led to its use at other times as well. In some instances, entire services and events are

---

[1]   Sister Rosie Sims, a member of St John Progressive Baptist Church, Austin, TX, one of the churches studied in Walter F. Pitts, *Old Ship of Zion: The Afro-Baptist Ritual in the African Diaspora* (Oxford University Press, 1993/1996), p. 27.

[2]   Pastor Marvin L. Winans, interview with the author, 14 January 2004.

[3]   *The Black Church* is a term which, according to C. Eric Lincoln and Lawrence Mamiya, has come to replace the term *The Negro Church* which was used by earlier scholars in discussing Christian churches in the US populated by people of African descent. They write: '[We] use the term as do other scholars and much of the general public as a kind of sociological and theological shorthand regarding the pluralism of Black Christian churches ... . In general usage any black Christian person is included in "the Black Church" if he or she is a member of a black congregation.' That is how I use the term in this chapter. See C. Eric Lincoln and Lawrence Mamiya, *The Black Church in the African American Experience* (Duke University Press, 1990), p. 1.

built around praise and worship music. This chapter presents an overview of the history of praise and worship music's proliferation within the Black Church, the recording artists, both Black and White, largely responsible for its introduction, and the ways specific congregations utilize the music. Special attention is given to three churches in Detroit, Michigan, a city known as a major centre for gospel music performed by Black artists.

While it would seem to be a benign set of rituals, especially since it is a church-oriented musical form, praise and worship has created its share of controversies. Some charge that praise and worship has sidelined age-old musical repertoires, along with middle-aged and elderly deacons in some denominations, and placed in the spotlight the under-40 praise team with its new sounds and terminology.

In reality praise and worship is neither as completely new as some would suggest nor as destructive to traditions as others assert. An examination of the music presented and the intentions expressed by those involved in praise and worship in Detroit's Black Churches as well as within the national gospel industry reveals that the perception that there has been a complete generational shift is incorrect. I argue that praise and worship leaders and teams frequently incorporate this genre as a 'new layer'[4] that enhances rather than replaces the African, African American and mainstream Christian rituals that already exist within the Black Church. The result is a devotional mode that meets the spiritual demands and musical needs of many contemporary Black congregations.

Biblical Antecedents of the Devotional/Praise and Worship Service

Although the individual words 'praise' and 'worship' are often spoken as if they are interchangeable, many who teach it or who are acknowledged worship leaders differentiate between the two. Pastor and author Myles Munroe writes that praise means commending, glorifying and otherwise 'putting God in first place'; however, he writes later that 'worship is what praise is all about: seeking God until He graces us with His presence.'[5] Praise and worship music, according to Consuella Smith, an evangelist and praise and worship leader at Greater Christ Temple Church in Detroit, is most often found at the beginning of the worship service so that the Spirit of the Lord can be ushered in. At the same time, worshippers can prepare themselves to experience the presence of God, she explained.[6]

While it is the contemporary Christian Church that has applied this inclusive label 'praise and worship' to a specific set of devotional rituals, the Old and New Testaments are filled with instances of God's people performing acts of praise and worship, often outside of temples or sanctuaries. For example, Leah praises

---

[4]   Carl B. Phillips, telephone interview with the author, 16 Feburary 2005.

[5]   Myles Munroe, *The Purpose and Power of Praise and Worship* (Destiny Image, 2000), p. 62.

[6]   Consuella Smith, personal interview with the author, 22 October 2004.

God when she gives birth to a third son, Judah, she can present to her husband Jacob in Genesis 29:35. Psalms 29, 30 and 47 respectively contain examples of the praises offered to God by David, the descendants of Korah and even anonymous individuals. And in Luke 19:36, the crowds praise God for the miracles they had seen Jesus perform on the day of his triumphal entry into Jerusalem.

The point at which Abraham prepares to sacrifice his son Isaac in Genesis 22:5 is one of the earliest mentions of the word 'worship' in the Old Testament. In Daniel 3, the three young men, usually called the Hebrew Boys within the Christian Church, who refused to bow down to the golden image made by King Nebuchadnezzar, demonstrated their unwillingness to worship anything or anyone other than their own God despite the threat of being thrown into a fiery furnace. In the New Testament, the references to worship include the description of the twenty-four elders who were seated on the throne and then fell on their faces and worshipped God in Revelation 11:16.

Besides these acts of praise and worship, there are a number of terms directly from the Old Testament/Hebrew Bible that have also found their way into the vocabulary of those involved in praise and worship. These terms are often alluded to in the instructions the praise and worship leader gives to the congregation. For example, when the leader says, 'Let's bless the Lord with a sacrifice of praise', she or he is referencing the term '*towdah*'. But almost as frequently, the Hebrew words themselves are included in instructions given to the audience, as in 'Let's *shabach* the Lord!' Some of the most popular praise and worship songs, such as the one entitled 'Shabach', include several Hebrew terms and their definitions within the lyrics, including *shabach* (praise with a loud, exuberant voice), *barak* (bless the Lord by remembering what God has done), *yadah* (praise with extended or raise hands) and others.[7]

The usage of these ancient terms from the Old Testament/Hebrew Bible means, among other things, that this movement within the Christian Church, thought by some practitioners to be the domain of those rebels perceived as bringing something brand new to the worship experience, has in reality pulled terminology to the forefront that is older than Christianity itself.

The Traditional Devotional Service

We cannot look at how praise and worship is practised within the contemporary Black Church without examining its African and African American predecessors. Pearl Williams-Jones provides several reasons for such an examination as she cites

---

[7] Tobias Fox, composer, 'Shabach', Full Gospel Baptist Fellowship, *A New Thing* (GospoCentric, Inc. 1995). Also see Walt Whitman and the Soul Children of Chicago, *Growing Up* (CGI/Platinum Entertainment, 1996) and Byron Cage, *Prince of Praise* (GospoCentric, 2003).

a variety of African retentions within the performance of gospel music.[8] Multiple generations of Africans had been sold and born into slavery before large numbers of slave owners decided to introduce them to Christianity in North America. It was also well into the 1700s that the enslaved Africans embraced Christianity in significant numbers. This slow acceptance was due in part to the fact that many practised the beliefs and rituals that had made the journey with them or their ancestors through the Middle Passage, much to the consternation of those who had tried to bring them the gospel for decades. The ring shout, spirit possession and other ecstatic/religious dance and rituals that existed before the founding of the Black Church, were valued links to a West African heritage that placed these expressive cultural elements at the very centre of life.[9]

Once Africans in America began to accept Christianity, they adapted the religion using their own spiritual and cultural values. This adaptation included giving birth to new musical forms, such as the Negro Spiritual, through which they addressed a range of earthly and heavenly concerns while praising God. Jackie Patillo, formerly General Manager of Integrity Gospel,[10] an industry leader in praise and worship music, says the roots of the genre were within the enslaved Africans: 'Though we have contemporary choruses that people define as praise and worship, I would say that our ancestors had praise and worship in the fields; we call that music "spirituals". Some were prayers asking for help. Some were moans. And some were songs worshipping God and acknowledging his greatness.'[11]

The cultural and religious rituals of these Africans in America persisted, not only during slavery but long after as they created the Black Church.[12] While there are some ceremonies that cross cultural and racial lines within the Christian Church, there are certain other practices that are widely viewed as synonymous with the traditional Black worship experience, even if not all branches of the Black Church include them. Among them is the devotional service, sometimes called 'devotion', which has been the opening segment of the traditional worship in several denominations of the Black Church.

Arthur Paris categorizes the major sub-segments of the typical opening service he observed for his study of the Black Pentecostal worship as opening song(s), scripture reading, requests for prayer, prayer, song service and testimony service.[13]

---

[8]   Pearl Williams-Jones, 'Afro-American Gospel Music: A Crystallization of the Black Aesthetic', *Journal for the Society of Ethnomusicology*, 19/3 (September 1975): pp. 373–85.

[9]   Robert L. Hall, 'African Religious Retentions in Florida', in Joseph E. Holloway (ed.), *Africanisms in American Culture* (Indiana University Press, 1990), pp. 107–11.

[10]   Patillo is currently the executive director of the Gospel Music Association.

[11]   Jackie Patillo, telephone interview with the author, 14 June 2004.

[12]   C. Eric Lincoln and Lawrence H. Mamiya, *The Black Church in the African American Experience* (Duke University Press, 1990), p. 1.

[13]   Arthur Paris, *Black Pentecostalism: Southern Religion in an Urban World* (University of Massachusetts Press, 1982), p. 54.

Similarly, Walter F. Pitts, Jr. writes that within the Afro-Baptist Church tradition, there are two ritual 'frames' or segments, the first of which is the devotional service; it consists of prayers, lined hymns, congregational songs and spirituals that precede the main 'frame' of the service in which the preaching and ecstatic elements of the Black Church ritual are to be found. He has identified these components throughout the African Diaspora and views them as tying disparate Black cultures to the African continent.[14] No matter which combination of building blocks is included, devotion not only signals the start of the service in the churches that practise these rituals, but it prepares the worshippers for the apex of the experience: the point at which the preacher delivers the sermon, or 'The Service of the Word', as Paris has labelled it.

Among the opening music generally found within the devotional service can be congregational songs ('I'm A Soldier in the Army of the Lord', for example), well known, easily sung gospel songs ('He's Sweet I Know'), and centuries-old hymns led or 'lined out' in a call and response mode ('I Love the Lord').

Congregants are expected to participate by singing, listening, testifying and praying silently along with the individuals leading the devotional service. At certain times, the congregation is directed to stand, sit or kneel, and they may be told to perform two or more of these actions during a single song. Though the gospel and congregational songs that are performed during devotional service can be spirited and fast-paced, the lined hymns, part of the Baptist tradition, are generally sung in a manner that is anything but jubilant in sound.[15] Lining out involves one individual, usually a deacon during a regular service, or perhaps a layperson during a testimonial meeting, chanting a line or two of a hymn and ending on a specific pitch. The congregation follows by singing that same passage with some variation on the tune. Practised in North America by early colonists, lining out later became a hallmark of hymn singing in Black churches, perhaps because of its similarities to call and response found throughout the African Diaspora.[16] Pitts observed during his research in the Afro-Baptist Churches that older members were singing along and younger member were often squirming.

The lack of engagement by the younger congregants could be due to the tempo, the fluctuations between major and minor keys, and the unaccompanied nature of the singing. Another reason many of a certain age group may have not gravitated toward these songs is offered by Dorgan Needom, minister of music at Detroit's Unity Baptist Church: 'Today's twenty-first century churchgoer doesn't

---

[14]   Walter Pitts, *Old Ship of Zion: The Afro-Baptist Ritual in the African Diaspora* (Oxford University Press, 1982), pp. 91–131.

[15]   An individual metered hymn that is performed in this style is also referred to as a 'Dr Watts', even if it was not written by Dr Isaac Watts, the prolific English hymn writer of the eighteenth century. The label came to refer to the style, not the composer. See http://www.negrospirituals.com/song.htm.

[16]   Eileen Southern, *The Music of Black Americans: A History* (W.W. Norton, 1997), p. 29.

understand its relevance. Deacons don't take time to explain it; they just [start singing] and expect people to join in.'[17]

Not only were many ignorant of the significance of the rituals, there were probably as many who could not comprehend the actual lyrics as they were being sung with elongated vowels over several beats and measures. Ironically, the old devotional service and the contemporary praise and worship service parallel one another in this area. For just as there were those younger congregants who felt left out of devotion because they did not understand the words being spoken and sung and were not drawn to the traditional music, today there are congregants who have not been schooled in the Hebraic terms, the new lyrics and music, and thus may not be fully engaged by the contemporary praise and worship songs and behaviours. Fortunately, the most skilful and sensitive praise and worship leaders have learned to accommodate these congregants, as will be discussed in the second part of this chapter.

The Emergence of Praise and Worship Music

The praise and worship movement arose, according to Robert R. Redman, among American Pentecostals and charismatics and was one of two 'sweeping changes in Christian worship' during the latter part of the twentieth century.[18] He outlines the worship experience: 'A typical service begins with twenty to thirty minutes or more of congregational singing, led by a worship leader, a band with a small ensemble of singers, and often a choir as well, modelled on the gospel choir in African American churches. Leaders encourage a wide range of physical expressions through clapping, raising hands, swaying and even dancing.'[19] The praise and worship services include 'participatory' sermons and Contemporary Worship Music (CWM), which is a considerable departure from traditional multi-verse hymns in that the songs are shorter and more focused on single themes or images. This allows the congregation to quickly learn and repeat the lines as is typical with praise and worship songs.[20] Another feature of this service may be 'singing in the Spirit' which the leader may encourage at the end of a quiet song if he or she wishes the congregation to focus on God's presence.[21]

---

[17]   Dorgan Needom, telephone interview with the author, 25 August 2004.

[18]   Robert R. Redman, 'Welcome to the Worship Awakening', *Theology Today*, 58/3 (Oct. 2001): pp. 369–83.

[19]   Redman, 'Welcome to the Worship Awakening', p. 369.

[20]   Redman, 'Welcome to the Worship Awakening', p. 369.

[21]   Redman describes 'singing in the spirit' this way: 'The last phrase or line of the song may be repeated several times as a way of setting up what follows, then one musician (often the keyboardist) will repeat a two or three chord progression, creating a drone-like musical effect. The congregation takes over singing freely either in tongues or repeating a phrase in English. This can last for a few minutes or until the worship leaders feel led to end it.' Redman, 'Welcome to the Worship Awakening', pp. 376–7.

Artists such as Twila Paris, Keith Green, Andrae Crouch, the 2nd Chapter of Acts and Danny Lee and the Children of Truth were performing music in the 1970s that could easily be called praise and worship music today. By 1981, there was a large enough pool of recording artists producing praise and worship music that the Gospel Music Association (GMA), whose artists primarily sing Contemporary Christian Music (CCM), presented its first Dove Awards in that category.[22]

The Praise and Worship Movement Grows

At the time the GMA initially created this category, the majority of those who were being nominated were white artists who performed for white congregations and consumers. Eventually there would be black singers, such as Alvin Slaughter, Ron Kenoly, Bob Bailey and Larnelle Harris, who would also perform in that style for predominately white audiences. Three different factors converged in order for the majority of black audiences to be exposed to praise and worship music. First, black churches heard the music via various media, including Christian television, movies, and radio. Second, several black artists, such as Min. Thomas Whitfield, West Angeles Church of God in Christ and Richard Smallwood performed and recorded praise and worship style music, even before most of their core audience was familiar with that designation. Third, record companies that specialized in the genre, including Maranatha! and Integrity, emerged and disseminated the music widely.[23]

How Praise and Worship Is Incorporated within the Black Church

Detractors see praise and worship music as a style threatening to replace the older gospel song repertoire; however, a closer examination of two influential gospel musicians shows that their approach to praise and worship is markedly eclectic, and that it often coexists with traditional songs and styles on gospel musicians' recordings.

Many praise and worship artists use a range of styles, creating songs that can combine 'world music', 'rhythm and praise',[24] hip hop, rock and/or other contemporary styles. In this category, of course, is Israel Houghton, whose music

---

[22]   The list of the artists who have won the Dove (now GMA) Award for praise and worship album of the year can be found on the GMW website: http://www.gmamusicawards. com/history/browse.cfm?cid=39.

[23]   Maranatha! Music, 'About Us', http://maranathamusic.com/about, accessed 22 October 2012; Integrity Media promotional materials, 2003–2004.

[24]   Anson and Eric Dawkins, who coined the term 'rhythm and praise' explain: 'Gospel rhythm and blues is an oxymoron .... So we wanted to have rhythm and praise.' It reflects what artists 'with a hip hop, R&B, urban flavor are doing'. Mark Christian Tilles, 'Interview', *Gospelflava.com* (1999).

is described by LaTonya Taylor as 'an eclectic, almost un-classifiable blend of Christian pop, gospel, worship, and other influences'.[25] Because their music is culturally expansive, Israel and New Breed point out in the song called 'I Hear the Sound' that trying to categorize what they do is difficult since it goes beyond racial musical profiling:

> It ain't a black thing
> It ain't a white thing
> It ain't a colored thing
> It's a kingdom thing[26]

They declare themselves to be 'a new breed' of worshipper and Christian warrior. They project a similar message that defines their identity in the chant found in 'Come in from the Outside':

> We're the generation
> That will give You praise and adoration
> Let Your kingdom come
> Let Your will be done
> Establish now Your throne, oh my Lord[27]

Here, they appear to draw a generational line in the proverbial sand – 'We're going to praise God in a way our forefathers did not.' That is what they appear to do, until we listen and look carefully at the refrain that follows:

> O my Lord
> Lord, Lord, Lord
> Praise You Lord
> Lord, Lord, Lord
> We love You Lord
> Lord, Lord, Lord
> O my Lord

The refrain, 'Oh my Lord, Lord, Lord', one of thousands of communally-created phrases and refrains within the Black sacred repertoire, first came to the attention of most movie fans in the 1989 release 'Glory', which is set in the 1860s during the Civil War. In the film, the refrain serves as a bridge between spoken testimonies by Black soldiers as well as a plea to The Almighty as the men willingly face possible annihilation in order to be seen by society as Black *men* fighting for their own freedom.

---

[25] LaTonya Taylor, 'Breaking Barriers', ChristianityToday.com (19 January 2004).

[26] Israel and New Breed, *Live from Another Level* (Integrity Gospel, 2004).

[27] Israel and New Breed, *Live from Another Level*.

As Israel and New Breed repeat the refrain, its melody, which they initially sing as simply as the Black soldiers perform it in the movie, takes on the complexity that is a hallmark of their contemporary sound. But their stacked, intricate harmonies in no way negate the fact that a centuries-old refrain is embedded within it. On the same CD, the infectious 'Friend of God' praise and worship song and chant leads to a 'Friend' medley that includes two of the venerable hymns of Christianity, 'No Not One' and 'What a Friend We Have in Jesus.'[28] That medley flows into several minutes of 'singing in the Spirit' in which audience and artists eventually move into spontaneous sounds of adoration that can often arise during a praise and worship experience. More importantly, it is the combination of the so-called old school and new school that brings this audience to a moment of high worship.

Fred Hammond, the acclaimed Detroit-based composer/musician/singer/ producer, does something similar as he juxtaposes traditional devotional songs and contemporary praise and worship music on CD's and in live performance settings. One of his most popular recordings of the last decade is 'Jesus Be a Fence', a traditional gospel song composed by Sam Cooke in the days when he was with the gospel quartet The Soul Stirrers. Hammond first recorded it on Bishop Carlton Pearson's *Live at Azusa III* (Integrity Music, 1999). He re-recorded it for Verity Records in 2000 on his own CD entitled *Purpose by Design* where it is listed among songs more readily placed within the praise and worship category, such as 'You Are the Living Word'.

Praise and Worship in Detroit's Churches

Based on what I have witnessed personally and have documented for this study, that 'sound of old gospel' is being incorporated in a number of Detroit's Black Churches that utilize praise and worship music. The responses provided by thirty-seven Detroit-area church musicians and ministers of music who completed my informal survey also reflect this mix of traditional and contemporary forms.[29] Almost eighty-four per cent (84%) reported that praise and worship music is performed during their worship services; 67% use it during all of their worship services, and 16% use it during most of them. That is virtually the same percentage (87.5%) that reported that traditional music is used at every service (75%) or at most services (12.50%).

---

[28]   Israel and New Breed, *Live from Another Level*.

[29]   On 10 September 2004, the co-founders of the Detroit Musicians' Fellowship allowed me to distribute my survey on the use of praise and worship music during the annual dinner. Although almost half of those present were serving at Baptist Churches, the balance represented a range of other denominations – Church of God in Christ, Disciples of Christ, Methodist (AME and UMC), Pentecostal, United Church of Christ, Spiritual – and non-denominational. Because of that diversity and the age range of those present, the results are another means of assessing the extent to which praise and worship music is used in Detroit's Black Churches.

This combination of the old and the new is also being duplicated in the churches specifically monitored for this research, Greater Christ Temple Church, Perfecting Church and St. James Missionary Baptist Church.[30] Though only one service is documented here for each, I have attended other services and events at these churches and at numerous others in the area which mirror what is reported here.

Praise and Worship at Greater Christ Temple Church

Greater Christ Temple Church, located in Ferndale, Michigan, is led by Bishop Carl E. Holland who became the congregation's pastor in 1969, five years after it was founded. The church was originally affiliated with the Pentecostal Assemblies of the World (P.A.W.). But in 2000 Bishop Holland founded the Pentecostal Assembly of Believers, Inc., consisting of churches in Michigan, Alabama, Georgia and Tennessee.

Carl B. Phillips, a former gospel radio announcer, is the minister of music for Christ Temple and for the denomination. He describes a watershed moment in 1998 that led to incorporating the new genre at Christ Temple: 'The choir was singing Kirk Franklin's "Now Behold the Lamb" and a spirit of praise and worship was created.'[31] Phillips wanted to see that the spirit envelop the church on a regular basis, so he asked the pastor's permission to slowly bring praise and worship to the church. He began with well-known gospel songs, such as 'God Is' and 'Can't Stop Praising His Name', as well as the music of Fred Hammond and Thomas Whitfield.[32]

Today, the church has five praise and worship leaders, each assigned to a different Sunday. According to Phillips, the two female worship leaders, who are also ministers, utilize more hymns and gospel songs; he and Evangelist Consuella Smith use a combination of contemporary praise and worship songs and traditional gospel music on their respective Sundays while the fifth and youngest leader uses almost all contemporary praise and worship songs.

Sunday morning worship is at 11:30 am, Bible Study is Wednesday at 7:30 pm, and choir rehearsals on Tuesday and Thursday evenings. The Praise and worship team rehearses monthly. The Sunday morning and evening services begin with praise and worship, as do revival services. Sunday night differs slightly, however, in that the opening period includes testimony service as well. All other church meetings and rehearsals begin with prayer.[33] To insure that the entire membership understands praise and worship, Evangelist Smith teaches its concepts and

---

[30]   In 2005, St James Baptist Church was renamed Shield of Faith Ministries. However, without any intention of disregarding this new designation, it will be referred to as St James within this text since the national recording history that drew me to investigate it as well as the fact that the research referenced here was completed while it was known as St James.

[31]   Kirk Franklin, 'Now Behold the Lamb', *Kirk Franklin: Christmas* (GospoCentric Records, 1995).

[32]   Carl B. Phillips, personal interview with the author, 22 October 2004.

[33]   Consuella Smith, telephone interview with the author, 23 March 2005.

terminology to the new converts; she was at the time of the research, one of the praise and worship leaders and the administrative assistant to the Bishop.

The Sunday morning worship I documented on 12 December 2002 is an excellent example of how praise and worship is conducted at Greater Christ Temple. The service began at 11:30 am with prayer by one of the church's ministers; it has been the custom at Greater Christ for the ministers, not the deacons, to handle the opening devotional services. This particular prayer included petitions for the worship service, the congregation and the pastor. The five-person praise and worship team for that Sunday at Greater Christ Temple began their portion of the service at 11:42. The worship leader, Evangelist Smith, began with an adapted Christmas carol, 'O Come All Ye Faithful', with additional verses that have been sung in the Black Church for decades ('For He Alone is Worthy', 'O Come and Lift Him Higher').

This seasonal song was followed by several praise and worship songs, 'With my Hands Lifted Up (and My Mouth Filled with Praise)', 'None Like You', and 'Lord, I Lift Your Name on High', one of the most popular songs of the genre, along with devotional songs 'Jesus, I'll Never Forget', 'There's A Storm Out on the Ocean', and the traditional gospel song 'Can't [Cain't] Nobody Do Me Like Jesus'.

Evangelist Smith selected music that conveyed a sense of the holiday season while simultaneously involving the congregation in the worship experience by including something for the varied musical tastes represented within the congregation: praise and worship music, traditional devotional music and gospel songs. As she explains it: 'Our congregation is in transition. Therefore your praise and worship has to be inclusive of music for a variety of ages and tastes.'[34] Her selections also coincide with the desires of Bishop Holland that the congregation maintain the hymns and apostolic music traditions.[35] Consequently, they are not only interwoven into most of the praise and worship segments, but they constitute the majority of what the congregation sings during the balance of the service.

Praise and Worship at Saint James Missionary Baptist Church

The St James Baptist Church was officially founded in 1921, but it was under the leadership of their third pastor, the Rev. W.C. Barnett (1938–72), that the church, then located on Mt Elliott and Pulford, earned its national reputation as the St James Young Adult Choir (later the St James Adult Choir) and released recordings that captured the sound and feel of the Black Baptist gospel choir. The church's organist at that time, Charles H. Nicks, Jr., later became its fourth pastor (1972–89). He and minister of music Jimmy 'J.D.' Dowell led the choir through their popular 'O Give Thanks' Thanksgiving week concerts, buzz-worthy Sunday night musicals, appearances before and with national and international figures,

---

[34] Consuella Smith, telephone interview, 16 June 2005.
[35] Carl B. Phillips, personal interview, 19 October 2004.

and recordings that were embraced throughout the gospel music community.[36] The current pastor, The Rev Dr James A. Jennings, Jr, who was installed in 1990, moved the church to its present location on Van Dyke in Detroit. He also changed the name to Shield of Faith Ministries. The reported membership at the time of my fieldwork was 3000.

The service I analysed at the St James Missionary Baptist Church was their annual Watch Night Service of 31 December 2002/1 January 2003.[37] That evening was filled with a mix of traditional gospel, congregational songs, and contemporary praise and worship music. Marcus Jennings and a team of six singers led the praise and worship service, which began at 9:07 pm. An organist and a drummer provided accompaniment for the three praise and worship songs: 'He Is Good', 'Let Jesus Fill This Place' and 'Wonderful (Yes He Is)'.

Next, minister of music Dowell introduced a children's liturgical dance troupe of six that performed to Fred Hammond's version of 'Jesus Be a Fence' discussed earlier. Two adult liturgical dancers followed the children, using a gospel-influenced version of the hymn 'O, To Be Kept'. Praise and worship ended with an upbeat congregational song, 'This Morning When I Rose', directed by Dowell.

As with the other spotlighted churches, both long-standing traditional songs and praise and worship songs were performed; the congregation was exhorted to offer praises to God orally and physically, regardless of the type of music being introduced at the time. Minister Jennings recalled during our interview that in his early days of introducing the form, there were senior members of the congregation who asked him to teach the praise and worship team specific traditional devotional songs they loved and missed. He admitted that his first response was a silent but emphatic 'no'. But after listening to pastor and recording artist Bishop Carlton Pearson explain that some of the older members will never become fans of praise and worship and that they need to be reached where they are, Jennings began to include more traditional songs.[38]

Praise and Worship at Perfecting Church

Perfecting Church is perhaps the best known of the three churches in the study because of the fame of its founder and pastor, Marvin L. Winans, singer, composer,

---

[36]   Read more about the Reverend Nicks, St James Baptist Church and their contributions to gospel music at http://museum.msu.edu/museum/tes/gospel/nicks.htm.

[37]   Watch Night Service is held in Black Churches across the country on December 31 as believers praise God for seeing them through the old year and ask for protection in the new one. But apparently the roots of the service can be traced to several non-religious occurrences of the 1800s. See John Hope Franklin, *Emancipation Proclamation* (Harlan Davidson, 1963/1995). Also see these websites: http://www.thestate.com/mld/thestate/news/local/4838480.htm; http://www.wsbrec-.org/blackfacts/WatchNight.htm; http://www.the state.com/mld/thestate/news/local/4838480.htm.

[38]   Marcus Jennings, personal interview, 2 January 2003.

musician and member of the Grammy Award-winning Winans family of Detroit. He also became noted in 2012 for preaching the eulogy for Whitney Houston. He held the initial meeting for Perfecting Church in the basement of his home with eight individuals, but the first official service for the church occurred at the Michigan Inn in Southfield, Michigan, on 27 May 1989. Because of the non-denominational church's rapid growth, the congregation moved several times before settling into their present edifice on E. Nevada in Detroit in March of 1996. The congregation's reported membership is 3000, a sizeable percentage of whom have taken some college courses or have earned college degrees and a median age between 30 and 40.[39]

Pastor Winans instituted praise and worship at Perfecting after he took a trip to Holland in 1990; there he heard a multicultural congregation perform `Lord, I Lift Your Name on High' for the first time. He knew immediately upon hearing it that he was going to bring it to Perfecting Church. Although pastoral duties are his primary focus, Marvin Winans continues not only to set policy for what music will be sung, but he participates in praise and worship, often playing the electronic piano and introducing a variety of songs during that part of the service just as he does throughout the rest of the worship experience. Perfecting has embraced praise and worship extensively as exemplified by the fact that all church services as well as the Bible Studies begin with it. The church has also devoted entire weekends to exploring praise and worship and related topics, with invited speakers, classes and a master songwriting course taught by Pastor Winans.[40]

Randy Short, the Director of the Department of Praise and Worship, oversees fifty individuals whose backgrounds range from having travelled the world as professional gospel singers to having served solely in the local church. There are two praise and worship leaders; the rest of the singers serve on six teams consisting of three sopranos, three altos and three tenors. The six-piece band that accompanies them includes organist, keyboardist, drummer, percussionist, bass and lead guitarists.

Perfecting Church's Tuesday evening Bible Study is conducted with virtually the same elements as their Sunday morning worship which is why a description of the Bible Study held on Tuesday, 12 August 2003, is indicative of how praise and worship music is utilized there. Pastor Winans came to the podium at 8 pm and led the congregation in the praise and worship song 'I Love You Lord', after which the praise team and leader took over with two more praise and worship songs, 'Hallelujah You're Worthy' and 'Shout unto God with the Voices of Triumph (Clap Those Hands, O Ye People)'. The exhortations from the praise

---

[39]   Pastor Marvin L. Winans, interview with the author, 14 January 2004. The Perfecting Church's website with more information on the church is www.perfectingchurch.org.

[40]   Beverly Ferguson (AKA 'Squeeze'), telephone interview with the author, 9 March 2005. The Member Auxiliary Coordinator for Perfecting Church, her duties include coordinating the annual Praise and Worship weekend.

and worship leader were placed between songs, just as they would be during the traditional devotional service.

Just before beginning the lesson/sermon for the evening, Pastor Winans led the congregation in the hymn 'Great Is Thy Faithfulness'. Because it contains lyrics that are as reverential as those of the more contemporary songs that were sung earlier ('Thou changest not, Thy compassions, they fail not'), the placement of this hymn before the most sacred moment of the worship experience is testament to the pastor's appreciation for a wide range of musical genres and his determination to make that eclectic mix a hallmark of Perfecting. Short elaborates: 'Pastor Winans has set an order for worship service. Our worship leaders incorporate hymns, praise and worship music in our services. We know what is expected in terms of musical content, so we choose music that edifies, speaks the truth, exhorts, and worships God.'[41] Pastor Winans later summarized the inclusive nature of the music that is offered: 'Again, Perfecting is different in that we'll go from "The Lord Is My Light" to "Halle, Halle, Hallelou". I mean, we'll go from the islands to slavery to Holland without missing a beat.'[42]

Closing Comments on Praise and Worship in the Black Church

Clearly, this model in which praise and worship music is intertwined with traditional songs can be found in a growing percentage of The Black Church. The reasons offered by the praise and worship leaders at the three churches profiled – a pastor's insistence that the traditional songs not be discarded, another pastor's penchant for mixing a variety of genres, and a praise and worship leader's sensitivity to the requests of the older members – provide insights into why the inclusive model is utilized in many congregations. Randy Short offers another explanation:

> The Bible speaks of not destroying the old landmarks. I don't believe you can just remove traditional music from worship service[s]. Modernize it, update it, whatever, but don't get rid of it . ... Revelation of praise and worship gives a better understanding of traditional music. I know why my mother and grandmother sang [those songs]. It gave them hope![43]

There are, of course, other models for incorporating this music, from using it exclusively to not using it at all.[44] But whichever model is utilized, this element is clearly something more than a 'fad' if the word means that which comes in and

---

[41]   Randy Short, email to the author, 5 May 2004.

[42]   Pastor Marvin L. Winans, 4 January 2004.

[43]   Randy Short, email to the author, 5 May 2004.

[44]   For discussion of Black churches that have resisted using praise and worship music in their services, see Deborah Smith Pollard, *When the Church Becomes Your Party: Contemporary Gospel Music* (Wayne State University Press, 2008), pp. 50–51.

leaves quickly. Gospel record stores have sections devoted to this music form, and in many, such as Detroit's God's World Store, it has been the best selling form since 2002, according to storeowner Larry Robinson. But since total sales for urban influenced gospel will usually be higher, there is clearly more to be considered in assessing the acceptance of praise and worship music than its ranking in the marketplace.

Those who would comprehend the widespread incorporation of the genre might want to turn their gaze to the church itself. There, they will find praise teams and congregations engaged in worship using music from top-selling recording artists, but they are also likely to hear the sounds that have been part of the Black Church experience for generations, evidence that despite the presence of innovation, there remains a place for 'the sound of old gospel',[45] at least for now.

References

Dove Award/GMA Award Winners: praise and worship album of the year category, http://christianmusic.about.com/od/doves/tp/doveworshiphistory. htm, accessed 22 October 2012.

Franklin, John Hope, *Emancipation Proclamation 1963* (Wheeling, IL: Harlan Davidson, 1995).

Franklin, Kirk, 'Now Behold the Lamb', *Kirk Franklin: Christmas* (GospoCentric Records, 1995).

Hall, Robert L., 'African Religious Retentions in Florida', in Joseph E. Holloway (ed.), *Africanisms in American Culture* (Bloomington: Indiana University Press, 1990).

Hammond, Fred, *Purpose by Design* (Verity Gospel, 2000).

Israel and New Breed, *Live from Another Level* (Integrity Gospel, 2004).

Integrity Media, promotional materials (2003–2004).

Lacy, Dwayne, 'Fred Hammond Worship Alive Concert Recap, October 10, 2004 in Houston, Texas', http://goo.gl/QVpA2, accessed 26 June 2005.

Lincoln, C. Eric and Mamiya, Lawrence, *The Black Church in the African American Experience* (Durham: Duke University Press, 1990).

McAllister, Judith Christie, 'This Is the Day', *Send Judah First* (Judah Music Records, 2001).

Maranatha! Music, 'About Us', http://maranathamusic.com/about, accessed 22 October 2012.

Munroe, Myles, *The Purpose and Power of Praise & Worship* (Shippensburg, PA: Destiny Image, 2000).

'Negro Spirituals', http://www.negrospirituals.com/song.htm, accessed 6 May 2005.

Nicks, Reverend Charles H, *Lest We Forget: Legends of Detroit Gospel,* http://museum.msu.edu/-museum/tes/gospel/nicks.htm, accessed 5 November 2004,

---

45   Marvin Winans, interview with the author, 2004.

Paris, Arthur, *Black Pentecostalism: Southern Religion in an Urban World* (Amherst: University of Massachusetts Press, 1982).

Pearson, Carlton, *Live at Azusa III* (Integrity Music, 1999).

'Perfecting Church', www.perfectingchurch.org, accessed June 2004.

Pollard, Deborah Smith, *When the Church Becomes Your Party: Contemporary Gospel Music* (Detroit: Wayne State University Press, 2008).

Pitts, Walter F., *Old Ship of Zion: The Afro-Baptist Ritual in the African Diaspora* (New York: Oxford University Press, 1993/1996).

Redman, Robert R., 'Welcome to the Worship Awakening', *Theology Today*, 58/3 (Oct. 2001): 369–83.

'Shabach', recorded by The Full Gospel Baptist Fellowship Mass Choir, *A New Thing: Experience the Fullness* (GospoCentric, 1995).

'Shabach', recorded by Walt Whitman and the Soul Children of Chicago, *Growing Up* (CGI Records, 1991).

Short, Randy, email to the author, May 5, 2004.

Southern, Eileen, *The Music of Black Americans: A History*, 3rd ed. (New York: W.W. Norton, 1971/1997).

Taylor, LaTonya, 'Breaking Barriers', *ChristianityToday.com*, http://goo.gl/TY23M, accessed 4 March 2005.

Tilles, Mark Christian, 'Interview with Dawkins and Dawkins', http://www.gospelflava.com/articles/-dawkins.html, accessed 24 April 2005.

Watch Night Service, http://www.thestate.com/mld/thestate/news/local/4838480.htm; http://www.wsbrec-.org/blackfacts/WatchNight.htm; http://www.thestate.com/mld/thestate/news/local/4838480.htm

Williams-Jones, Pearl, 'Afro-American Gospel Music: A Crystallization of the Black Aesthetic', *Journal for the Society of Ethnomusicology*, 19/3 (September 1975): 373–85.

Interviews

Paul, Allen, personal interview, Detroit, Michigan, 21 January 2004.

Ferguson, Beverly, telephone interview, 9 March 2005.

Jennings, Marcus, personal interview, Detroit, Michigan, 2 January 2003.

Needom, Dorgan, telephone interview, 25 August 2004.

Patillo, Jackie, telephone interview, 14 June 2004.

Phillips, Carl B., telephone interview, 19 October 2004.

Phillips, Carl B., personal interview, Detroit, Michigan, 22 October 2004.

Smith, Consuella, personal interview, 22 October 2004.

Smith, Consuella, telephone interview, 16 February 2005.

Smith, Consuella, telephone interview, 23 March 2005.

Smith, Consuella, telephone interview, 16 June 2005.

Winans, Marvin L., personal interview, Detroit, Michigan, 14 January 2004.

Chapter 3

Tune Your Music to Your Heart: Reflections for Church Music Leaders

June Boyce-Tillman

Tune thy music to thy heart
Sing thy joy with thanks, and so thy sorrow;
Though devotion needs not art
Sometimes of the poor, the rich may borrow.

John Dowland

The question this chapter addresses is how 'tuning music to the heart' in the context of church worship might best be done. One of the dilemmas related to musical value is illustrated by a story told of John Wesley in a lecture in 1862:

> One good man sang out of tune, to the offence of Mr Wesley's delicate ear, 'George' said he 'you do not sing in tune.' The man stopped but soon began again. The rebuke was repeated, 'Please, sir, I sing with my heart,' was the sufficient reply. 'Then sing on'. Said Mr W.[1]

This anecdote contrasts singing in tune and singing with the heart, with Wesley ultimately evaluating the latter as the more important of the two. How do different value systems play out in a church community context? The act of singing in ritual collective contexts has been acknowledged as vital to the transformational power of congregational music. In the passage above, George's singing was 'out of tune' harmonically but was in tune with his emotional world. This chapter explores the complexity of musicking and how the totality of the experience needs to be taken into account by those in charge, particularly clergy and music leaders. Like Wesley, we need to recognize that the ultimate goal of hymnody is that the singers, subjects and songs all must be 'in tune'. I will argue that the performed theology of singing in church must be sufficiently in tune with the thinking/singing of a church community to enable spiritual nurture and growth. This chapter is written as a practice-as-research[2]

---

[1]   Quoted in Timothy Dudley-Smith, *A House of Praise: Collected Hymns 1961-2001* (Oxford University Press, 2003), ix.

[2]   R. Nelson, 'Modes of Practice-as-Research Knowledge and their Place in the Academy', in L. Allegue, B. Kershaw, S. Jones and A. Piccini (eds), *Practice-as-Research in Performance and Screen* (Palgrave, 2009), pp. 112–31.

reflection by a female Anglican priest/hymnwriter. My faith was nurtured by rural Anglicanism, fed by Oxford University Anglicanism, and influenced by experimental Methodist ministry in Notting Hill – after the late-1950s Race Riots, when folk music in worship was becoming popular. Later, as a leader of an Anglican church in South London during the time in which pressure to ordain women in Anglicanism and Roman Catholicism was growing, my musical and religious experiences combined worship in an urban Anglican context with the development of small, in general, private, feminist liturgical groups. This chapter's frame is that of John Dewey[3] who saw art as experience with the aesthetic residing in collaboration between the experienced and experiencer rather than as an essential property of the work of art itself. I will examine how the power of congregational song is created within the context of liturgy and the factors that influence this. This approach draws attention to the totality of the experience rather than simply the notated music (the subject of traditional musicology) or the context (the focus of sociology). I will use Christopher Small's term musicking to describe the use of singing in liturgical contexts:

> To music is to take part, in any capacity, in a musical performance, whether by performing, by listening, by rehearsing or practicing, by providing material for performance ... or by dancing .... It is *de*scriptive, not *pre*scriptive .... It takes place in a physical and a social setting ... [with it] we can ask the wider and more interesting question: *What's really going on?*[4]

Small helpfully sees the experience as one of encounter, an aspect that I have explored elsewhere in relation to the work of Martin Buber.[5] For, as Small has pointed out:

> The act of musicking establishes in the place where it is happening a set of relationships, and it is in those relationships that the meaning of the act lies. They are thought to be found not only between those organized sounds which are conventionally thought of as being the stuff of musical meaning but also between the people taking part, in whatever capacity, in the performance; and they model, or stand as metaphor for, ideal relationships as the participants in the performance imagine them to be: relationships between person and person, between individual and society, between humanity and the natural world and even perhaps the supernatural world.[6]

---

[3]   John Dewey, *Art as Experience* (Minton Balch and Co., 1934).

[4]   Christopher Small, *Musicking: The Meanings of Performing and Listening* (Wesleyan University Press, 1998), pp. 19–23.

[5]   June Boyce-Tillman, 'Music as Spiritual Experience', *Modern Believing: Church and Society*, 47/3 (July 2006): pp. 20–31; June Boyce-Tillman, *A Rainbow to Heaven* (Stainer and Bell, 2006); June Boyce-Tillman, *Unconventional Wisdom* (Equinox, 2007).

[6]   Small, *Musicking*, p. 30.

This chapter pulls these threads of the complex musical experience together using my own research and varied participation in the area of congregational singing that I hope practitioners within Christian congregational musicking will find helpful.[7]

Musicking as Performed Theology

In congregational singing in the Church of England and beyond, we employ a combination of poetry and music intended for public communal performance. C.S. Lewis calls hymns 'an extreme case of literature as an applied art'.[8] Or, in the words of liturgist Linda Clark, a hymn can be understood as 'a highly complex set of images, both verbal and aural, set in motion through singing'.[9] The hymn's existence as a composite art is both a source of considerable power and tension. The combination of words and music has sometimes produced a conflict of values. As Jenkins has conceded:

> Reason demands that the text of the hymn is of primary importance in all contexts and the music is secondary. But long practice, experience and human nature decree otherwise. The success, the memorability and the popularity of the hymn ... are almost invariably due to its music.[10]

But the hymn is not merely a potent combination of music and text that exists on the page; it is embodied in performance. As Linda Clark memorably puts it, 'A hymn does not *tell of* the faith, it *tells* it, declares it, bodies it forth.'[11] Because of this, the hymn/chant/song requires sufficient commitment on the part of the assembled congregation to engage in the performative act of singing.[12] Although the communally-said parts of worship in a formal liturgical tradition such as Anglicanism have a similar function, the act of singing requires an increased level

---

[7] For additional reflections on the connections between music and spirituality, see Boyce-Tillman, 'Music as Spiritual Experience'; Boyce-Tillman, *A Rainbow to Heaven*; Boyce-Tillman, *Unconventional Wisdom*.

[8] C.S. Lewis, *The Clark Lectures* (Clarendon Press, 1944), p. 105.

[9] Linda J. Clark, *Music in Churches: Nourishing Your Congregation's Musical Life* (The Alban Institute, 1994), p. 5.

[10] Kathryn Jenkins, *Redefining the Hymn: The Performative Context, Occasional Paper Third Series* 4 (Hymn Society of Britain and Ireland, 2010), pp. 9–10.

[11] Clark, *Music in Churches*, pp. 6–7.

[12] Harry Eskew, 'Hymns in the Church's Teaching Ministry'. This article was originally given as a faculty address at New Orleans Baptist Theological Seminary and subsequently published in spring 1978 issue of *Theological Educator*, the journal of the seminary faculty. http://singwithunderstanding.com/wp-content/uploads/2012/06/hymns-in-the-church.pdf, accessed 20 August 2008.

of bodily engagement. This may be the underlying meaning of the oft-quoted encouragement of Augustine of Hippo: 'Those who sing pray twice.'

The intensity of the embodied theological experience means that the theology of sung texts enters the being of the participant in a very significant way. It moves the interpersonal into the intrapersonal. It is for this reason that hymn writers such as Isaac Watts often see teaching as important in their work. In Watts's day, hymns were then often learned by heart.[13]

Their role of the hymn in spiritual formation makes the theology of the sung text of immense significance. However, in some traditions, like in many English Anglican churches, older hymns are often used to the exclusion of the new because they are considered easier to sing. As a result, hymnody does not keep up with contemporary theological developments. Congregations may unwittingly be affirming theological tenets that they no longer believe or replicating discourses now understood as problematic in their songs. Recently John Hull, in dealing with developments in the theology of disability, highlighted how damaging hymn texts can be for blind people where blindness is seen as a metaphor for failing to perceive the Gospel fully. Hull suggested changing the last line of the first verse of 'Amazing Grace' to:

> I once was lost and now am found
> Was bound and now am free.[14]

An understanding of singing as performed theology demands awareness of the sensitivities within congregations as a necessary skill for those managing musicking in congregational contexts. If particular groups feel excluded by the words, including the metaphors, in sung texts, the musicking will not create the desired sense of community.

Musicking as Communal Engagement

In his analysis of ritual, Victor Turner developed the notion of *communitas* – a shared experience that takes the participants out of everyday life into a liminal space; because of its powers of nourishment and purification, ritual is potentially transformative.[15] Similarly, psychiatrist Anthony Storr describes the main purpose of music in human society as being to create community.[16] The experience of unity that music enables is not only between the human participants but also between

---

[13]   Eskew, 'Hymns in the Church's Teaching Ministry'.

[14]   John Hull, speaking at the *Opening the Roof* conference, St Martin-in-the-Fields, 20 October 2012.

[15]   Turner, Victor, *The Ritual Process: Structure and Anti-structure* (Penguin Books, 1969/1974).

[16]   Anthony Storr, *Music and the Mind* (HarperCollins, 1993).

humans and the Divine. Hildegard of Bingen sees this unity as uniting heaven and earth:

> Music is the echo of the glory and beauty of heaven.
> And in echoing that glory and beauty, it carries human praise back to heaven.[17]

Lois Holzman, drawing on Vygotsky, sets out the notion of 'people collectively constructing environments in which to act on the world'.[18] This chapter examines some of the domains that have to be explored to enable such an environment to be created. In this way, music becomes part of the formative environment in which people are transformed in order to bring about transformation in the world. Ideally, this is what a church community is.

An Evaluative Frame for Musical Experience

We have seen that musicking is both performed theology and unifying ritual; Christian clergy and music leaders must take care to perform the theology that accurately reflects the beliefs of the church and in order to promote unity rather than division. The rest of the chapter will put forth a practical frame which music leaders and clergy can use to understand and evaluate the totality of musical experience in worship. Over the course of my own research and praxis, I have drawn a phenomenographic[19] map of the musical experience identifying four main domains:[20]

- Expression – the perceived emotional/feelingful content of the musical event
- Materials – what is used to make the sound
- Construction – the way form is structured
- Values – the ethics embraced by a particular church community

The model sees all these domains as interacting to create the musical experience in its entirety. Church leaders need to pay attention to each element in order that the transformational character of hymn singing may be enhanced.

Expression

For many theorists and music lovers, emotional expression is the heart of the musical experience: as philosopher Suzanne Langer wrote, 'music is a tonal

---

[17] Robert Van der Weyer (ed.), *Hildegard in a Nutshell* (Hodder and Stoughton, 1997).

[18] Lois Holzman, *Vygotsky at Work and Play* (Taylor and Francis, 2008).

[19] Ference Marton and Shirley Booth, *Learning and Awareness* (Lawrence Erlbaum Associates Publishers, 1997).

[20] Boyce-Tillman, *Unconventional Wisdom*.

analogue of emotive life.'[21] The expressive domain is concerned with the evocation of mood, emotion (individual or corporate), images, memories and atmosphere on the part of all those involved in the musical performance. These expressions may be very various, since music is able to 'give rise to a complex and infinite web of interpretants',[22] and the subjectivity of composer/author and the congregation members intersect powerfully. There is much debate in this area, but I am in the position of Lucy Green, who sees feelingful meaning as residing partly in the music itself (in such areas as speed and volume) and partly in the minds of the musickers.[23] (The way in which these may or may not operate transculturally is a matter for longer debate than this chapter allows.)

For our purposes, congregational singing is an area where the congregation member often brings extrinsic meaning to the music – that is, expressive meaning drawn from the congregation members' previous experiences. Extrinsic meaning is an immensely important component and often associated with hymns learned in childhood, a stage where useful tools for managing adult life can be learned.[24] So hymnody becomes a form of folk poetry passing on wisdom in a way that will only be fully comprehended in adult life. This is also true of hymns that are associated with significant rites of passage. Hymns like 'Praise My Soul the King of Heaven' often have many associations both beautiful and difficult for the generation of English Anglicans born in the first half of the twentieth century when it was often associated with events like baptisms and weddings.

Despite their communal use, many hymns are concerned with the feeling of personal devotion of the author with much use of the personal pronouns 'I', 'me' and 'my', exemplified in the Lutheran traditions of the seventeenth century with hymns like Johann Scheffler's (1624–77) 'O Love Who Formedst Me to Wear' with the powerful line of personal faith: 'O Love, I give myself to thee.'[25] This hymn type persisted in Protestantism with hymns like Isaac Watts's (1674–1748) 'When I Survey the Wondrous Cross' and Frances Ridley Havergal's (1836–79) 'Take My Life and Let It Be'. In the African American tradition there is 'Were You There When They Crucified My Lord?' These outpourings of private devotion marked 'the discovery that the personal cry of one may also be the voice of many'.[26] The personal becomes communal; people are not alone and so congregational

---

[21]   Suzanne Langer, *Philosophy in a New Key* (Harvard University Press 1942/1951), p. 27.

[22]   Jean-Jacques Nattiez, trans. Carolyn Abbate, *Music and Discourse: Towards a Semiology of Music* (Princeton University Press, 1990), p. 17.

[23]   Lucy Green, *Music on Deaf Ears: Musical Meaning, Ideology and Education* (Manchester University Press, 1988).

[24]   Glennella Key, *Experiences with Hymnody* (Convention Press, 1972), p. 131.

[25]   June Boyce-Tillman and Janet Wootton (eds), *Reflecting Praise* (Stainer and Bell, 1993), p. 25.

[26]   Pauline M. Parker, 'The Hymn as Literary Form', *Eighteenth Century Studies*, 8/4 (1975): p. 393.

songs become a source of hope. It is in this domain that personal identity is often constructed – an identity formed of being part of a particular culture. Simon Frith's observations about the power of music to express and form self-identity and cultural identity simultaneously applies particularly well to church music:

> Identity is thus necessarily a matter of ritual, it describes one's place in a dramatized pattern of relationships – one can never really express oneself 'autonomously'. Self-identity is cultural identity; claims to individual difference depend on audience appreciation, on shared performing and narrative rules .... But what makes music special – what makes it special for identity – is that it defines a space without boundaries (a game without frontiers). Music is thus the cultural form best able both to cross borders – sounds carry across fences and walls and oceans, across classes, races and nations – and to define places; in clubs, scenes, and raves, listening on headphones, radio and in the concert hall, we are only where the music takes us.[27]

This is well illustrated in a moving letter from the First World War showing how singing was used to strengthen the cultural roots of a young soldier who was aged twenty-five just before he died of his wounds on 7 September 1918:

> Dear Mother and Sister,
>
> I received you kind letter safely today and also the newspaper. ... Well, Mam, I understand that you are rather down hearted. Here we try to keep our spirits up through all the firing. We have short services here in the trenches and in all the mud. I turn to sing the verses that I learnt at dear Mynydd Gwyn. I hope that I will be back there soon ....
>
> Goodnight,
>
> Griffith[28]

In much of the literature, participation in community singing is seen as a source of empowerment.[29] And it is within this power that the healing power of congregational singing resides. This account comes from the archives of the Alister Hardy Trust and is a middle-aged woman recounting her experience:

---

[27]   Simon Frith, 'Music and Identity', in Stuart Hall and Paul du Gay (eds), *Questions of Cultural Identity* (Sage Publications, 1996), p. 126.

[28]   I am indebted to John Roberts for this translation from the Welsh of a letter from Griffith Roberts written 3 September 1918, quoted in full in June Boyce-Tillman, *Constructing Musical Healing: The Wounds that Sing* (Jessica Kingsley, 2000).

[29]   Melva Wilson Costen, *African American Christian Worship* (Abingdon Press, 1993), p. 25.

> After the address came the hymn 'All hail the power of Jesus' name'. During the
> singing of it I felt the power of God falling upon me. My sister felt it too, and
> said 'Floie, you're going to walk.' The Lord gave me faith then.[30]

Musical expression should not be limited to the positive; there is also a need for
hymns concerned with healing and the problematic nature of pain and suffering.
People have a variety of emotions and feelings to express – both happiness and
sadness. There are times in my life when an over-happy mood in worship leaves
me out in the cold because it is too far from where I am. In some of my hymns I
have attempted to achieve a balance between sadness and joy, such as the chorus
of my paraphrase of the hymn 'Thine Be the Glory':

> Christ our companion gloriously alive,
> We can share your darkness, we can share your light.[31]

When I used this hymn for a service a member of the congregation who had cared
for a son with severe epilepsy all her life said 'That is the first time that my life
experience has been present in a hymn in church.' These are verses I wrote for the
hymns for healing project:

> 2. Lord, in a world abusive and rejecting,
> Blood flows from wounds in children, trees and soil.
> We sit alone; our bodies ache with retching;
> Yet in Your hands we sense a healing oil.
>
> 3. Lord, when we walk in death's dark vale of shadows,
> Your Wisdom leads as tiny lights within
> Feeling Your counsel, all our pain is hallowed,
> To Your Unknowing, Lord, we say Amen.[32]

In transmitting a communal history, hymns like this can be an important source of
the identity of a particular church. Congregational singing thus becomes a domain
where devotion, empowerment, healing, empathy and identity play a significant part.

Materials

The second important domain for consideration of congregational singing is that
of Materials. All music making consists of organizations of concrete materials
drawn both from the human body and the environment. These include physical

---

[30]   Religious Experience Research Centre Archives.
[31]   Boyce-Tillman, *A Rainbow to Heaven*, p. 11.
[32]   June Boyce-Tillman, to the tune 'Lord of the Years' (Unpublished, 2010).

spaces of congregational music making, musical instruments of various kinds and the infinite variety of tone colours associated with the human voice.

The material that could be considered foundational material for congregational singing is the human body, particularly the voice. The sound of the singing voice is in great part culturally conditioned; different traditions value quite distinct vocal and instrumental colours, illustrated by the distinctions between the 'pure' timbres of the Anglican choral tradition and the idiosyncratic timbres of the Pentecostal gospel traditions. In a South London Anglican church in which I served, there were regularly debates about the tone colours used by members of the congregation from different ethnic backgrounds and the appropriateness of these within the Anglican choral tradition.

Into this domain as well comes the use of the body in worship and what gestures are validated in a tradition. These vary markedly from crossing in its various forms of the Roman Catholic and Orthodox traditions to the raised hands of the charismatic traditions. The hymnbooks of the literate hymn traditions restrict bodily movement while the more oral traditions (or those using technology to project the words) often include a much freer approach to the movement of the body. The use of dance is fraught with all Christianity's theological problems with the body, particularly the woman's body (though some contemporary hymn writers are reclaiming it).[33] Circle dance finds a regular place in feminist liturgy groups. These are sometimes dictated by the space being used and its acoustics and sometimes by the predilections of a particular church community.

Extending outward from the body, musical instruments are a second category that is a very important material consideration for congregational singing, and one that has generated a great deal of debate over the centuries of Christian music. Church communities are often defined by the instruments they use or do not use. In Calvin's view, the metrical psalms were to be sung only in unison and without instrumental accompaniment. Unaccompanied singing characterized the singing of the small feminist liturgy groups when material was often pitched to suit the musical capabilities of the participants. For the English Anglican tradition, the use of the organ for material from traditions other than the Anglican choral tradition is often problematic. Small feminist groups with which I have worked have been loath to use the organ, even when they were in situations where there was one and they had someone who could play it, as they saw it as patriarchal. An inflexible attitude toward what the organ symbolized led to the failure to introduce a music group into the Anglican church in South London because the community defined itself by using the organ.

A third important but often-neglected material consideration for congregational singing is the acoustics of the worship space. The relationship of worship bodies to these spaces has changed significantly in Western Protestant worship; now, sometimes it seems that musicians and singers interact in these spaces as though

---

[33] Louise Mary Bringle, *Joy and Wonder, Love and Longing: 75 Hymn Texts* (GIA 2002), p. 128.

worship were a private act, rather than a public one. Richard Sennett, in his concept of 'the intimate society', claims that we now create the illusion of a public society; in other words, that people act in the public arena as if they were surrounded by a bubble or shell of privacy.[34] This means that while we must do certain things in public settings, we do not see these acts as public acts. We are unaware of being part of a society that is larger than the intimate circle of family and friends, and that establishes our hesitancy to participate in wider social life. The person in the intimate society functions as a silent passive observer when in public or projecting private imagery onto public spaces.

The reconceiving of public Christian worship as a private event mirrors developments in the wider society.[35] In the modern West, we have come to think of the church building as a place to be alone with God. Kiefert sees this as dating from Victorian theatre and occurring in the 1980s when the audience stops being involved in the action and becomes a passive spectator of those who can do it.[36] The acoustic design of these churches reproduce a living room or den with wall-to-wall carpeting, where actors, with a great sound system, act on the stage. He critiques the separation between the minister and music group (the prime actors) from the passive audience. This reduces the role of the entire congregation in re-enacting the Christian drama.

Construction

In the domain of construction, musical and verbal ideas are debated and explored; as Phil Bohlman has noted, 'As a linguistic system, sacred music depends on the *dialectic* [author's italics] between written tradition, notably hymnody, the textuality of religious song, and oral tradition, usually liturgy and ritual.'[37] Construction is a domain dependent on how much is repeated and how contrast and development is achieved; these aspects differ widely, as I will illustrate, within literate and orate traditions. What musical constructions are considered appropriate for worship is an area often carefully regulated by the elders of the various traditions – be they the organists and hymn societies of the Anglican tradition or the worship leaders of the more charismatic traditions or the music ministers of the black Pentecostal traditions.

---

[34]   Richard Sennett, *The Fall of the Public Man* (W.W. Norton, 1976), p. 15, referenced in Ina Zwerger and Armin Medosch, 'Goodbye Privacy! Welcome Publicity?', http://thenextlayer.org/GoodbyePrivacyText, accessed 21 August 2011.

[35]   Terry K. Boggs, 'A Pastor's View of Acoustics and Meaningful Places for Worship', in *Acoustics for Liturgy, Meeting House Essays, No. 11* (Liturgical Training Publications, 1991), pp. 53–4.

[36]   Patrick R. Kiefert, 'Guess Who's Coming to Worship? Worship and Evangelism', *Word and World*, 9/1 (Winter 1989): pp. 46–51.

[37]   Bohlman, 'Music in American Religious Experience', p. 9.

The vast majority of the music considered 'hymnody' in the English Anglican tradition has a strophic construction. It is the strophic construction of Anglican hymnody that sets it apart from other areas of the Western classical song tradition. Traditional Anglican hymnody, although mainly originating with theological elite, often becomes 'the ordinary man's [sic] theology'[38] insofar as the drama is played out in the pattern of verse stanzas. Jenkins characterizes its structure as comprising careful metrical planning; skilled use of repetition and contrast; mnemonic devices; linguistic coding via exclusive diction and metaphor; and a direct and simple style to convey the material to the hearts and minds of the audience.[39]

Other traditions including the worship song, the spiritual or the repeated chant do not share a strophic structure. In the worship song traditions the tune sometimes needs regular adaption to accommodate metric variation from verse to verse. The more circular repetitive structures of orate traditions resurfaced in both Anglicanism and the feminist liturgy groups with the advent of repetitive meditative chants often drawn from the repertoire of the Taizé community. The spirituals of the Black tradition use a great deal of repetition both within a song and from one song to another. Lines like 'Yes we'll gather by the river' and 'I looked at my hands and they looked new' occur in a variety of contexts and constitute a bank of phrases that can be used to create new pieces in a semi-improvised process. In the spiritual tradition we meet an essentially orate tradition that has become literate as it enters the hymnbooks of English Anglicanism. A similar process happened when material originating in the folk in worship movement (such as Sydney Carter) entered Anglican worship. The reverse process of making orate also can occur when hymns from the literate traditions are taken into more orate cultures.[40] The processes of construction are different in literate and orate traditions.[41]

Olu Taiwo sets out the differences between the ways the beat functions in literate (metric) and orate (return beat) traditions. He describes the metric beat as linear and static and the return beat of the orate traditions as curved and dynamic and sees the literate beat as focused on past and future and the return beat on the present. The principles and terminologies developed in the Western classical tradition have often been applied to these more orate traditions, without sufficient regard for how musicians within those traditions have regarded their own processes of construction. The more cyclical repetitive structures of improvised traditions often sit uneasily with the structures associated with the more linear notated traditions.

---

[38] George Sampson, Warton Lecture on English Poetry at the British Academy, in *Proceedings of the British Academy*, 29 (1943): p. 37.

[39] Jenkins, *Redefining the Hymn*, p. 20.

[40] Costen, *African American Christian Worship*, p. 98.

[41] Walter Ong, *Orality and Literacy: The Technologizing of the Word* (Methuen, 1982).

But which structures are acceptable and which are not depend on the traditions of a particular church and a particular culture. Incorporating material from other traditions can cause ridicule or misunderstanding. Timothy Rommen sees these conflicting views as being an on-going issue for a church community.[42] Rommen sees the negotiation of these differences of judgement in musical construction and processes of hybridity as symptomatic of underlying changes in a community, arguing that musical change can be seen as 'secondary symptoms of the deeper, ethical projects that these artists and the communities they live in are pursuing'.[43] He sees how the debates in the Construction domain interact with those of Values in what he calls the 'ethics of style', stating that 'ethics is the antecedent of aesthetics'.[44] In my experience, aesthetic decisions are often made according to the values of those who hold positions of authority in particular contexts. Crossing traditions can cause ridicule or misunderstanding. Timothy Rommen sees these conflicting views as being an on-going issue for a church community:

> It follows that the style (and the discourse surrounding it) is a polarizing and insistent reminder of the impossible struggle for unity or, in Habermasian terms, of the struggle to arrive at the norm (consensus).[45]

In the time I have spent with both the feminist liturgy groups as well as in a South London Anglican church, I observed clear discourses of power driving some of the debates and disputes. Both of these groups also were in a situation where they needed to maintain an identity that also had other expressions, for example through fashion, art and speech. Matters of construction can lead to tensions within a church community that need careful negotiation as they often represent debates of a deeper level.

Values

The domain of Values is related to the wider community in which it is set – the context of the music-making experience – the macro area of culture and the micro area of a particular event.[46] Musical events contain value systems that are both internal (within the musicking itself) and external (the communal context of the music making). Notions of internal values for music are the subjects of debate

---

[42]   Timothy Rommen, *'Mek Some Noise': Gospel Music and the Ethics of Style in Trinidad* (University of California Press, 2007), p. 45.

[43]   Rommen, *'Mek Some Noise'*, p. 171.

[44]   Rommen, *'Mek Some Noise'*, p. 37.

[45]   Rommen, *'Mek Some Noise'*, p. 45.

[46]   For further discussion of musical values, see Boyce-Tillman, *Unconventional Wisdom.*

in musicological circles[47] but in singing, the presence of text can make them more explicit. One increasingly important value in English Anglicanism has been inclusivity. Over the last quarter century many groups have made bids for inclusion in the Anglican church's theology and worship – women, different ethnic groups, people with disabilities, gay, lesbian and transgender groups and theologians of the earth. However, historic liturgy and hymns of the English Anglican church have been less than inclusive.[48] Attempting to reconcile the value placed on inclusivity with the value of singing time-honoured hymns that often exclude certain groups creates a dilemma: Are we always to sing what we agree with or what the dominant culture throughout the majority of the church's past thinks we should believe? Should a hymn be a statement of universal agreement or a place for debate and challenge? Here the teaching role of congregational singing rises to the surface as the extra-personal potentially becomes intrapersonal. Timothy Rommen helpfully distinguishes between private morality and public ethics in congregational musical performance.[49]

For Rommen, public ethics declared in its sung texts may influence private morality. Individual morality may be different from public ethics; that is my experience in South London Anglicanism. With a firm belief in inclusive language for all excluded groups I find myself recently singing in the well-worn favourite 'Thou Whose Almighty Word' the words 'sight to the inly blind' and 'mankind' and extolling the expulsion of chaos which theologically, in my opinion, needs embracing. I deal with this frequent experience as an occasion for reflection on the extrapersonal environment in which my own history was formed and the intrapsychological effects of this.

And yet I believe to be truly catholic (which I interpret to mean fully inclusive) these debates need to be addressed and older, out-of-date attitudes challenged and abandoned. Can congregational singing be a place of protest against mainstream society? Janet Wootton has characterized women in the past as restricting their protest to writing, but not hymnody.[50] Today there is a tradition of justice-seeking

---

[47]   Susan McClary, *Feminine Endings: Music, Gender, and Sexuality* (University of Minnesota Press, 1991); Susan McClary, *Conventional Wisdom: The Content of Musical Form* (Ernest Bloch Lectures) (University of California Press, 2001).

[48]   For further analysis of gender within Christian liturgical traditions, see Teresa Berger, *Women's Ways of Worship: Gender Analysis and Liturgical History* (The Liturgical Press, 1999); Teresa Berger, *Dissident Daughters: Feminist Liturgies in Global Contexts* (Westminster John Knox Press, 2001); Janet H. Wootton, *Introducing a Practical Feminist Theology of Worship* (Sheffield Academic, 2000); Brian Wren, *What Language can I Borrow?* (SCM Press, 1989). For a disability studies approach to evaluating hymnody, see John Hull, '"Sight to the Inly Blind"? Attitudes to Blindness in the Hymnbooks', *Theology*, 105/827 (September/October 2002): pp. 333–41.

[49]   Rommen, *'Mek Some Noise'*, pp. 39–40.

[50]   Wootton, unpublished interview with author, 2003.

hymns from such writers as Sydney Carter with *Standing in the Rain*, Shirley Erena Murray[51] and the author herself.

One of the problems with hymnody in the English Anglican tradition is that most hymnbooks in common use are museums of past glories and as such may not be able speak to a new context. What do we do with the past? How can we sing 'Onward Christian Soldiers' when if a group sang 'Onward Muslim Soldiers' they would be arrested? Changing the past through altering songs is difficult because of the metrical constraints of hymnody, clearly illustrated by trying to substitute human being for man in Cardinal Newman's hymn 'Praise to the Holiest in the Height'. Some hymns are changed in collections like the Unitarian/Universalist hymnbook,[52] which contains many fine examples of how the past can be reworked. The fine prophetic hymn 'Turn back, O Man' becomes 'Turn Back, Turn Back'. However, there are painful decisions to be made:

> [The processes of peace] involve learning new skills and expanding the meaning of concepts, often 'unlearning' what was formerly believed to be true. Through performance, communities are finding ways of seeking truth and also recognizing its multiple faces.[53]

John Thornburg includes in his music ministry values: openness to God, humour, enthusiasm, empowerment, respect and finally asks congregations to

> ... invite people into a new way of thinking about the music of the church, not based on 'playing and singing the music I like' (which will always produce winners and losers) but rather based on the congregation's shared identity ('I will sing this song because it speaks of what God is calling us to do') and on solidarity. ('Though this song is not my favourite, I will sing it because it may be saving the life of the person sitting next to me.')[54]

So ideally hymnody in a church reflects a tolerance of diversity, retaining some of the old but looking to creating the new and critically asking which Values from the past need jettisoning.

---

[51]   Shirley Erena Murray, *In Every Corner Sing* (Hope Publishing, 1992).

[52]   Unitarian/Universalist Hymnbook Resources Commission, *Singing the Living Tradition* (Beacon Press, 1993).

[53]   Cynthia Cohen, 'Music: A Universal Language?' in Pliver Urbain (ed.), *Music and Conflict Transformation: Harmonies and Dissonances in Geopolitics* (I.B. Tauris, 2008), p. 31.

[54]   John Thornburg, '"Nobody Booed" is Not Good Enough: *The Transforming Power of Worship*', http://www.congregationalsinging.com/essays/essay04.htm, accessed 20 August 2011.

Conclusion

This chapter has examined congregational singing as embodied theology and participatory activity capable of creating unity. To help clergy and musical leaders consider the various roles music plays, this chapter has used a phenomenographic map of congregational musicking based on the experience of the author as a member and sometimes leader of both South London Anglican and feminist liturgical groups and a hymn/song/chant writer. I hope to have demonstrated the expressive power of communal singing at an intrapersonal level and how this interacts with the extra- and inter-personal aspects of worship. By showcasing the diversity of materials available for producing and accompanying music, the musical consequences of developments within church acoustics and how the body can be used while singing have been highlighted. In focusing on construction, I have contrasted orate and literate traditions and shown how aesthetic judgements are formed and how discourses of power interact in complex ways with an ethics of style. The domain of Values has presented the dilemmas of gaining consensus on contemporary ethical issues. The musicking experience shapes a church community and leads to this question: how far can the diversity in all these domains be embraced to create a church community that is transformative by virtue of its inclusivity? I hope that this reflective chapter will help leaders and congregants evaluate their own particular situation in their quest for building a just community.

Bibliography

Berger, Teresa, *Women's Ways of Worship: Gender Analysis and Liturgical History* (Collegeville, MN: The Liturgical Press, 1999).

Berger, Teresa, *Dissident Daughters: Feminist Liturgies in Global Context* (London: Westminster John Knox Press, 2001).

Boggs, Terry K., 'A Pastor's View of Acoustics and Meaningful Places for Worship', in *Acoustics for Liturgy, Meeting House Essays, No. 11* (Boston: Liturgical Training Publications, 1991).

Bohlman, Philip V., 'Introduction: Music in American Religious Experience', in Philip V. Bohlman, Edith L. Blumhofer and Maria M. Chow (eds), *Music in American Religious Experience* (Oxford: Oxford University Press, 2006).

Boyce-Tillman, June, *Constructing Musical Healing: The Wounds that Sing* (London: Jessica Kingsley, 2000).

Boyce-Tillman, June, 'Music as Spiritual Experience', *Modern Believing: Church and Society*, 47/3 (July 2006): 20-31.

Boyce-Tillman, June, *A Rainbow to Heaven* (London: Stainer and Bell, 2006).

Boyce-Tillman, June, *Unconventional Wisdom* (London: Equinox, 2007).

Boyce-Tillman, June and Wootton, Janet (eds), *Reflecting Praise* (London: Stainer and Bell, 2003).

Bringle, Mary Louise, *Joy and Wonder, Love and Longing: 75 Hymn Texts* (Chicago: GIA Publications, 2002).

Clark, Linda J., *Music in Churches: Nourishing Your Congregation's Musical Life* (Herndon, VA: The Alban Institute, 1994).

Cohen, Cynthia, 'Music: A Universal Language?', in Olivier Urbain (ed.), *Music and Conflict Transformation: Harmonies and Dissonances in Geopolitics* (London: I.B. Tauris, 2008).

Costen, Melva Wilson, *African American Christian Worship* (Nashville: Abingdon Press, 1993).

Dewey, John, *Art as Experience* (New York: Minton Balch and Co., 1943).

Dudley-Smith, Timothy *A House of Praise: Collected Hymns 1961-2001* (Oxford University Press, 2003).

Eskew, Harry, 'Hymns in the Church's Teaching Ministry', article originally given as a faculty address at New Orleans Baptist Theological Seminary, http://singwithunderstanding.com/wp-content/uploads/2012/06/hymns-in-the-church.pdf.

Frith, Simon, 'Music and Identity', in Stuart Hall and Paul du Gay (eds), *Questions of Cultural Identity* (Thousand Oaks, CA: Sage Publications, 1996).

Green, Lucy, *Music on Deaf Ears: Musical Meaning, Ideology and Education* (Manchester: Manchester University Press, 1998).

Holzman, Lois, *Vygotsky at Work and Play* (New York: Taylor and Francis, 2008).

Hull, John, '"Sight to the Inly Blind"? Attitudes to Blindness in the Hymnbooks', *Theology*, 105/827 (September/October 2002): 333–41.

Jenkins, Kathryn, *Redefining the Hymn: The Performative Context – Occasional Papers – Third Series 4* (Hymn Society of Britain and Ireland, 2010).

Key, Glennella, *Experiences with Hymnody* (Nashville: Convention Press, 1972).

Kiefert, Patrick R., 'Guess Who's Coming to Worship? Worship and Evangelism', *Word and World*, 9/1 (Winter 1989): 46–51.

Langer, Suzanne, *Philosophy in a New Key* (Cambridge, MA; Harvard University Press, 1942/1951).

Lewis, C.S., *The Clark Lectures* (Oxford: Clarendon Press, 1944).

McClary, Susan, *Feminine Endings: Music, Gender and Sexuality* (Minneapolis: University of Minnesota Press, 1991).

McClary, Susan, *Conventional Wisdom: The Content of Musical Form* (Ernest Bloch Lectures) (Berkeley: University of California Press, 2001).

Marton, Ference and Booth, Shirley, *Learning and Awareness* (Mahwah, NJ: Lawrence Erlbaum Associates: Publishers, 1997).

Mayhew, Kevin, *Anglican Hymns Old and New* (Stowmarket, UK: Kevin Mayhew, 2008).

Murray, Shirley Erena, *In Every Corner Sing* (Carol Stream, IL: Hope Publishing, 1992).

Nattiez, Jean-Jacques, trans. Carolyn Abbate, *Music and Discourse: Towards a Semiology of Music* (Princeton: Princeton University Press, 1990).

Nelson, R., 'Modes of Practice-as-Research Knowledge and their Place in the Academy', in L. Allegue, B. Kershaw, S. Jones, A. Piccini (eds), *Practice-as-Research in Performance and Screen* (Basingstoke: Palgrave, 2009).

Ong, Walter, *Orality and Literacy: The Technologizing of the Word* (London: Methuen, 1982).

Pauline, Parker M., 'The Hymn as Literary Form', *Eighteenth Century Studies*, 8/4 (1975): 392–419.

Rommen, Timothy, *'Mek Some Noise' Gospel Music and the Ethics of Style in Trinidad* (Berkeley: University of California Press, 2007).

Sampson, George, 'Warton Lecture on English Poetry at the British Academy', in *Proceedings of the British Academy*, 29 (1943): 37–64.

Small, Christopher, *Musicking: The Meanings of Performing and Listening* (Middleton, CT: Wesleyan University Press, 1998).

Storr, Anthony, *Music and the Mind* (London: HarperCollins, 1993).

Taiwo, Olu, *The Return Beat*, unpublished email, 2012.

Thornburg, John, '"Nobody Booed" is not Good Enough: *The Transforming Power of Worship*', http://www.congregationalsinging.com/essays/essay04.htm, accessed 20 August 2011.

Turner, Victor, *The Ritual Process: Structure and Anti-structure* (Baltimore: Penguin Books, 1969/1974).

Unitarian/Universalist Hymnbook Resources Commission, *Singing the Living Tradition* (Boston: Beacon Press, 1993).

Van der Weyer, Robert (ed.), *Hildegard in a Nutshell* (London: Hodder and Stoughton, 1997).

Wootton, Janet H., *Introducing a Practical Feminist Theology of Worship* (Sheffield: Sheffield Academic, 2000)

Wootton, Janet, unpublished interview with author, Union Chapel Islington, July 2003.

Zwerger, Ina and Medosch, Armin, 'Goodbye Privacy! Welcome Publicity?', http://thenextlayer.org/GoodbyePrivacyText, accessed 21 August 2011.

Chapter 4
Jazz and Anglican Spirituality?
Some Notes on Connections

Martyn Percy

I was watching (TV) one night, and they were interviewing a man about jazz music. He said jazz music was invented by the first generation out of slavery. I thought that was beautiful because, while it is music, it is very hard to put on paper; it is so much more a language of the soul. It is as if the soul is saying something, something about freedom. I think Christian spirituality is like jazz music. I think loving Jesus is something you feel. I think it is something very difficult to get on paper. But it is no less real, no less meaningful, no less beautiful ...[1]

Connections between music, theology and ecclesiology are not difficult to make. Historically, the rather raucous local musical ensembles that provided musical accompaniment to English church services in the early seventeenth century were gradually replaced by one single instrument – the pipe organ – in the eighteenth century. Were notes of harmony sounded by the accompanists, or was the noise made one of tuneful discord? Or was there another message? However one interprets the arrival of the pipe organ, the result was, invariably, an order and discipline applied to services that clergy themselves could not have orchestrated. The pipe organ, in other words, eventually provided a musical order and *discipline* to services that complemented the liturgy. This, in turn, was developed by the rise of hymnody in the late eighteenth and nineteenth centuries. Church services, from being times and occasions that could be contested, became far more coherent. Nowadays in the Church of England, one can occasionally catch a glimpse of what the local musical anarchy in churches might have sounded like three hundred years ago. Simply tune in to how the bells toll for services – and see if the bell-ringers stay for the service they have just announced.

This chapter is, however, neither a historical nor theological exploration of the connections between music and ecclesiology. Writers such as Jeremy Begbie[2] have contributed significantly to our understanding of the connections between theology and music. The work of many church historians – including Keith

---

[1] Don Miller, *Blue Like Jazz* (Thomas Nelson Publishing, 2003), p. 239.

[2] Jeremy Begbie, *Theology, Music and Time* (CUP, 2000); Jeremy Begbie, *Resounding Truth: Christian Wisdom in the World of Music* (Baker Books, 2008).

Thomas[3] – testifies to the unusual and complex history of musical accompaniment down the ages in our English parish churches. That has tended to be more of a history of disconnections and reconnections. In contrast, the connections I want to explore in this chapter are somewhat tendentious, and rooted in a kind of metaphorical reconstruction. And, more generally, the observations made in this chapter are grounded in the principal concerns and approaches I take to the study of the church, and to Christianity and contemporary culture. Here, I am usually shaped by two intellectual genealogies. The fusion of the two is, in itself, a 'jazz-like' combination: making space for improvisation, but also forming views, analysis and ideas through a tense synthesis of style and genre.

The first genealogical stream is broadly a fusion of sociology and anthropology. The legacy of Clifford Geertz, and indeed the more recent work of David Martin, for example, is constantly in the background. The second genealogical stream is theological, and shaped by writers such as James Hopewell, Jim Nieman, Denham Grierson and Nicholas Healy – contextual theologians of varying hue and colour. And these two intellectual genealogies produce a kind of 'binocular' approach to the study of the church, with all that this metaphor implies. Some things, in the distance, come in to view; only a few things are focused upon, but in order to extrapolate a larger picture. So, as someone working with a framework of sociology and anthropology, I am naturally wary (some might say suspicious) of the ways in which structures and practices are legitimized by appeals to fundaments – be they biblical or drawn from the 'tradition'. And one must be equally wary of the idea that the development of structures and practices can be further legitimized by appeals to the work of the Holy Spirit. That said, the theological element to the 'binocular' is receptive to revelation, and to ways in which the body of Christ grows and develops in local contexts – denominations, places and times, and amongst people genuinely and truly seeking to live authentic and faithful Christian lives that correspond to God's revealed will for the world. It is has been my practice, in studying and writing on contemporary ecclesiology, fundamentalism and revivalism, and together more generally with Christianity and contemporary culture, to deploy this 'binocular' approach. I regard it as a complementary trajectory, and not a competitive impulse. And as I stated earlier, there is more than a hint of a 'jazz-like' methodology in bringing the two together to create a harmony, rhythm and sound from two streams or sources that usually, at first sight, do not appear as though they belong together.

This chapter is a reconstructive enterprise, an attempt – tenuous in places, granted – to suggest some new and potentially illuminating connections between ecclesial polity and jazz music. And I must own up to a personal interest here – in jazz, generally, and in *bossa nova* particularly – with which this chapter is concerned. I am, of course, aware of some of the potential pitfalls in attempting such a chapter. In characterising jazz, I am aware that there can be a tendency to engage in 'ethnic essentialism' (e.g., on rhythms) when trying to describe the

---

origins of music,[4] and I have tried to avoid this where possible. The purpose of this chapter is, however, twofold: namely, to make a general argument for jazz as a good metaphor for understanding Anglican ecclesial polity (or at least the ideal and caricatured forms of its English behaviourist proclivities); and from that, to infer something more particular about *bossa nova* in relation to Anglican polity. What I will be attempting to sketch, therefore, are the connections between a certain kind of jazz and the cadences and timbre of Anglican ecclesial polity, using jazz as a metaphor, to explore a kind of 'morphological mood'. In suggesting such a thing, I am mindful of the links that some authors – writing in the field of ministerial formation and spiritual development – have already made between music and ecclesiology; even though these are often more implicit than explicit.

Thirty years ago, two theologians, Daniel Hardy and David Ford, in their seminal collaborative work,[5] suggested that it might be fertile to think of the Trinity as music – and most especially as jazz. Their metaphor offers an insight into the Trinitarian nature of God: the composer-performer-listener linkage can resonate with the Father, Son and Holy Spirit. Music is also created in time, and yet creates its own time. It also involves law and freedom, and its practice always reveals 'more than there is'. The authors also went on to suggest that ecclesial life has something of the 'jazz factor' about it. Again, truth is comprehended through combinations. Hardy and Ford also suggested that between order and disorder in worship, there is a third way: non-order. Non-order is, for Hardy and Ford, not a compromise between order and disorder, but rather a different way of seeing ecclesiology – something with an open, yet composed texture. They use the analogy of jazz to celebrate the freedom of worship (in effect, an orthodox, liberating theology of praise), by pointing out that that jazz combines the two principal modes of musical expression in the West: composition and improvisation.

In jazz, they suggest, the two come together to create something that is fleeting, original, novel, harmonic and spontaneous, and yet also recognizable and memorable. In using this analogy, Hardy and Ford find an expression of praise that is resonant with their doctrine of God: free and liberating, yet also known through specific types of agency such as liturgy and sacraments. The theology that they articulate makes room for the novel and the innovative, whilst at the same time affirming the traditional and the concrete.

Hardy and Ford are therefore suggesting that music changes us, by wooing us into participation. Music is 'a harmonic language' that is attentive to mood: sadness, celebration, reflection and dynamism are 'caught' in music. Moreover, music is a gift, and as we learn to read it, understand it and use it, we learn more about the God who has given it. Gifts express the giver. In thinking about the Trinity metaphorically as jazz music, one becomes mindful of its combinations: its formal dimensions married to its innovative nature, and its capacity to cover a spectrum of needs from celebration to commiseration. Moreover, there are the

---

[4]   On this, for example, see Cornell West, *Race Matters* (Beacon Press, 1993), pp. 150–51.

[5]   David Ford and Daniel Hardy, *Jubilate: Theology in Praise* (DLT, 1984).

many different sounds that make up *one* sound. Music is ultimately both purity and a blend; it is enriched by the singular and the symphonic. Like an ecclesial community, the distinctive and the different remain, even in the midst of diversity.

This might allow us to say that divine music is simultaneously scripted yet improvised; formal, yet free. When the Church (in all its breadth) corresponds to the Trinity in worship and appreciation, it becomes an *orchestra* of praise and participation. Likening the Trinity to jazz is perhaps not so strange. Jazz is a genre of music that is normally associated with both freedom of expression and a lesser degree of formality; where improvisation and composition meet. It is simultaneously transforming yet traditional; never predictable, and yet reliable. Order and freedom coexist, with passive listening turned into participation and communion. From an apparently tense synthesis of composition and improvisation, the fruits of inspiration, liberation and dance can issue. To understand the Trinity through a jazz-like metaphorical lens is not to understand each note and sequence, nor is it to deconstruct the score: it is to listen, learn and participate.

But what might this mean in more ecclesial and concrete terms, specifically in terms of worshippers and ecclesial communities? Donald Schon remarks that 'internalised knowledge arises in, and informs, current action', and that this is what happens when 'good jazz musicians improvise together'.[6] Something is made in the togetherness. Just suppose for a moment that one was to liken the life of the church, as a community of teaching and learning, to *music* in the first instance? To be sure, it seems strange, especially as one prominent sociologist of religion recently noted that 'the grand symphony of Christendom' is over; all that is left are 'enthusiastic music makers'.[7] The implication is that the cancer of secularism has consumed most of the territory of belief; the body of Christ may twitch a little, but it is basically dying.

Naturally, as head of an Anglican theological school, I do not agree with this. In England at least, Christianity remains the dominant paradigm of religion that gives focus and articulation to the innate spiritual inklings of its people. True enough – and to continue with the musical metaphor – fewer and fewer may attend regular recitals, but knowledge of and appreciation of the musical score remains much as it has always done. The task of the church remains much as it has always been: the offering of religion in response to wonder, awe, grief, vernacular religion, operant faith and praxis and 'common spirituality'.

The advantage of the jazz metaphor is that it hints that theology – teaching and learning about God – is probably more than just thinking about God. It is art, dance, liturgy, protest and practical. It is an *activity*. As Paul van Buren reminds us, it is the movement of people 'struck by the biblical story, in which they undertake to revise continually the ways in which they say how things are with their present

───────────

[6] Donald Schon, *The Reflective Practitioner: How Professionals Think in Action* (Basic Books, 1983), p. 55.

[7] Steve Bruce, *Religion in the Modern World* (Oxford University Press, 1996), p. 234.

circumstances, in the light of how they read that story'.[8] Where the story strikes there is power, response and religious community: the body of God, the church. To return to the musical metaphor, one can see that you do not have to choose between the symphony on the one hand, or the banal and enthusiastic music-makers that Steve Bruce offers on the other.

There may be another, better way of seeing this. The striking work of Jan Garbarek and the Hilliard Ensemble,[9] which mixes the ordered ancient polyphony with the spontaneity of modern jazz saxophone, suggests a sociological and theological solution to Bruce's antinomy. The music alluded to here is a marriage of two fundamental practices in Western music: improvisation and composition, and alluded to earlier – though this is, here, jazz and plainchant together. Even though they are separated by centuries, the synthesis suggests, at least metaphorically, that order and freedom can co-exist in harmony; indeed, in a harmony that is not tense, but inspiring and liberating. So we should perhaps pause at this point and reflect that jazz is arguably one of a number of the only art forms that is genuinely American in origin – where freedom is celebrated in many spheres of cultural, political and public life. And jazz remains, curiously, one of the few art forms banned by the Nazis in Germany. The capacity of this form of music to inspire freedom and liberation should not be underestimated.

Garbarek's work is not the only example of forms and expression of freedom interweaving with more formal composition, and creating new senses of possibility. Orlando Gough's speculative 'Latin Jazz' achieves the same effect through a different musical genre.[10] Still with jazz, *bossa nova* and Samba rhythms convey an order and mellowness that simultaneously carries a message of orthodoxy and liberalism. One could say that the jazz tradition, in many ways, is liberalism set to music (here I am especially thinking of Billy Taylor's 'I Wish I Knew How it Would Feel to be Free'[11]). To briefly depart from the jazz metaphor here, and were one to extend the analogy further, from passive listening to active participation, the idea of a Ceilidh gets close to the sort of socio-theological reflexivity envisaged here. In a Ceilidh, patterns and improvisation co-exist: each form of dance is recognizable, yet the atmosphere is one of freedom rather than slavish correspondence. The dances must be taught, true enough. But this does not constrain participants: it enables them, liberating all who join in the harmony that is created by music and movement. This was something Sydney Carter understood in his folk hymn 'Lord of the Dance', which is set to an old Shaker dancing tune.

Given these general remarks about orchestration, ecclesiology, spirituality and jazz, I now want to move into a more intentional reflection on Anglican polity and jazz, and, specifically as this discussion develops, the genre of jazz known as *bossa nova*. One of the reasons the reflection is legitimate is that Anglicanism,

---

[8]   Paul van Buren, *The Burden of Freedom* (Harper, 1976), p. 51.

[9]   See *Officium* (ECM Records, 1994).

[10]   *Message from the Border* (Atalyst Records, 1995).

[11]   *Billy Taylor and the Billy Taylor Trio* (Capitol Records, 1964).

like jazz, and as we noted earlier, is often described as a tense synthesis, with improvisation and composition, which when performed, is primarily harmonious. Here, for example, is how Brian McLaren describes Anglican polity:

> Generous orthodoxy is the practice of dynamic tension: you can resist the reductionist temptation to always choose one thing over another, and you learn to hold two or more things together when necessary ... . Anglicans have demonstrated this both/and beautifully in relation to scripture ... it is never *sola* [scripture] – never the only factor. Rather, scripture is in dialogue with the tradition, reason and experience ... . None of them *sola* can be the ultimate source of authority ... . When these [the four] agree, Anglicans more forward with confidence ... . When they don't agree, Anglicans seek to live with the tension and the tolerance, believing that better outcomes will follow if they live with the tension rather than resolve it [prematurely?] by rejecting one of the four values ... all are gifts from God, and none should be rejected ... . Compromise ... Anglicans make room for one another when scripture, reason, tradition and experience don't line up for everyone the same way ... .[12]

The jazz-like overtones hardly need spelling out. And one can go further still in comparison. Anglicanism, whether encountered locally in any context, or globally as a Communion, is, like jazz, incomplete – not formally scripted like a grand symphony (it does not claim any unique Christian fundaments), it is only understood more fully when performed. As a genre or denomination, it is still evolving, albeit slowly. It begins in the middle. It is a *via media*. Indeed, it often expresses itself in antinomies that embody dynamic and creative tensions: passionate coolness; feint conviction; Catholic and Protestant; Synodical and Episcopal; 'open', yet 'defined'. Others go further (one detects a hue of the 'blues' here): 'faithful doubt?'; 'truthful duplicity'; 'troubled commitment'; 'un-decidability'; concrete and fluid; solid, yet reflexive. As the writer Urban Holmes III expressed it, it can hardly ever resist the pairing of two three letter words: 'Yes, but ...'. Anglicanism seems to have an 'in-built' reflexivity which is almost part of its DNA. Moreover, it is a kind of peaceable polity in which 'speaking across differences' matters; indeed, one might say that style is as important as substance. It is a relaxed, mellow polity: the very idea of 'passionate coolness' is a guide not only to its approach to mission and polity, but also to its dominant cadence and timbre. The heartbeat of Anglicanism is, in some respects, and perhaps ideally (or maybe a caricature?) slow, chilled and steady; but can also work at pace, and can be given to exuberant spiritual excess and overflow, whether that be modern or traditional worship.

The idea of a genre of music born out of fusion – indeed any fusion, morphologically – being a metaphor for Anglicanism is potentially illuminating. And some of the more compelling ideas located in the jazz-Anglican metaphor are rooted in improvisation, responsiveness and openness. But we might also suggest

---

[12]   Brian McLaren, *Generous Orthodoxy* (Zondervan, 2004), p. 85.

that incompleteness is a virtue to attend to here as well. Moreover, this leadership comprehends that much of Anglican polity is open; and although has a shape, is nonetheless unresolved. It is, like a body, replete with creative dilemmas; checks and balances; the reactive and proactive. For example, and in terms of resolving ecclesial conflict, or in inhabiting theological dilemmas, one can see that the Anglican desire and need to sometimes reach settlements that do not achieve closure is actually a deep formational habit of wisdom that has helped to form Anglican polity down the centuries. It is embodied liturgically, but can also be traced in pastoral, parish and synodical resolutions that cover a range of issues. Put another way, there is a tension between being an identifiable community with creeds; whilst also being a body that recognizes that a whole range of other issues are essentially un-decidable.[13] In terms of jazz, Don Miller expresses this in a similar vein:

> I never liked jazz music because jazz music doesn't resolve. But I was outside the Bagdad Theater in Portland one night when I saw a man playing the saxophone. I stood there for fifteen minutes, and he never opened his eyes. After that I like [sic?] jazz music. Sometimes you have to watch somebody love something before you can love it yourself. It is as if they are showing you the way. I used to not like God because God didn't resolve.[14]

Essentially, the calling to lead in many expressions of Anglican polity is often about inhabiting the gap between vocation, ideals, praxis and action. Often, no neutral or universally affirmed settlements can be reached on a considerable number of issues within the church. But settlements have to be reached that allow for the possibility of continuing openness, adjustment and innovation. Inevitably, therefore, consensus is sometimes a slow and painful moment to arrive at, and even when achieved, usually involves a degree of provisionality. This is, of course, a typical Anglican habit, embodying a necessary humility and holiness in relation to matters of truth, but without losing sight of the fact that difficult decisions still need to be made. This is the nature of the body.

In some respects, and not unlike the work of Garbarek mentioned earlier, these ideas have resonance with other forms of music that have emerged as a result of jazz fusions. For example, even a brief history of jazz and Indian music reveals that jazz pioneers like John Coltrane and Miles Davis both embraced this fusion at various stages of their careers, and elements of it can also be found in the popular music of the day (e.g., the Beatles in 'Norwegian Wood', 1965; and later 'Within You Without You', 1967, in which George Harrison used the *sitar*, *tambura* and other instruments such as the *tabla*, *dilruba*, and *swarmandel*, accompanied by four London-based Indian musicians). Generally, the jazz fusion that emerged in

---

[13]   On this, see Stephen Pickard, 'Innovation and Undecidability: Some Implications for the *Koinonia* of the Anglican Church', *Journal of Anglican Studies*, 2/2 (Dec. 2004): pp. 87–105.

[14]   Miller, *Blue Like Jazz*, p. 237.

the work of Davies and Coltrane has tended to be indebted to Indian Karnatic music – elaborations that are much faster in tempo and shorter than their equivalents in Hindustani music. The unusual harmonies, rhythmic flourishes and syncopation of this form of Indian music allowed greater latitude for jazz musicians in developing forms of composition that could meander when performed, and allowed the musicians greater freedom in their interaction with audiences and context. There is something of this residually, for example, in Dave Burbreck's 'Take Five'[15] in which the melodies and polyrhythm both conflict and combine. In terms of contemporary Indian music and jazz fusions, Nitin Sawhney, an award-winning British composer, producer and performer of Indian origin, remains a pivotal figure.[16]

But why might *bossa nova* be a potential 'fit' for comparison here? Can a genre of jazz really be likened to an established form of ecclesial polity that predates it by several centuries? I do not mean to suppose that such a comparison should be anything other than an aid to reflection here. But I hold that such comparisons can be illuminating, and, as we shall see, helpful in a degree of self-understanding for Anglicanism – or indeed any Christians thinking about the morphological mood of their polity and the denominational proclivities that mark their identity.

Bossa nova is essentially a fusion of samba and earlier forms of jazz. It gained a significant following in the 1960s, and like many musical genres, has grown to become widespread and diffuse, finding its way into the repertoire of the Beatles ('And I Love Her', 1964), George Michael ('Jesus to a Child' – a song dedicated to his former lover, Anselmo Feleppa, who died in 1993), the Black-Eyed Peas ('Mas Que Nada' on Sérgio Mendes's album *Timeless*, 2006) or the work of Nitin Sawhney (for example, see 'Homelands', 2006; or 'Distant Dreams', featuring Roxanne Tataei, 2010). The word 'bossa' itself is Brazilian slang for doing something with particular charm, natural flair or innate ability. Akin to the term 'sprezzatura' (i.e., a certain nonchalance, concealing all art and effort), which is drawn from Castiglione's *The Book of the Courtier* (published in 1528) we are instantly reminded of the effortless, understated composure of Anglican polity. Although that has been tested in recent decades by a succession of debates on gender and sexuality, Anglicanism remains a quintessential distillation and expression of effortless ecclesial polity: harmony at ease with diversity. It is an enchanting faith; but not given to brashness or bridling. *Bossa nova* is Brazilian, though, and not from Central America. Yet some of its roots – for example in the liberationist hints occurring in the music also remind us of the subtle ways that liberation theology shapes Anglican thinking on social justice and theological method – are arguably also discernible.

The *bossa nova* musical style evolved from samba,[17] but is much more complex harmonically and less dependent on percussion and therefore less rhythmically-

[15] Sony Records, 1974.

[16] http://www.nitinsawhney.com, accessed 25 September 2012.

[17] See for example Chris McGowan and Ricardo Pessanha, *The Brazilian Sound: Samba, Bossa Nova and the Popular Music of Brazil* (Temple University Press, 1998).

driven than its ancestor, thereby creating the distinctive 'relaxed' sound. Whereas samba evolved in the favelas, *bossa nova* grew out of the more middle-class beachside neighbourhoods of Rio de Janeiro. The later transferability of *bossa nova* to California (what later became to be known as 'cool jazz') is comprehensible in this respect: the east coast of South America to the West Coast of North America is not the largest cultural gap for a musical genre to traverse, though some mutation on the journey was bound to be inevitable. Early exponents of the genre in Brazil included Johnny Alf, Antonio Carlos Jobim and João Gilberto. The internationally acclaimed 1959 film *Orfeu Negro* ('Black Orpheus', with the score written by Luiz Bonfá) brought *bossa nova* some significant public and critical attention. American jazz artists such as Charlie Byrd and Stan Getz cemented its popularity, leading to the global success in the early 1960's of Gilberto and Getz. Numerous 'pasteurized' versions of *bossa nova* followed, with Ella Fitzgerald and Frank Sinatra arguably leading the way. The Getz and Gilberto recording of 'The Girl From Ipanema' (1964) remains one of the best-known and most-covered *bossa nova* songs of all time.

Bossa nova music is, as we noted earlier, an unusual fusion of styles. Samba is influential, but without imputing its percussive dominance. But perhaps what makes *bossa nova* most distinctive is its use of the classical guitar, to pick up the melodies and counter-melodies. The piano is also a feature of the genre, often serving as stylistic bridge between *bossa nova* and more conventional jazz melodies. The singing too, is often soft and deep, with the voice of the performer often singing with a slightly husky, intimate, sensual cadence; almost a tender whispering, at times. The singing is, in other words, personal and relational (but not overtly sexual, I think), and reminiscent of the intimate Anglican poetry of John Donne and George Herbert, and the rich tradition of Anglican mysticism. For the singing seems to woo the listener; but it does not force itself on the hearer. The softness of the voices closes the gap between the performer and audience; this is music that comes alongside the listener, and gently raises the spirits (which no doubt accounts for why so much of it is played as background music in large public spaces). Thus, cross-pollination of style, substance and rhythm are rooted in the blend of instruments used, including those of percussion – though the latter is usually performed in a deliberate yet under-stated way. The more orchestral styles of *bossa nova* – Dusty Springfield's 'The Look of Love' (1967, and written by Burt Bacharach) comes to mind – give the genre a unique aural texture. In a comparable vein, one finds influences in the mellowness of Miles Davis and Charlie Byrd. There is a certain level at which *bossa nova*'s aural texture both soothes and elevates, in much the way that worshippers at Choral Evensong might describe their sentient experience. This idea of Anglican identity as a *fusion*, therefore, is quite compelling. As one recent writer has noted:

> The blend of concern for ordered ministry (and thus ordered worship), freedom from an uncritical affirmation of hierarchical ecclesiastical authority, with the appeal to Scripture at the heart of this, and the rooted belief that the forms of common worship were the most important clues about what was held to

be recognizably orthodox teaching – this blend or fusion came to define the Anglican ethos in a growing diversity of cultural contexts. Catholic, yes, in the sense of seeing the Church today as responsible to its history and to the gifts of God in the past, even those gifts given to people who have to be seen as in some ways in error. Reformed, yes, in the sense that the principle remains of subjecting the state of the Church at any given moment to the judgment of Scripture – though not necessarily therefore imagining that Scripture alone offers the answer to every contemporary question. And running through the treatment of these issues, a further assumption that renewal in Christ does not abolish but fulfils the long-frustrated capacities of human beings: that we are set free to sense and to think the texture of God's Wisdom in the whole of creation and at the same time to see how it is itself brought to fulfilment in the cross of Jesus.[18]

So what metaphorical connections between *bossa nova* jazz and Anglican spirituality might be implied for us here? Anglicanism, as we have noted, can be narrated as a relaxed, mild, temperate form of ecclesial polity, not easily given to extremes. Rather like the climate of the nation that gave birth to its national church, it is often overcast, but also occasionally sunny; mild, with warm spells. We imagine meteorological extremes, but they are, in reality, merely trifles. As Bill Bryson observes in his *Notes from a Small Island*,[19] the world is somewhat puzzled when our newspapers have headlines like 'Phew, what a Scorcher', or, more risibly 'Britain sizzles in the 70's'. In most parts of the Americas and the Continent, that is a cue to fetch the cardigan – not strip off and sit down with an ice cream.

We have already noted the caricature of Anglicanism being a tension or fusion of opposites: a matter of 'passionate coolness'. But like jazz itself, I rather like this stylistic interpretation of the Anglican mood, since it suggests an actual energy for temperate ecclesial climes. But it has a weakness too, which is that people can often dwell on the actual comfort that the accommodation and temperance bring. And temperance can be an over-rated virtue, if it is allowed to dictate moderation and exclude the excess of passion. If it sets the tempo all the time, then the radical of excess, which drives religion, is inhibited.

One of the characteristics that marked out the early architects of Anglicanism such as John Donne and George Herbert is that they understood faith to be passion. Faith, in terms of discipleship, is often not reasoned coolness. It is passion that spills over; the love that is stronger than death. It might be thought through. It may even be willed reason. But it has to be willed with the very fibre of your being. I mention this because it is sometimes easy to misunderstand the place of religion in the modern world, and for people of faith to collude – unintentionally, and sometimes naively – with secular reasoning. For example, excessive, passionate

---

[18]   Rowan Williams, from the Preface to Martyn Percy, Mark Chapman, Ian S. Markham and James Barney Hawkins IV (eds), *Christ and Culture: Communion After Lambeth* (SCM-Canterbury Press, 2010), p. 5.

[19]   Bill Bryson, *Notes from a Small Island* (HarperCollins, 1996).

faith is not the same as extreme faith. The former is intemperate and immodest; but it abounds in energy and love because it cannot spring from the liberty of God. It is released as a kind of raw energy, precisely because it breaks the chains of inhibition, and springs forth from spiritual encounters that can border on ecstasy. But this is not, as I say, extremism. It is merely passion resulting from encounter, conversion, conviction, resurrection and transformation.

The Enlightenment and the legacy of modernity has made religion into some kind of 'subject' that is essentially apart from 'ordinary' life. It is as though being religious was specious, atypical and abnormal. We talk too easily of having a 'religious' or 'spiritual' experience, as though all other kinds of experiences were 'normal'. But if you turn the phrase around for the moment, you might ask yourself what might it mean to have a 'secular experience'? It would be an odd phrase to use – even in conversation with an atheist. Yet most religious people have accepted the goalposts being moved all too easily. Religions have allowed themselves to be marginalized and particularized, and have even naively participated in the progressive programme of modernity's de-normalization. Religious passion, then, is often narrated as extremism – in the media especially. Religious experience is seen as 'specious', when in fact spiritual feelings and intimations of the divine are perfectly normal and very commonplace. But under such prevailing and reigning secular conditionality, spiritual restraint quickly becomes a virtue that services the controlling of religion: 'all things in moderation', as the English say.

But I'd like to suggest that this understanding of temperance is actually an abuse of the term. Temperance is not about control from without. It is rather, the deep spiritual exercise of restraint for the sake of the self and the other. It is a spiritual discipline and a virtue that can only be exercised in proportion to the energy and passion that wells up from the same source. It is not a dainty refusal to take an extra portion. It is, rather, a steely and willed act of moderation or self-control that emerges out of passionate convictions, grace and love. That's why the list of the fruits of the Holy Spirit from *Galatians* (5: 22ff) is so important. Love, joy, peace, patience, kindness, self-control, humility, gentleness and faithfulness are all rooted in the passion of Christ – a putting to death of our desires, and seeing them reconfigured through the Holy Spirit into the heart of God. So excess and abundance are of God; extremism, however, is of the flesh.

In terms of the metaphor of jazz in relation to Anglican spirituality, these observations are important for several reasons. First, spiritual passion is not just about the expulsion of energy. It also has another meaning in religion which is concerned with the absorption of pain, sacrifice and suffering – like the passion of Christ. Here, passion is absolutely for the other; but it is passion that is almost entirely configured in its receptivity. Much like the passion of a parent or a lover, God's passion is sometimes spoken in eloquent silence; in sacrifice and in endurance. God 'speaks' in the apophatic (i.e., absence, silence, spaces, etc.) and in the kataphatic (i.e., expressive, passionate, etc.). It is in both, and in the fusion of the two: in solidarity and in suffering; in patience, kindness, self-control, humility and gentleness. Indeed, in the unresolved and the incomplete: jazz and Anglicanism are one of soul and mind here. The resonance of the samba roots in *bossa nova*, and the more general context of oppression in the formation of the music, and yet its ultimate mellowness and gentleness, hardly need spelling out here.

Second, it is perhaps important to remember that the example of the architects of Anglicanism – those people that inspire the faith – is often to be found in the delicate combination of passion, practice and reason. One of the qualities I sometimes look for in seminarians is their restraint and mellowness; the very ability to *contain* their passion – for the church, for Christ, and for others. Anglican spirituality is not about being liberal, conservative, or even somewhere in the middle. It is about knowing your place before God, and being directionally passionate for the possibility of the kingdom.

Third, temperance – which is good and rightful for ecclesial life and spirituality – should not be allowed to blunt the energy and enthusiasm that flows from living the gospel. To be sure, ordered-ness and calculation have their place. But if they are allowed to control and marginalize passion, then there is a great danger that temperance can become totalitarian. The excess of energy, at this point, is almost guaranteed to be narrated as extremism. But religion, of course, is about extremes. Extreme love; extreme sacrifice; and extreme selflessness that go beyond reason. Religion in moderation is, arguably, a contradiction in terms. It should offend, cajole, probe and interrogate. Like jazz, and more colloquially, one might say that a faith that does not cause you to move is hardly worth the candle.

As Hardy and Ford knew, when they first drew attention to the metaphor of jazz and spirituality, passion for God, even though it is often misunderstood, is about the excess and abundance that God intends for all who suffer and struggle. But it is not about extremism. The work of the fruit of the Spirit is about producing a deeper response. As Anglican spirituality frequently testifies, the kingdom will not be known for moderation, but for liberation. The gospel is a new power; it is foolishness; it is offence. It is, in its purest form, a radical expression of the in-temperate – God's radical risk in Christ. A love that is stronger than death. This is why the language of the bible is sometimes stark; just as jazz is sometimes extremely surprising, and even occasionally unsettling. The manna that rains down from heaven does not drizzle – it rains. The Lord appears in a dazzling cloud, and in fire; not in a mid, overcast afternoon. Anglican spirituality, rather like *bossa nova*, revels in the passionate and excessive, but is not extreme or uncontained. It is passionate; and yet compassionately held in such a way as to be persuasive rather than repellent. Strange though this seems, but I happen to think that the Church of England might just be on to something here. It is easy to despair of its tepid nature; and its interminable vacillations; the softness of the timbre of its *bossa nova* soul. And yet, it is full of the fruits of God's Spirit – exactly the kinds of abundance and generosity listed in *Galatians*.

Indeed, let me say a little more at this point.[20] I love the Church of England because it is patient. It does not expect the world to change in an instant, or to be bludgeoned into belief, because it knows that certain things take centuries. I love it because it is kind. It is kind enough to welcome strangers, whatever their beliefs, and shake their hands, and offer them a coffee after church. I like the fact that it is neither envious of more flamboyant or successful-at-proselytizing faiths, nor boastful. I like the fact that it is not normally arrogant or rude. I like the fact that it does not insist on its own way, but is genuinely tolerant of other religious beliefs – and none. I like the fact that it does not rejoice in wrongdoing, but quietly presents an ethical framework of kindness. I like the fact that it believes in the values of the New Testament, and of St Paul's description of love; but also believes that it is more important to embody them than to quote them. I like the fact that it doesn't speak like a child, think like a child, or reason like a child. I like the fact that it is mature enough to value faithful doubt. I like the fact that it is calm. Indeed, this is something of what faith, hope and charity are all about. As Paul says of the fruits of the Spirit, there are no laws against such things.

Ultimately, all we have attempted in this chapter is to establish some playful connections between a certain kind of jazz and the cadences and timbre of Anglican ecclesial polity, and, using jazz as a metaphor, to explore a kind of 'morphological mood'. Perhaps as Burt Bacharach might have said, and so far as spirituality is concerned, it has 'the look of love' about it. And so far as Anglicanism as a whole is concerned, it is a polity neither of order nor disorder; it is an abductive faith, after all – composed, yet open. It has something of the *bossa nova* spirit; one that sees that improvisation and composition belonging together. True, this may be said of jazz more broadly, together with many other genres of music from around the world. But perhaps what is so distinctive about *bossa nova* specifically, and jazz more broadly (as opposed to other genres of music that combine improvisation and composition), and that is particularly helpful in this analogy, is the attention that it brings to mellowness and openness, which I hold to be deeply Anglican dynamics.

As George Herbert said of spirituality and prayer, in its ideal Anglican spiritual form, it is 'softness, and peace, and love, and blisse … the milkie way; the bird of paradise'. But let the last word go to Don Miller's homage to jazz and spirituality, and scripted towards the close of Steve Taylor's film (Lionsgate, 2012) of the book. Don, the subject of the book and film (and played by Marshall Allman in the film) sums it up like this:

> Sometimes you just have to watch someone love something before you can love it yourself. Penny (my girlfriend) loves Jesus. My dad loves jazz. He told me jazz is like life because it doesn't resolve. And he gave me his record collection to prove it. And I have been listening to those records, over and over. But every time I put on John Coltrane's 'A Love Supreme' (1964, Impulse Records)

---

[20]   Here, I am paraphrasing Christina Patterson's 'Thank God for the Church of England', *The Independent* (25 July 2009): p. 28.

I swear I can hear something my father says isn't there. I hear a resolution. Resolution. A final end to the story? I know not everyone hears the universe this way. But what if Penny is right? What if God is trying to compose something? And what if all these stars (above us) are just notes on a page of music, swirling in the blue, like jazz?

Bibliography

Begbie, Jeremy, *Theology, Music and Time* (Cambridge: Cambridge University Press, 2000).

Begbie, Jeremy, *Resounding Truth: Christian Wisdom in the World of Music* (Grand Rapids: Baker Books, 2008).

Bruce, Steve, *Religion in the Modern World* (Oxford: Oxford University Press, 1996).

Bryson, Bill, *Notes from a Small Island* (London: HarperCollins, 1996).

Ford, Daniel and Hardy, David, *Jubilate: Theology in Praise* (London: Darton, Longman and Todd, 1984).

McGowan, Chris and Pessanha, Ricardo, *The Brazilian Sound: Samba, Bossa Nova and the Popular Music of Brazil* (Philadelphia: Temple University Press, 1998).

McLaren, Brian, *Generous Orthodoxy* (Grand Rapids: Zondervan, 2004).

Miller, Don, *Blue Like Jazz* (Nashville: Thomas Nelson Publishing, 2003).

Patterson, Christina, 'Thank God for the Church of England', *The Independent* (25 July 2009): 28.

Pickard, Stephen, 'Innovation and Undecidability: Some Implications for the *Koinonia* of the Anglican Church', *Journal of Anglican Studies*, 2/2 (December 2004): 87–105.

Schon, Donald, The Reflective Practitioner: How Professionals Think in Action (New York: Basic Books, 1983).

Thomas, Kieth, *Religion and Decline of Magic* (London: Penguin, 1971).

van Buren, Paul, *The Burden of Freedom* (New York: Harper, 1976).

West, Cornell, *Race Matters* (Boston: Beacon Press, 1993).

Williams, Rowan, Preface to Martyn Percy, Mark Chapman, Ian S. Markham and James Barney Hawkins IV (eds), *Christ and Culture: Communion After Lambeth* (London: SCM-Canterbury Press, 2010).

Discography

Billy Taylor and the Billy Taylor Trio (London: Capitol Records, 1964).

Officium (Munchen, Germany: ECM Records, 1994).

Message from the Border (London: Atalyst Records, 1995).

'Nitin Sawhney', http://www.nitinsawhney.com, accessed 25 September 2012.

PART II
Interplay of Identities

Chapter 5
Making Borrowed Songs: Mennonite Hymns, Appropriation and Media

Jonathan Dueck

Introduction

For some time ethnomusicologists have mostly agreed with Hobsbawm's idea that traditions are 'invented', a helpful idea discrediting the belief that musical traditions are really, authentically tied to origins.[1] And ethnomusicologists have criticized and played with that phrase, 'the invention of tradition', a great deal.[2] But after all that, at least among ethnomusicologists interested in 'identity', there remains a strong interest in the 'Otherness' of cultures and their musics – in studying identity, we

---

[1] Eric Hobsbawm and Terence Ranger, *The Invention of Tradition* (Cambridge University Press, 1983).

[2] For example, see Adelaida Reyes Schramm, 'Music and Tradition: From Native to Adopted Land Through the Refugee Experience', *Yearbook for Traditional Music*, 21 (1 January 1989): pp. 25–35; Christopher Waterman, 'Our Tradition Is a Very Modern Tradition': Popular Music and the Construction of Pan-Yoruba Identity', *Ethnomusicology*, 34/3 (1990); David B. Coplan, 'Ethnomusicology and the Meaning of Tradition', in Stephen Blum, Philip Vilas Bohlman and Daniel M Neuman (eds), *Ethnomusicology and Modern Music History* (University of Illinois Press, 1991), pp. 35–48; Barbara Kirshenblatt-Gimblett, 'Theorizing Heritage', *Ethnomusicology*, 39/3 (1 October 1995): pp. 367–80; Ruth Davis, 'Cultural Policy and the Tunisian Ma'lūf: Redefining a Tradition', *Ethnomusicology*, 41/1 (1 January 1997): pp. 1–21; Paul Sant Cassia, 'Exoticizing Discoveries and Extraordinary Experiences: "Traditional" Music, Modernity, and Nostalgia in Malta and Other Mediterranean Societies', *Ethnomusicology*, 44/2 (1 April 2000): pp. 281–301; Shannon Dudley, 'Tradition and Modernity in Steel Band Performance', in Frances R. Aparicio and Candida F. Jaquez (eds), *Musical Migrations, Volume I: Transnationalism and Cultural Hybridity in Latin/o America* (Palgrave Macmillan, 2003), pp. 147–60; Shzr Ee Tan, 'Manufacturing and Consuming Culture: Fakesong in Singapore', *Ethnomusicology Forum*, 14/1 (2005): pp. 83–106; Imani Sanga, 'Music and Nationalism in Tanzania: Dynamics of National Space in Muziki Wa Injili in Dar Es Salaam', *Ethnomusicology*, 52/1 (1 January 2008): pp. 52–84; K.B. Schofield, 'Reviving the Golden Age Again: "Classicization", Hindustani Music, and the Mughals', *Ethnomusicology*, 54/3 (2010): pp. 484–517. The concept also appears in writings on Mennonites: see for example Kimberly D. Schmidt, Diane Zimmerman Umble and Steven D. Reschly, *Strangers at Home: Amish and Mennonite Women in History* (Johns Hopkins University Press, 2002).

often look for the ways musical cultures 'resist' or 'subvert' the musical interventions of outsiders.[3] This kind of analysis depends on the tacit belief that musicians are protecting *something prior and something purer* – in other words, in practice, ethnomusicologists continue to believe that origins, or something like them, matter.[4]

There are two problems emerging from this curious dissonance between ethnomusicology's analytic interests in identity and its acceptance that tradition is 'invented': first, our acceptance of Hobsbawm's now-*passé* critique means we can no longer easily invoke the 'authenticity' of music. This deprives us of a vocabulary commonly used to index deep and meaningful *feelings* engendered by music we encounter as 'real' or 'true'. Second, our interest in the ways invented traditions can *help* communities musically 'resist' the powers that be doesn't leave enough space for complicity and ambivalence in our music makers. Our oft-chosen analytic positions and theoretical frames, in other words, can prompt us to de-emphasize beauty and feeling in music, and to simplify (to make too morally 'neat') the relationships between musical cultures and their Others.

For ethnomusicologists interested in Western church music, like myself, these problems are especially acute. As a global music, Western church music is tied to Euro-colonialism and to missions – that is, to unequal power relationships and sometimes to the displacement of local musical traditions. As a 'local' music in North America, Western church music is a hodgepodge of songs from a wide variety of sites of origin in Europe and elsewhere, and it has always been a tradition that depends on media. Church musical media (at first print media, but now also a variety of recorded and digital media) of course, replicates and circulates – it does not circumscribe or protect origins. And yet, church music in North America is also a wide variety of oral traditions, ways of singing learned and remembered person-to-person. And the appropriated songs that make up North American Christian collections – hymnals, praise and worship songs, Native American hymnody, Christian contemporary music record catalogues, gospel repertoires, and on and on – are sometimes deeply, feelingfully owned by the communities that sing them, remake them, and pass them on.

Here, then, I want to propose an alternate framework for thinking of 'musical tradition', a framework that relies not on 'invention' but on the much more

---

[3]   For a fuller discussion of this line of thinking, see Jonathan Dueck, 'Binding and Loosing In Song: Conflict, Identity, And Canadian Mennonite Music', *Ethnomusicology*, 55/2 (27 May 2011): pp. 229–54.

[4]   Élite Mennonite musicians also value origins; see for example Mary Oyer's quoted comments on 'soundpools' and her article using the concept in Anna Groff, '606: When, Why and How Do Mennonites Use the Anthem?', *The Mennonite* (18 March 2008), http://www.themennonite.org/issues/11-6/articles/606_When_why_and_how_do_-Mennonites_use_the_anthem, accessed 24 November 2012; Mary K. Oyer, 'International Mennonite Music-Making as Cross-Cultural Experience', in Maureen Epp, Carol Ann Weaver, Doreen Klassen and Anna Janacek (eds), *Sound In The Lands: Mennonite Music Across Borders* (Pandora Press, 2011), pp. 125–40.

everyday acts of borrowing pieces and putting them together. I will argue that the most characteristic musical activities are acts not of 'invention', but of historically situated cobbling together, of fabrication from the musical materials we have at hand in a particular place and time. The materials available to us – musical gestures, instruments and music technologies, particular songs – are not only raw materials but also constraints, *limits* on the musics and identities we can make. And the fact that those musical elements are tied to structures of power and meaning means *we* are also complicit with those structures in making music. This aspect of my argument resonates with Lysloff and Gay's arguments that music – of many time periods and places – can be imagined as a historically and materially grounded 'technoculture'.[5] Music, then, can be imagined as a historically situated and materially produced object that bears the imprint of its social and material environment; I am calling music, imagined this way, a musical 'artefact', here.[6] The word 'artefact' recalls Clifford's critique of ethnographies as collections of bits of culture, curated and aestheticized – things appropriated; and also of 'artifice', that is, desired truth-effects; and 'artisans', that is, *bricoleurs*.[7]

If the 'artefact' is a kind of musical object, by making such a musical-object-in-the-world, I argue, we also become a particular kind of musical *subject*.[8] Music made this way can, in other words, *still* be deeply authentic for us, by which I mean experientially and feelingfully real. Marx's understanding of the way non-alienated labour allows us to become human, to become a social subject in the world, underlies my pairing of a 'musical artefact' as object with (artefactual) subjectivity in this chapter. This is not the place for an extended reading of Marx's thinking on alienation, and concomitantly on the relationship between acts of making objects and the production of subjects – but it is worth noting that music appears in Marx's discussions of alienation as 'really free' labour through which 'self-realization'

---

[5] Renée Lysloff and Leslie C. Gay, *Music and Technoculture* (Wesleyan University Press, 2003); Leslie C. Gay, Jr., 'Before the Deluge: The Technoculture of Song-Sheet Publishing Viewed from Late Nineteenth-Century Galveston', *American Music*, 17/4 (1 December 1999): pp. 396–421.

[6] The term in its American spelling, 'artifact', more simply shows its etymological overlap with the other cognate terms I mention here. My usage of the term also recalls Silverstein and Urban's use of the term 'text-artifact', a physical inscription bearing text; their term draws on Ricoeur. See Michael Silverstein and Greg Urban, *Natural Histories of Discourse* (University of Chicago Press, 1996), pp. 1–3.

[7] James Clifford, 'On Collecting Art and Culture', *The Predicament of Culture* (Harvard University Press, 1988), pp. 215–51.

[8] I began exploring the idea of a musical 'subject' related to the object of the musical artifact in an article on Russian Mennonite *Kernlieder*: Jonathan Dueck, 'Mennonite Choral Music Recordings of the West Coast Mennonite Chamber Choir (Sound Review Essay)', *Journal of American Folklore*, 121/2 (2008): pp. 348–60. My ongoing research on *Kernlieder*, and on the songs of Cheyenne Mennonites will, I hope, continue the project outlined in this paragraph.

can happen.[9] My argument here, then, both proposes a theoretical construct – the musical artefact (an object) and its subjects – and constitutes a push away from our ethnomusicological tendency to rely on 'identities' and 'cultures', with their dependence on origins, in thinking about how music comes to be meaningful to us.

I will build this idea by exploring the borrowing, making and feelingful ownership that accompany a particular Mennonite hymn, the doxology 'Praise God From Whom All Blessings Flow', which appeared first in the 1969 Mennonite *Hymnal*. Mennonites are a Protestant group that emerged in sixteenth-century Central and Western Europe, on the Radical left of the Reformation. Mennonites' pacifist beliefs did not endear them to their governments, and following intense persecution, some (now called Swiss Mennonites) fled Switzerland to North America, and others (now called Russian Mennonites) fled the Netherlands to Prussia, then Russia, then Canada. Mennonites have pursued missions since the mid-nineteenth century, and there are now more Mennonites in Latin America, Asia and Africa than in Europe and North America.[10] On their long diasporic journeys, Mennonite groups have borrowed and repurposed many musics, including 'Praise God from Whom All Blessings Flow', which began its life in the Mennonite repertoire as a tune borrowed from other nineteenth-century tunebook sources, then making its way into the *Harmonia Sacra*, a Swiss Mennonite shape note book from the Shenandoah Valley of Virginia.

Before embarking upon my exploration, two brief caveats are necessary: first, I write as someone who grew up a Canadian Russian Mennonite – a useful position for investigating (Mennonite) musical subjectivity because of the access it provides, both to subjectivity itself and, through long experience, to at least one Mennonite practice of singing the hymns about which I write.[11] But, as Burnim

---

[9] Karl Marx, *Selected Writings*, trans. and ed. David McLellan (Oxford University Press, 1977), p. 368. This argument also reflects critical writings on media: new media forms shape certain kinds of subjectivity, as McLuhan pointed out that print culture produced sight-centric, linear-thinking subjects; Adorno prophesied that industrial cultural objects produced the willing subjects of hegemonic power and Nestor García Canclini further suggests that new media forms produce not only subjectivities but also sociabilities bonded by the imagined co-consumption of media, often in private and atomized settings, and not by the face-to-face sharing of public space: Marshall McLuhan, *The Gutenberg Galaxy; the Making of Typographic Man* (University of Toronto Press, 1962); Max Horkheimer and Theodor W. Adorno, *Dialectic of Enlightenment* (Herder and Herder, 1972); Nestor García Canclini, *Consumers and Citizens: Globalization and Multicultural Conflicts* (University of Minnesota Press, 2001).

[10] For a basic introduction to Mennonites and their history, see C.J. Dyck, *An Introduction to Mennonite History: A Popular History of the Anabaptists and the Mennonites* (Herald Press, 1993). For an introduction to European Mennonite history in particular, see Claude Baecher et al., *Testing Faith and Tradition: Global Mennonite History Series: Europe*, ed. John A. Lapp and C. Arnold Snyder (Good Books, 2006).

[11] See Chou Chiener, 'Experience and Fieldwork: A Native Researcher's View', *Ethnomusicology*, 46/3 (2002): pp. 456–86.

noted, group identities and scholarly insidership relate in rather complex ways; I write as an insider to Russian and Swiss Mennonite ethnicity and to a shared Mennonite religious identity, but not as an insider to the Shenandoah Valley Swiss Mennonite community.[12] My case study is in part autoethnographic, working to understand my own experience of borrowed Mennonite songs; but it does so by exploring the ways the histories and experiences of others intersect with my own.

Second, this case study is organized around a central song with strong significance for particular Mennonite communities, but traces broader collections (a hymnal, a shape note book) in which the song can historically be placed. One might question if particular pieces can 'stand in' for the broader experiential qualities of collections. I acknowledge that this metonymic structure is not without problems – among them, slippage between the very particular qualities of the songs under discussion and the more general qualities of songs within a collection. But, I will argue, the qualities of borrowing and 'making' which I trace can characterize both pieces and collections. Both 'Praise God from Whom All Blessings Flow', and its collection, the *Harmonia Sacra*, are imprints of compiler Joseph Funk's borrowing of musical and material elements from the German and Scotch Irish communities of the nineteenth-century Shenandoah Valley. And, as Kropf and Nafziger's discussion of the Mennonite hymns that represented 'home' for their interviewees suggest, for singers, particular songs do at times stand in as the 'core' of a repertoire of hymns, lending particular meanings to the whole.[13]

'606' as Mennonite 'Anthem' and the Virginia *Harmonia Sacra*

The central idea of this paper started to take shape for me when, in 2000, I first encountered the *Sacred Harp* and *Harmonia Sacra* shape note books. Shape note books are a nineteenth-century form of musical media, oblong books of tunes that were used for social singing in the (Christian) public culture of the American South and the Western frontier. Shape note tunebooks contributed and circulated many tunes that are now familiar hymns for Mennonites and other Protestants, but the books themselves were used in 'singing schools' that travelling singing school teachers held in many communities. They are presently mostly used in 'singings' or 'sings', social gatherings to sing tunes together. The books present a wide array of tunes using a total of either four or seven different shapes including triangles, squares and diamonds in place of the round note-heads that are familiarly used in Western music notation; these shapes represent the syllables of a solmization system and, unlike preceding hymnals which typically presented hymn texts but not tunes, were therefore an aid to learning new tunes. Shape note tunebooks are

---

[12]   Mellonee Burnim, 'Culture Bearer and Tradition Bearer: An Ethnomusicologist's Research on Gospel Music', *Ethnomusicology*, 29/3 (1985): pp. 432–47.

[13]   Marlene Kropf and Kenneth Nafziger, *Singing: A Mennonite Voice* (Herald Press, 2001), pp. 19–44.

still in use today – all over the Anglophone world, in the case of the *Sacred Harp*, the most famous of tunebooks.[14] The *Harmonia Sacra* is still sung from regularly in the Shenandoah Valley of Virginia, primarily by Mennonites, and in a related New Year's sing held in Elkhart, Indiana.

The most widely known *Harmonia Sacra* tune, among Mennonites, is the anthem 'Praise God from Whom All Blessings Flow', known by its tune name, 'Dedication Anthem' in *Harmonia Sacra*, and as '606' from its initial appearance in the 1969 *Mennonite Hymnal*.[15] The song presents Thomas Ken's well-known 1695/1709 doxology text, set not to the tune Old Hundredth but rather to a polyphonic anthem by Samuel Stanley that appeared in Lowell Mason's *Boston Handel and Haydn Society Collection* (9th edition, 1830) before it made its way into the *Harmonia Sacra* (and into the Virginia Mennonite repertoire) two years later.[16] The 1969 *Hymnal* was used by two North American denominations: the General Conference Mennonite Church (GC) and the Mennonite Church (MC), which in 2002 joined and formed two similarly named national conferences, Mennonite Church USA and Mennonite Church Canada. The 1969 *Hymnal* itself represented an important link between the groups; previously, the MCs and GCs sang from different books.[17] Among Mennonites of these denominational backgrounds, the song is very widely sung. It is sometimes even humorously called 'The Mennonite National Anthem', a term that makes particular sense when the song is sung at denominational conference meetings by thousands of Mennonites, *a cappella*.[18] Indeed, after the hymnal was introduced in the 1969 *Mennonite Conference* in Turner, Oregon, Mary Oyer, a centrally important Mennonite music leader and a

---

[14]   For good introductions to shape note books and singing, see Buell E. Cobb Jr., *The Sacred Harp: A Tradition and Its Music* (University of Georgia Press, 2004); John Bealle, *Public Worship, Private Faith: Sacred Harp and American Folksong* (University of Georgia Press, 1997); Kiri Miller, *Traveling Home: Sacred Harp Singing And American Pluralism* (University of Illinois Press, 2008). All of these books focus on *Sacred Harp* but address the broader world of shape note singing.

[15]   Joseph Funk and Sons, *The Harmonia Sacra: A Compilation of Genuine Church Music*, ed. James Nelson Gingerich (Good Books, 1993); Joint Hymnal Committee, ed., *The Mennonite Hymnal* (Scottdale, PA; Newton, KS: Herald Press; Faith and Life Press, 1969).

[16]   Handel and Haydn Society (Boston MA.), The Boston Handel and Haydn Society Collection of Church Music: Being a Selection of the Most Approved Psalm and Hymn Tunes, Anthems, Sentences, Chants, &C.: Together with Many Beautiful Extracts from the Works of Haydn, Mozart, Beethoven, and Other Eminent Composers, Harmonized for Three and Four Voices, with a Figured Base for the Organ and Piano Forte (Richardson, Lord and Holbrook, 1830).

[17]   Oyer, 'International Mennonite Music-Making', p. 127.

[18]   See for example: Alyssa Cable, 'The Ghosts of Conventions Past', *Mennocon.com*, 2012, http://www.men-nocon.com/featured/the-ghosts-of-conventions-past/, accessed 24 November 2012.

Figure 5.1   Opening bars of *Dedication Anthem*

member of the *Hymnal* committee, recalls that the song became the 'immediate favourite' and soon after was known by its number, 606.[19]

Alan Stucky, a Mennonite pastor, recorded and shared on YouTube a performance of '606' from the 2011 Mennonite Church USA conference in Pittsburgh that is a good representation of performance practice for the song in many congregations.[20] Stucky chooses a wide shot showing hundreds of Mennonite singing together in the large, dark hall, for the most part leaving the songleader out of the frame. Figure 5.1 presents the opening six bars of the song. The songleader intones the tenor and soprano notes that open the song, and the 'congregation' of conference attendees launch into these opening bars of the song at a rapid clip (about 85 half note beats per minute), singing loudly with vibrato, with sharp rhythmic attacks on each part entry. Phrases are shaped around the musical gestures rather than the text, with dynamics rising as staggered voices enter at increasing pitch levels (see Figure 5.2). The overall effect is robust, full-throated and declamatory – rather more emphatically anthemic than a baseball-game performance of *The Star Spangled Banner*, for example.

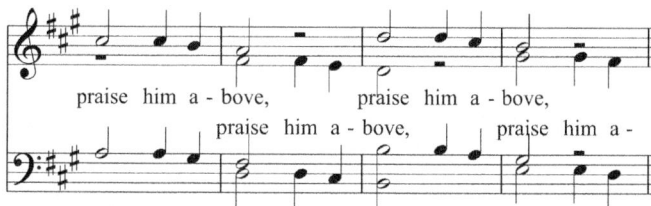

Figure 5.2   Staggered voice entries in *Dedication Anthem*

---

[19]   Oyer, 'International Mennonite Music-Making as Cross-Cultural Experience', p. 128. When the 1992 *Hymnal: A Worship Book* changed the number of the song to 118, members of one Ohio congregation 'booed and hissed the announcement', and most still call the song '606': Kropf and Nafziger, *Singing: A Mennonite Voice*, p. 37.

[20]   Alan Stucky, 'Praise God from Whom at Pittsburgh 2011', *Youtube.com*, 8 July 2011, http://www.youtube.com/-watch?v=jp_cBS031PQ, accessed 24 November 2012.

The *Harmonia Sacra* was compiled by Joseph Funk, a Mennonite of Harrisonburg, Virginia. Harrisonburg is in the Shenandoah Valley, the Northern tip of the American South, a meeting-place for Scotch-Irish Americans and German-speakers, including Mennonites; both groups had migrated there from Pennsylvania in the early 1700s.[21] This migration brought so many German speakers that Virginia published its laws in German in addition to English at that time. Both camp meetings and singing schools were part of a public space shared by the Mennonites and other Valley residents, and Funk's tunebooks reflect a common stock of Valley musical materials.[22] In 1816 Funk compiled *Choral-Musik,* a German-language book featuring the chorales and psalm tunes that many German-speakers in the area sang, printed with four-shape type borrowed from fellow Valley native Ananias Davisson, who in the same year compiled *The Kentucky Harmony.*[23] Its introduction contains words of welcome from the local Reformed Church minister, and area Lutherans also used the book.

In 1832, as the German-speakers of the Valley increasingly began to speak English, Funk compiled a new English four-shape tunebook called *Genuine Church Music*, eventually republished in seven shapes as *Harmonia Sacra.*[24] This included American folk tunes, camp meeting songs, and New England-composed tunes – the collection of Anglo-American popular and folk musics found in the Valley, similar (considered broadly) to Davisson's earlier tunebook. Funk promoted the volume not only to Mennonites but also to the plurality of religious and ethnic communities in Virginia, offering hundreds of singing schools throughout the Blue Ridge mountains.[25] But the book remains in use today through its continuous practice by Shenandoah Valley (Virginia) Mennonite groups for singings.[26] With their entry into the 1890 *Hymns and Tunes*, and later into the 1969 *Hymnal*, several tunes from the *Harmonia Sacra* travelled much further than the

---

[21]   Harry Lee Eskew, 'Shape-Note Hymnody in the Shenandoah Valley' (PhD diss., Tulane University, 1966), p. 3.

[22]   Ibid., 15–16.

[23]   Ibid., 76–81.

[24]   Ibid., 97–8.

[25]   John W. Wayland, 'Joseph Funk, Father of Song in Northern Virginia', in Joseph Funk and Sons (eds), *The New Harmonia Sacra* (Ruebush-Kieffer Co., 1923), p. 3; Eskew, 'Shape-Note Hymnody in the Shenandoah Valley', p. 74; Richard John Stanislaw, 'Choral Performance Practice in the Four-Shape Literature of American Frontier Singing Schools' (DMA diss., University of Illinois at Urbana-Champaign, 1976), p. 128.

[26]   Warren Steel, 'Shape-Note Singing in the Shenandoah Valley', 1997, http://www.mcsr.olemiss.edu/~mudws/-shenandoah.html, accessed 24 November 2012. Its longevity and use among area Mennonites is significant, as it was not the only Mennonite tunebook available; James Hall lists six Mennonite tunebooks produced between 1800–1820 alone: James Williams Hall, Jr., 'The Tune-book in American Culture: 1800–1820' (University of Pennsylvania, 1967), p. 204.

book itself did, covering the breadth of MC and GC Mennonite communities all over North America.[27]

The *Sacred Harp* and Singing Diasporas

The *Harmonia Sacra's* initial trajectory – in which a geographically bounded Mennonite community preserved the book through curation and local use, but a much broader Mennonite community accessed its repertoire through the placement of its songs in a new piece of media, the *Hymnal* – presents a strong contrast to that of the *Sacred Harp*. B.F. White, the *Sacred Harp*'s compiler, not only travelled to promote his book as Funk did; he also set up the Southern Musical Convention, a gathering that drew singing school teachers from all over Georgia and Alabama. In so doing, he created broad networks across the South for the distribution and use of his tunebook. White helped to found and shape singing traditions through spelling out singing school rules and guidelines, many of which characterize even present-day shaped-note singing, in the rules of the Southern Musical Convention.[28] Singing school teachers fanned out geographically and produced their own conventions, with their own constitutions (modelled on White's). Through the singing and the teaching activities of the members of this group, and later the Chattahoochee Musical Convention, the *Sacred Harp* became popular throughout the Southeast and has remained so to the present day. Kiri Miller explored the ways in which the social form of the 'singing', with its particular ways of organizing singing procedurally and spatially, travelled and became owned by a large diaspora in the Northern and Western US (and, though this is not Miller's focus, in other Anglophone parts of the world).[29] In other words, White produced a popular medium not only for the music but also the social occasion of shape note singing, both of which proliferate today in a diaspora that spans the English-speaking world.

These two tunebooks' networks of social forms and musical practices – arguably overlapping in earlier days – have begun to re-articulate recently. A group of singers in Elkhart, Indiana, a Midwestern Mennonite institutional centre about eleven hours drive from Harrisonburg, began holding *Harmonia Sacra* singings in the 1980s.[30] Many of these Mennonite singers first came to the shape note tradition through 'Mary Oyer and the 1969 *Hymnal*'. In the 1980s James Nelson Gingerich,

---

[27]   Rebecca Slough and Shirley Sprunger King (eds), *Nurturing Spirit Through Song: The Life of Mary K. Oyer* (Cascadia, 2007), p. 244.

[28]   See Charles Ellington, 'The Sacred Harp Tradition of the South: Its Origin and Evolution' (PhD diss., Florida State University, 1969), p. 43. Bealle's fourth chapter in *Public Worship, Private Faith* offers a very useful account of the spread of *Sacred Harp*.

[29]   Miller, Traveling Home.

[30]   Published minutes begin, however, in 1998, at the group's site: http://harmoniasacra.org/minutes/.

a Mennonite physician living in Goshen (near Elkhart), began attending *Sacred Harp* singings in the area with singers 'heavily influenced by Chicago *Sacred Harp* folks', and began to travel South to singings. They began to hold quarterly *Harmonia Sacra* singings, and Gingerich worked closely with Mary Oyer and the Mennonite-owned publishing house, Good Books, to reprint the oblong *Harmonia Sacra* (which was then out of print).[31]

To show what's significant about this Indiana gathering and its connections to *Sacred Harp*, I'm going to first recount a Shenandoah Valley singing I attended at Dayton Mennonite Church on 3 July 2005 and then contrast it with the Elkhart singing. In the early evening midsummer warmth, the church parking lot was filled with vehicles indexing a spectrum of Swiss Mennonite groups from the Shenandoah Valley: Japanese sedans and American pickup trucks for mainstream Mennonite Church USA folk; dark-coloured cars for conservative Mennonite groups; and buggies for Old Order Mennonites. Once inside the church, men and women, and young and old, sat together in the church pews, facing forward towards the leader – not in the 'hollow square' formation with the leader in the centre, typical of *Sacred Harp* singing. Nearly everyone held the 'Legacy Edition', the 24th edition of the *Harmonia Sacra*. This book is not in landscape format as are the *Sacred Harp* and all other editions of the *Harmonia Sacra* (including the 25th edition with which Gingerich was closely involved); it is instead a portrait format book, similar in its dimensions to a hymnal. It was set in shape notes by hand by Lydia Ann Beery, a Conservative Mennonite woman; unlike most nineteenth century shape note books, the melody is presented in the soprano rather than the tenor line. Beery's editorial choice reflects Virginia practice for all *Harmonia Sacra* tune-books: at the singings I attended, sopranos were told to sing from the tenor line in the 'long book', and tenors to sing the soprano line. At Dayton, we opened the singing with prayer. When we sang '606' at Dayton, it was introduced by its tune name, 'Dedication Anthem', along with its numbers in the 'Long Book' and the 'Legacy'. My recording of the singing shows some commonalities with the Mennonite Church USA Pittsburgh meeting recording referenced earlier; there is some vibrato, and a good deal of dynamic variation – long crescendos in each section. But each phrase, too, even in the declamatory 'Hallelujah' section that concludes the piece, is shaped gently, swelling, receding dynamically. In contrast to Pittsburgh, the tempo is flexible and much slower (about 62 beats per minute). Some sing non-vibrato as conserving Mennonite groups often do. The effect as a whole is considerably gentler than the Pittsburgh conference performance.

The Elkhart New Years' Day singing in 2007, which I attended, on the other hand, presented a middle ground between Mennonite Church USA singing practices and those of the *Sacred Harp*. The singing happened in the symbolic centre of Mennonite Church USA ecclesial identity: the chapel of Associated Mennonite Biblical Seminary (AMBS), the denomination's main seminary. AMBS is the

---

[31]   James Nelson Gingerich, 'Re: Questions Re: Elkhart H.S. Singing', email message to author, 25 February 2003.

institutional home of Rebecca Slough, editor of the 1992 Mennonite *Hymnal: A Worship Book* from which the Pittsburgh convention sang '606'. Mary Oyer sat in the back row of the Chapel at this singing. Nametags identified the singers, some of whom had travelled from Chicago, Pennsylvania, or even California to attend the singing; this lengthy travel characterizes *Sacred Harp* singing practice, and a number of the singers at this gathering were *Sacred Harp* singers, including Ted Mercer, a well-known *Sacred Harp* singer and composer. Others were Northern Indiana Mennonites who are primarily Mennonite church hymn singers. James Nelson Gingerich, near the beginning of the singing, offered an erudite and brief history of the *Harmonia Sacra* and its seven shapes for the (four-shape) *Sacred Harp* singers in attendance. In the midst of the singing, one singer complained that a tune's text was not the same as it was in the *Sacred Harp*; James answered, 'but we're singing from *this* book today'.

Elkhart's singers sat in a 'hollow square' as *Sacred Harp* singers do, each side singing a different voice part. My recording of 'Dedication Anthem' in Elkhart resonates with both *Sacred Harp* and Mennonite church singing practice. There's a heterogeneous sense of ensemble in the recording, with distinctly audible voice parts – reflecting both the arrangement of singers in a 'hollow square' and the diversity of vocal tones employed by the singers. Some sing with a tone reminiscent of *Sacred Harp* singings, loudly, non-vibrato in a penetrating bright tone. Some sing with more warmth and vibrato. The tempo is fast and regular, as characterizes both the Pittsburgh performance I mention above and typical *Sacred Harp* performance practice for 'fuging tunes', with imitative counterpoint similar to portions of 'Dedication Anthem'.

In correspondence with me, Gingerich characterized Elkhart singing practice as both tied to and distinct from *Sacred Harp* practice:

> … we in Elkhart County have always sung *Harmonia Sacra* more in *Sacred Harp* style. But we certainly don't sing it like we sing *Sacred Harp*. With its sweeter harmonies and more refined sound (more Mason, Bradbury, and Hastings), we tend to sing it less loudly, and with a less straight beating style. *Sacred Harp* singers would not confuse it with their book. But Virginian *Harmonia Sacra* singers would probably think it more raw than they are used to.[32]

Gingerich's comments suggest, for me, both commonly held aesthetic principles that distinguish the two singing traditions (which I have tried to reflect in my commentary above), but also the ways that he, as a person whose own experience and work ties the two traditions together, makes sense of the 'ownership' singers feel for both traditions.

---

[32]   Ibid.

Linking Shape Note Songs and Mennonite Hymns as Musical Artefacts

My reading of these two singings here suggests some of the ways in which *Harmonia Sacra* and 'Dedication Anthem'/'606' link – through shared repertoires and markedly divergent performance styles – a wide spectrum of Mennonites, and the diaspora which emerged from (Anglophone) Southern shape note singing. The echoes of this link are still resounding: the August 2006 *Harmonia Sacra* singing in the Old Hamburg Church near Luray, Virginia was attended by mid-Atlantic Sacred Harpers, who led songs and demonstrated *Sacred Harp* singing. And Mennonite Church USA and Canada congregational singing in local churches often involves songs of shape note origin. For example, when I led a 2007 hymn sing at an urban, Washington DC-area Mennonite church, nearly half of the songs congregational members asked to sing were from shape note sources. The congregation sang them as though from memory, in some cases ignoring the tempi that I set but arriving, perfectly together, on their own downbeat. And in Edmonton, Alberta (Canada), nearly the opposite end of the North American continent, when, in 2001, I was asked one evening to talk about the *Harmonia Sacra*, some older congregational members surprised me by laughing as I named the shapes and reminisced about singing schools in rural Alberta which used its tunes.[33]

These shape note books are for me the paradigm of what I'm here calling the musical 'artefact'. The term draws attention to the making of this kind of social and musical link – the formation of a musical object from locally available materials, the journeyman-like arrangement of those materials, the artifice of such an arrangement which tries to produce particular effects for particular audiences and the contingent persistence over time of such a musical object and its circulation to other audiences. An 'artefact' like Funk's book might be imagined as a material embodiment of what Stuart Hall has called an 'articulation': literally made between things, it links and differentiates groups and bodies of texts at once.[34] The stories of the *Harmonia Sacra*'s making, and its shared circumstances of production and repertoires with other shape note books like *Kentucky Harmony* and *Sacred Harp*, are still wrapped round it, and as the book and its songs persist over time, these stories become new materials conditioning its travels and its articulations for the communities who remake and use it.

Concluding Reflections

If the borrowed musical objects of Western Christian hymnody – what I have here called the 'musical artefact' – are viewed from the admittedly particular

---

[33]   Some of the members of this Alberta Mennonite community arrived in the mid-twentieth century in Canada from Virginia and Pennsylvania.

[34]   See David Morley and Kuan-Hsing Chen (eds), *Stuart Hall: Critical Dialogues in Cultural Studies* (Routledge, 1996).

vantage point of the story of '606', then, they have two key characteristics.[35] '606' and the *Harmonia Sacra* were made from local musical, cultural, and physical materials at hand. These borrowed, remade, songs still formed perfectly usable ties to (Virginia, and much broader Mennonite) musical subjectivities. '606', then, means something because of the set of relationships, memories and so forth, which it actualizes, reimagines and remakes. It is not primarily oppositional, critical or resistant. Instead, it is multiple, polyphonic, poetic and literary; it is a very recursive cobbling together of stories. Looking at songs like '606' in their historical particularity, in their smallness, their materiality allows for contradiction and complexity in the way those songs articulate with musical cultures and identities. I am arguing, then, that thinking ethnomusicologically about church music needs to begin not with origins but with the retelling and trading of stories of how songs are borrowed and remade, how they are used, and how these kinds of movement and *bricolage* help make them meaningful for faith and people that are also, always, on the move.

Acknowledgements

I would like to thank Duke's Thompson Writing Programme for their support as I wrote this chapter. I would also like to thank Anna Nekola, Doreen Klassen, Wesley Berg, Peter Letkemann, John Plunkett, Kimberly Schmidt, Carl Urion and David Graber for their helpful feedback on the chapter, as I worked on it. Finally I'd like to thank Kiri Miller, Jeffers Engelhardt, Byron Dueck and Martin Daughtry for discussions that were very useful in thinking through the idea of the 'artefact' with these cases in mind.

References

Lapp, John A. and Snyder, C. Arnold (eds), *Testing Faith and Tradition: Global Mennonite History Series: Europe* (Intercourse, PA: Good Books, 2006).
Bealle, John, *Public Worship, Private Faith: Sacred Harp and American Folksong* (Athens, GA: University of Georgia Press, 1997).
Burnim, Mellonee, 'Culture Bearer and Tradition Bearer: An Ethnomusicologist's Research on Gospel Music', *Ethnomusicology*, 29/3 (1985): 432–47.

---

[35] See Engelhardt's work on 'ecumenicity' for a strongly complementary understanding of church-musical circulation in Europe; on Mennonites, Schmidt makes a similar case concerning material cultures outside of music – sewing circles. Jeffers Engelhardt, 'Late-and Post-Soviet Music Scholarship and the Tenacious Ecumenicity of Christian Musics in Estonia', *Journal of Baltic Studies*, 39/3 (2008): pp. 239–62; Schmidt, Umble and Reschly, *Strangers at Home*.

Cable, Alyssa, 'The Ghosts of Conventions Past', *Mennocon.com*, 2012, http://www.mennocon.com/featured/the-ghosts-of-conventions-past/, accessed 24 November 2012.

Canclini, Nestor García, *Consumers and Citizens: Globalization and Multicultural Conflicts* (Minneapolis: University of Minnesota Press, 2001).

Cassia, Paul Sant, 'Exoticizing Discoveries and Extraordinary Experiences: 'Traditional' Music, Modernity, and Nostalgia in Malta and Other Mediterranean Societies', *Ethnomusicology*, 44/2 (1 April 2000): 281–301.

Chiener, Chou, 'Experience and Fieldwork: A Native Researcher's View', *Ethnomusicology*, 46/3 (2002): 456–86.

Clifford, James, 'On Collecting Art and Culture', in *The Predicament of Culture* (Cambridge, MA: Harvard University Press, 1988).

Cobb, Jr., Buell E., *The Sacred Harp: A Tradition and Its Music* (Athens: University of Georgia Press, 2004).

Coplan, David B., 'Ethnomusicology and the Meaning of Tradition', in Stephen Blum, Philip Vilas Bohlman and Daniel M Neuman (eds), *Ethnomusicology and Modern Music History* (Urbana: University of Illinois Press, 1991).

Davis, Ruth, 'Cultural Policy and the Tunisian Ma'lūf: Redefining a Tradition', *Ethnomusicology*, 41/1 (1 January 1997): 1–21.

Dudley, Shannon, 'Tradition and Modernity in Steel Band Performance', in Frances R. Aparicio and Candida F. Jaquez (eds), *Musical Migrations, Volume I: Transnationalism and Cultural Hybridity in Latin/o America* (New York: Palgrave Macmillan, 2003).

Dueck, Jonathan, 'Mennonite Choral Music Recordings of the West Coast Mennonite Chamber Choir (Sound Review Essay)', *Journal of American Folklore*, 121/2 (2008): 348-360.

Dueck, Jonathan, 'Binding and Loosing in Song: Conflict, Identity, and Canadian Mennonite Music', *Ethnomusicology*, 55/2 (27 May 2011): 229–54.

Dyck, C.J., *An Introduction to Mennonite History: A Popular History of the Anabaptists and the Mennonites* (Scottdale, PA: Herald Press, 1993).

Ellington, Charles, 'The Sacred Harp Tradition of the South: Its Origin and Evolution' (PhD diss., Florida State University, 1969).

Engelhardt, Jeffers, 'Late- and Post-Soviet Music Scholarship and the Tenacious Ecumenicity of Christian Musics in Estonia', *Journal of Baltic Studies*, 39/3 (2008): 239–62.

Eskew, Harry Lee, 'Shape-Note Hymnody in the Shenandoah Valley' (PhD diss., Tulane University, 1966).

Funk, Joseph and Sons, *The Harmonia Sacra: A Compilation of Genuine Church Music*, ed. James Nelson Gingerich (Intercourse, PA: Good Books, 1993).

Gay Jr., Leslie C., 'Before the Deluge: The Technoculture of Song-Sheet Publishing Viewed from Late Nineteenth-Century Galveston', *American Music*, 17/4 (1 December 1999): 396–421.

Gingerich, James Nelson, 'Re: Questions Re: Elkhart H.S. Singing', email message to author, 25 February 2003.

Groff, Anna, '606: When, Why and How Do Mennonites Use the Anthem?' *The Mennonite*, 18 March 2008. http://www.themennonite.org/issues/11-6/articles/606_When_why_and_how_do_-Mennonites_use_the_anthem, accessed 24 November 2012.

Hall, James Williams Jr., 'The Tune-book in American Culture: 1800–1820', University of Pennsylvania, 1967.

Handel and Haydn Society (Boston, MA), *The Boston Handel and Haydn Society Collection of Church Music: Being a Selection of the Most Approved Psalm and Hymn Tunes, Anthems, Sentences, Chants, &C.: Together with Many Beautiful Extracts from the Works of Haydn, Mozart, Beethoven, and Other Eminent Composers, Harmonized for Three and Four Voices, with a Figured Base for the Organ and Piano Forte* (Richardson, Lord and Holbrook, 1830).

Hobsbawm, Eric and Terence Ranger, *The Invention of Tradition* (Cambridge: Cambridge University Press, 1983).

Horkheimer, Max and Theodor W. Adorno, *Dialectic of Enlightenment* (New York: Herder and Herder, 1972).

Joint Hymnal Committee (ed.), *The Mennonite Hymnal* (Scottdale, PA; Newton, KS: Herald Press; Faith and Life Press, 1969).

Kirshenblatt-Gimblett, Barbara, 'Theorizing Heritage', *Ethnomusicology*, 39/3 (1 October 1995): 367–80.

Kropf, Marlene and Nafzinger, Kenneth, *Singing: A Mennonite Voice* (Scottdale, PA: Herald Press, 2001).

Lysloff, Renée and Gay, Leslie C., *Music and Technoculture* (Middletown, CN: Wesleyan University Press, 2003).

Marx, Karl, *Selected Writings*, trans. and ed. David McLellan (Oxford: Oxford University Press, 1977).

McLuhan, Marshall, *The Gutenberg Galaxy; the Making of Typographic Man* (Toronto: University of Toronto Press, 1962).

Miller, Kiri, *Traveling Home: Sacred Harp Singing And American Pluralism* (Urbana: University of Illinois Press, 2008).

Morley, David and Chen, Kuan-Hsing (eds), *Stuart Hall: Critical Dialogues in Cultural Studies* (London: Routledge, 1996).

Oyer, Mary K., 'International Mennonite Music-Making as Cross-Cultural Experience', in Maureen Epp, Carol Ann Weaver, Doreen Klassen and Anna Janacek (eds), *Sound In The Lands: Mennonite Music Across Borders* (Kitchener, ON: Pandora Press, 2011).

Sanga, Imani, 'Music and Nationalism in Tanzania: Dynamics of National Space in Muziki Wa Injili in Dar Es Salaam', *Ethnomusicology*, 52/1 (1 January 2008): 52–84.

Schmidt, Kimberly D., Umble, Diane Zimmerman and Reschly, Steven D., *Strangers at Home: Amish and Mennonite Women in History* (Baltimore: Johns Hopkins University Press, 2002).

Schofield, K.B., 'Reviving the Golden Age Again: "Classicization", Hindustani Music, and the Mughals', *Ethnomusicology*, 54/3 (2010): 484–517.

Schramm, Adelaida Reyes, 'Music and Tradition: From Native to Adopted Land Through the Refugee Experience', *Yearbook for Traditional Music*, 21 (1 January 1989): 25–35.

Silverstein, Michael and Urban, Greg, *Natural Histories of Discourse* (Chicago and London: University of Chicago Press, 1996).

Slough, Rebecca and King, Shirley Sprunger, *Nurturing Spirit Through Song: The Life of Mary K. Oyer* (Telford, PA: Cascadia, 2007).

Stanislaw, Richard John, 'Choral Performance Practice in the Four-Shape Literature of American Frontier Singing Schools' (DMA diss., University of Illinois at Urbana-Champaign, 1976).

Steel, Warren, 'Shape-Note Singing in the Shenandoah Valley,' http://www.mcsr. olemiss.edu/-~mudws/shenandoah.html, accessed 24 November 2012.

Stucky, Alan, 'Praise God from Whom at Pittsburgh 2011', *Youtube.com*, 8 July 2011, http://www.youtube.com/watch?v=jp_cBS031PQ,aAccessed 24 November 2012.

Tan, Shzr Ee, 'Manufacturing and Consuming Culture: Fakesong in Singapore', *Ethnomusicology Forum*, 14/1 (2005): 83–106.

Waterman, Christopher, 'Our Tradition Is a Very Modern Tradition': Popular Music and the Construction of Pan-Yoruba Identity', *Ethnomusicology*, 34/3 (1990).

Wayland, John W., 'Joseph Funk, Father of Song in Northern Virginia', in Joseph Funk and Sons (eds), *The New Harmonia Sacra* (Dayton, VA: Ruebush-Kieffer Co., 1923).

Chapter 6

New Music for New Times?: Debates over Catholic Congregational Music in Hungary

Kinga Povedák

As we know, there is no single religion that creates music on its own. They all use various forms and tools offered by contemporary cultural realities.[1] The position of the Catholic Church in Hungary regarding the status and reception of Christian popular music differs in many respects from Protestant churches and, in particular, Pentecostal or Charismatic denominations. The latter churches are more open to contemporary culture due to the fact that they appeared in Hungary mostly after the 1989 political turn; also, as they were established during the late modern period, they lack corresponding antecedents in Hungarian church music history they could build on, as there were no prevalent traditions.

In contrast to the Protestant Church, which during the nineteenth and twentieth centuries generally embraced advances in technology (especially media and communication), the Catholic Church displayed much more ambivalence. For the Catholic Church, however, industrial revolutions, technological modernization, the spread of liberal political ideas and the processes of social mobility of the nineteenth and twentieth centuries have presented a far greater challenge – and still do. The Catholic Church was forced to respond to these radical social and technological changes and other processes that threatened its authority and status as no thorough reforms had been instituted before the Second Vatican Council (1962–65), while spontaneous reactions could be observed among believers as part of a grassroots movement which spread continually and grew diverse as a result of a lack of regulation or clear guidelines. Ambivalence toward modernity has characterized the post-Vatican II era.[2]

Naturally, Vatican II has been unable to regulate all areas of vernacular religiosity. Of these, the most prominent is the issue of church music: should sacred music based on rock and roll be permitted during the Mass or should it be limited to use outside of the church? Since religious popular music is an especially apt tool for reaching younger generations, the significant debates that emerged should not only be understood within this conflict; they should also be interpreted in a

[1] Benjámin Rajeczky, 'Gregorián, népének, népdal' [Gregorian, Folk Hymn, Folk Song] in Ferenc Bónis (ed.), *Magyar Zenetörténeti Tanulmányok Szabolcsi Bence 70. születésnapjára.* (Zeneműkiadó, 1969), p. 46.

[2] John F. Baldovin, *Reforming the Liturgy* (Liturgical Press, 2008).

significantly broader context, which is nothing less than the relationship between religion and modernity, religion and change, and religion and mass culture.[3]

It is safe to say that church music in the Hungarian Catholic Church and perhaps in the global Catholic Church of our day represents a diversity on a scale never before witnessed; indeed, musical traditions of various ages and levels of culture live side by side today with the fashionable popular music of recent times. This type of diversity as a rule impacts each believer differently and has also led to the emergence of powerful controversies on the level of vernacular religiosity. As a consequence, the Church has been forced to respond to an increasing number of influences that it encounters in a rapidly changing era, while the amount of time available to deliberate and phrase its response and to consider potential consequences has shrunk.

As a rule, therefore, dissenting points of view have been increasing, and conflicts between various parties representing various interpretations have deepened about the aesthetic level of Christian popular music and whether it should be used during the Catholic liturgy. In this postmodernist relativist age, however, the view on church music is complicated further by the fact that prevalent aesthetic canons have crumbled, thus creating more space for different understandings and opposing views of varying trends.

The purpose of this chapter is to outline the political and aesthetic preferences as a result of which the reception and opinion of popular music in the Church were shaped in socialist-era Hungary and after the country's regime change (in 1989–90). This study demonstrates that criticism in connection with music was primarily based on aesthetic and not religious considerations, and that debates on theological content in fact reflect the aesthetic preferences of the opposing parties.

Political Circumstances

The situation of the Catholic Church is especially complex in the countries of the former socialist bloc, where Christian churches represented the greatest ideological threat to the openly atheist political powers. As in most socialist countries, the Hungarian political powers forced churches into a dependent position. Following the forceful action taken against the churches, the socialist state signed an 'agreement' with the Christian churches in 1950, in which they mandated the dissolution of religious orders, the confiscation of church property, and the

---

[3]   It is important to note, however, that throughout history, church music has never been static, homogeneous or constant; rather, it has been a heterogeneous and syncretic phenomenon that integrates various traditions and musical worlds. We should not think, therefore, that debates over church music style are exclusive to this age. For further discussion, see Rajeczky, 'Gregorián'; see also Andrew Wilson-Dickson, *Fejezetek a kereszténység zenéjéből* [*A Brief History of Christian Music: From Biblical Times to the Present*] (Gemini Budapest Kiadó, 1998).

subjugation of the churches to the state.[4] The period was marked by regular show trials, arrests and intimidations.[5] The social presence and role of the churches were rendered insignificant and confined to the officially sanctioned work of the clergy. Not only churches, but all social organizations and activities came under party and state control.[6] As of 1957, the 'soft dictatorship' or 'Goulash communism' of János Kádár[7] implemented the so-called 3 Ts ideology after the Hungarian words: *támogat* (support), *tűr* (tolerate) and *tilt* (prohibit). Religion was situated on the borders of toleration and prohibition.[8] Under these circumstances, products of Western popular culture, including rock and roll, immediately encountered the filter of censorship. Thus, a unique situation developed. Rock and roll transformed Hungarian popular music and fashion and created new subcultures that presented a threat to the political powers. As a result, governmental powers took forceful action against it and attempted to force it within controlled limits[9] since the strictly regulated nature of the system did not provide space for social self-organization. The centrally directed and controlled culture did not embrace small community initiatives[10] since, as Ferenc Tomka noted, the party leadership was aware of the fact that 'community represents strength because it may be the source of an independent way of thinking and perhaps even resistance'.[11]

The musical style primarily regarded as a kind of counter-culture by the political powers emerged within the realm of religion, which already represented counter-culture in and of itself. Religious leaders usually tolerated the incipient Christian popular music and the small communities formed around it but were not pleased with and rarely supported either of them, a circumstance which might partly be due to the fact that the churches had been forced into a dependent position by the

---

[4]   Pál Gerő Bozsóky and László Lukács (eds), *Az elnyomatásból a szabadságba. Az egyház Magyarországon 1945–2001 [From Oppression to Freedom: The Church in Hungary 1945–2001]* (Vigilia Kiadó, 2005), pp. 57–87.

[5]   Ferenc Tomka, *Halálra szántak, mégis élünk! [We Were Sentenced to Death. But We Are Alive!]* (Szent István Társulat, 2005).

[6]   Tibor Valuch (ed.), *Magyar társadalomtörténeti olvasókönyv 1944-től napjainkig [Sources for the Social History of Hungary from 1944 to Present Days]* (Argumentum–Osiris, 2004), p. 149.

[7]   János Kádár (1912–89) was the General Secretary of the Hungarian Socialist Workers' Party who ruled Hungary from 1956 to 1989.

[8]   In order to gain international acceptance after the oppression of the 1956 revolution, Hungary enhanced the image of religious freedom both at home and in international affairs. In 1964, Hungary signed a 'partial agreement' with the Vatican. Consequently, Hungary became a positive model for state-church relationships in the socialist bloc.

[9]   Attempts were made to regulate this by law. According to Decree 61/1971 issued on 17 December 1971 by the Ministry of Culture, 'dance music and lyrics shall not fall within the category of socially valuable literary and artistic products.' Cited by Kőbányai, *Beatünnep*, p. 75.

[10]   Valuch, *Magyar*, p. 149.

[11]   Tomka, *Halálra*, p. 173.

political system and thus had to follow the state's lead on tolerating or prohibiting certain social phenomena. As a consequence, members of the Conference of Catholic Bishops kept a clear distance from grass-roots religious festivals for young people, which often included Christian popular music. Therefore, it is due primarily to political reasons that the festival that has taken place in Nagymaros near Budapest since 1971 and that mobilized thousands of Catholic youth was not officially recognized by the head of the Catholic Church in Hungary, László Cardinal Lékai, until he had visited Pope John Paul II in 1980. It was only after this event that he made a public appearance at the festival,[12] which is to say that the festival then only become officially tolerated – not approved – by the Church.[13]

While during the twentieth century the Catholic Church in Hungary and in Central Eastern Europe had generally been closed to musical styles that originated from the West – for example, believers encountered neither gospel music nor jazz in the church context – it did not form an opinion or a strategy on musical modernization. This trend was exaggerated during the Cold War by the attempt to entirely cut off cultural influences from the West, including all elements of Western popular culture of the 1960s; along with rock and roll, these were all considered dangerous. The musical trends within mass culture, however, conquered young people – including religious young people – at a rapid speed. It therefore posed a threat to numerous religious people and political leaders.

Christian popular music was, therefore, an alternative trend in several ways. First of all, in terms of politics, it formed part of the counter-culture launched by rock and roll music; its counter-cultural status also came from being religious, since religion under the socialism of the Kádár era represented a form of opposition to the political system. Second, this political position was reinforced by the fact that this movement was regarded as a sort of alternative religiosity within the institutional Church that presented a danger to traditions.[14] And third, because of its liberal roots, the movement had the potential to alter the frameworks and rituals of religious life, among other things.[15]

---

[12]   For greater detail, see Kinga Povedák, 'Catholicism in Transition', in Giselle Vincett (ed.), *Christianity in the Modern World: Changes and Controversies* (Ashgate, 2013), in press.

[13]   Tomka, *Halálra*, p. 196.

[14]   Another reason why Cardinal Lékai did not support Christian popular music was that he considered small groups organized around music to be a threat to state-church relations.

[15]   I do not mention the decrees issued during Vatican II in the section on historical antecedents although they are clearly related to the social climate I describe because of the renewal of the Church and the transformation of its new language and rites. However, they emerged in Hungary's Catholic religious life and practices with a significant delay. Thus, I would not list them among the antecedents, but rather among circumstances that contributed to the strengthening of Christian popular music in the 1970s. Fr Miklós Blanckenstein described the period between 1968 and 1972 as follows: 'This period was marked by the

Debates before the Political Turn in 1989

The debates triggered by the appearance of Christian popular music largely parallel those within the 'worship wars' in the United States, for example, over the meaning of musical style and the commodification of sacred music.[16] However, a unique feature of Hungarian Catholic disagreements over music is located in these debates' characteristic of blending or failing to recognize mass cultural boundaries, cultural layers and religious denominations. Since the 1960s, new trends were taking root at the same speed among both religious and non-religious cultures, including the Catholic, Calvinist and Lutheran denominations in Hungary.[17] The new style and the accompanying consequences of changing church music transcended denominational boundaries, and young people from different denominations often sang the new songs together. One of the obvious reasons behind this was an overarching religious content that was acceptable to everyone primarily because it was openly tied to Christianity. The denominational ties within Christianity were secondary from the point of view of music in most cases. The second reason was the attraction of music owing to new trends and a new stylistic language that enabled young people at the time to identify with religious music. Now they were able to communicate in their own musical language and not in that of their grandparents, and this, in most cases, was far more important than the denomination-specific content. According to Bodnár, '[t]his new music had a community-forming power; those who heard it felt even more that the liturgy belonged to them'.[18]

In addition, the *samizdat* quality of the manner in which this music spread in the region brought about this ecumenism: certain songs without the author's name indicated spread like folklore and were often transcribed the way they were heard; it was therefore frequently unclear for members of young choirs and bands

---

emergence of the new type of Christianity that happened to coincide with the beat movement of the 1960s. Although the opening-up created by Vatican II was much more influential on theology than on the Hungarian Church, it led to a change in lifestyle in the seminary as well, for example, lay clothing, playing the guitar, and beat masses.' István Kamarás, *Lelkierőmű Nagymaroson [Spiritual Power-plant at Nagymaros]* (VITA, 1989), p. 38.

[16]   See, for instance, Anna E. Nekola, *Between This World and the Next: The Musical 'Worship Wars' and Evangelical Ideology in the United States, 1960–2005* (PhD diss., University of Wisconsin-Madison, 2009).

[17]   The religious map of Hungary indicates that the country has been continually dominated by what are known as the *historical* Christian churches, i.e., those that have played a significant role in Hungarian history and culture. The period after the regime change differed from the 1960s and 1970s in that a variety of new religious groups, the Protestant Charismatic movements and various forms of implicit religiosity emerged. See István Kamarás, *Kis magyar religiográfia [A Little Hungarian Religiography]* (Pro Pannonia, 2003).

[18]   Dániel Bodnár, *Lélektől lélekig [From Soul to Soul]* (Múzik Bt., 2002), p. 29.

to which denomination a particular song with a religious message was primarily tied.[19] According to one informant,

> After I got to Budapest, it was my job to collect music sheets since Jenő and his friends' reputation had even reached Szeged. Each time I went home, Aunt Emese would ask me, 'So, have you brought any new songs?' ... In Budapest, they didn't tell you too much. They didn't tell you whose song it was, who wrote it, why he wrote it, what he wrote it for.[20]

Besides this, information about various events and new songs naturally spread by word of mouth. According to Bodnár, 'songs spread from place to place from one person to another'.[21] Fr. Sándor Sebők, a parish priest in the town of Fót near Budapest, said that 'we taped [Jenő Sillye's] songs and spread them in parishes throughout the country'.[22]

Though many were enthusiastic about the new songs, another attitude was also in evidence during the Hungarian debates about church music. That is, critics who rejected the new musical styles found reception across denominational affiliations. This rejection, therefore, constituted a unifying force among the clergy and critics. Certain writers used the same arguments about aesthetics to attack the new musical style.

These aesthetic criticisms are similar to Adorno's in connection with the fashionable popular music of his day, in which he considers modern music to be void of any artistic value. For Adorno, 'as the current musical consciousness of the masses can scarcely be called Dionysian, so its latest changes have nothing to do with taste. ... [T]he current musical condition of the masses [is] one of "degeneration."'[23] In Hungary, criticism of an aesthetic nature is primarily associated with László Dobszay and György Czigány.[24] As one of the significant

---

[19]   Kinga Povedák, '"Did you bring new songs?" The role of Contemporary Catholic Music in Hungary', *Acta Ethnographica Hungarica*, 56/1 (2011): pp. 31–41.

[20]   Sz. L., 54 year-old man, Szeged (2009).

[21]   Bodnár, *Lélektől*, p. 26.

[22]   Bodnár, *Lélektől*, p. 29.

[23]   T.W. Adorno, 'On the Fetish-Character in Music and the Regression of Listening', in R.D. Leppert (ed.), *Essays on Music: Theodor W. Adorno* (University of California Press, 2002), pp. 288–317.

[24]   Professor László Dobszay (1935–2011) was a music historian, chorister, respected scholar of chant and early Christian church music, and president of the Hungarian Church Music Association. György Czigány (1931–) is a poet, writer, musical editor and presenter and has been a music producer at Hungarian Television and Hungarian Radio for decades.

It is also important to note that these debates essentially about musical aesthetics are not specific to Hungarian Catholics. See Walter Kohli, *Rockzene és keresztyén életvitel. A XX. század legnagyobb zenei forradalma* [*Rock Music and Christian Way of Life: The Biggest Music Revolution of the 20th Century*] (Evangéliumi Kiadó, 1984); Corrado Balducci,

proponents of the revitalization of Gregorian chant in Hungary and a guiding force in Hungarian church music, Dobszay was of the opinion that church songs from the sixteenth century onward had been characterized by a continual homogenization that lead to a subjective, moralizing and pietist tone gradually dominating the songs. With regard to modern religious music, he concluded that 'songs almost exclusively by dilettante composers ... cannot be said to be modern or valuable musically or religiously'.[25] In agreement with Dobszay, Czigány argues that Christian popular music is not suited to evangelization. He sees the reasons for this in the low standard and unfinished quality of the songs, which he calls kitsch. According to Czigány,

> [w]hat is primitive spreads, dilettante improvisation conquers ... . This is the responsibility of clergy who think that they can use any cheap means to attract young people to the altar or who themselves possess such a low level of musical culture that they might even consider 'beautiful' these attempted hits and disco songs fit for small town coffee shops (in the worst sense of the word) ... . It is truly sacred music that must be brought into the churches, rather than bad music.[26]

Török[27] wishes to strengthen the subjective aesthetic criticism using the *Motu Proprio* and the decrees issued during Vatican II. The latter stress that the Church approves of all forms of artistic expression that comply with desired conditions – i.e., that they are sacred, universal and true art – and provides a space for them during the Mass.[28] For his part, Török declares that beat, pop and other forms of music have no place in the liturgy since 'if something is different by its nature, then its basic characteristics cannot be changed through individual ideas or inappropriate practices. None of the three requirements (that music be artistic, sacred and universal) is met by these kinds of songs.'[29]

In addition to attacking the music's aesthetic value, critics also point to what they see as a lack of theological content in the new songs. Baptist Jenő Bányai and Calvinist Kálmán Csomasz Tóth maintain that Christian popular music has only

---

Sátánizmus és rockzene [*Satanism and Rock Music*] (Bencés-Piemme Kiadó, 1992); and Ratzinger, Joseph, *Új éneket az Úrnak!* [*Sing a New Song to the Lord!*] (Jel Kiadó, 2007).

[25] László Dobszay, *A magyar népének 1* [*Hungarian Folk Hymn 1*] (Veszprémi Egyetem, 1995).

[26] György Czigány, 'Lehet-e szent, ami rossz?' [How can it be saint if it's bad?] *Távlatok*, 3/1 (1993): p. 115.

[27] József Török (1946–) is a professor of Catholic Liturgy and Church History at the Pázmány Péter Catholic University.

[28] József Török, *Adoremus – Az egyház liturgiájának ismerete az egyházzenét művelő fiatalok részére* [*Adoremus. About Church Liturgy to Young Church Musicians*] (Ecclesia, 2004), p. 193.

[29] Török, *Adoremus*, p. 201.

appealed to young people because of the rhythm of the music and not its religious content. As Csomasz Tóth puts it,

> [t]he church must consider the global musical dialect of young people as a phenomenon and as a task. We cannot chase illusions; the alienated generation is interested in dance music, not in Jesus Christ. A person with a Christian responsibility and mission, however, can only serve Christ, who attracts sinners, and not dancing feet.[30]

Bányai also notes that 'popular music affects the nervous system, not the mind and the soul'.[31]

Mass entertainment and the music industry did not emerge in socialist-era Hungary as it did in the West in terms of its scale and business interests. Instead, Hungary saw an 'entertainment industry' which was kept in check through powerful central censorship and whose scale and possibilities were determined by control from the centre. Nevertheless, from the outset, the same criticism was voiced in Hungary of the secularization and commodification of music as was done in the US.[32] It is also important to bear in mind that performers of Christian popular music in Hungary earned no income from their performances before 1989 and practically worked as volunteers.[33] No sound recordings were released before

---

[30]   Kálmán Csomasz Tóth, 'Jazz az egyházban?' [Jazz in the Church?], *Református Egyház*, 21/5 (1969): p. 102.

[31]   Bányai, *Könnyűzene*, 'Könnyűzene templomainkban? Hozzászólás az egyházi zene mai problémáihoz' [Popular Music in our Churches? Comments on the Contemporary Problems of Church Music], *Theológiai Szemle*, 12/7–8 (1969): p. 224.

[32]   In the United States, Christian popular music, as I have already noted, has made use of the opportunities of mass culture from the outset; the same criticism of music in mass culture, therefore, has also been used against Christian popular music. Steven Miller paraphrases aptly the view of Christian rock's detractors: 'Christian rock artists admit to imitating the world's styles and using them for godly ends. But adopting the world's methods and using them for God is blatant compromise. The biblical mandate in Romans 12,2 is clear: 'Do not be conformed to this world. ... You can have your contemporary music or the Bible, but not both.' In Steve Miller, *The Contemporary Christian Music Debate: Worldly Compromise or Agent of Renewal?* (Tyndale House Publisher, 1993), p. 43.

In addition, many objected to the materialism that it seemed to borrow from consumer culture, which stood in opposition to the teachings of Christianity. Romanowski puts this as follows: 'But as the CCM [Christian contemporary music] industry became more successful and popular, it began to draw criticism from two groups: on the one hand, from those who believed that the original evangelistic ideals were being compromised, and on the other, from those, who felt the industry was limiting the performers' artistic and commercial potential.' Romanowski, 'Evangelicals', p. 45.

[33]   Jenő Sillye, who became one of the best-known popular music influenced church music songwriters, is described as '[f]ully devoted, working for Jesus' cause – and also eight hours a day! – first he travelled around the country by train because there was an

1984 when *Kristályóriás* ('Crystal Giant') by Jenő Sillye was released. Even at the end of the 1990s, homemade CDs and cassette tapes were the most common. Nevertheless, Jenő Bányai criticized the mass industry that ran secular popular music as early as 1969, as a natural result of which he not only deemed Christian popular music as unfit for the liturgy, but he also outright condemned people who even listened to it. As he put it,

> [i]f places of worship become loud from the same music which faithfully imitates the commercial products of the music entertainment industry in every significant aspect, this means that people driven by instincts expect and serve, even in the church, that which is otherwise suited to places of entertainment … . Due to our Gospel-inspired approach, we may doubt if the whole existence (the psyche and soma) of those who support this music of instincts is in fact 'the temple of God' … . In our understanding, a man who is born again (John 3:7) distances himself even in his home from this music, which is not worthy of him and does not further his spiritual development.[34]

In addition, we can also find people who, although accepting Christian music as evangelizing or worshipful communal music, reject its use within the church service. As one contributor to an e-forum puts it, '[i]f nothing else, during catechism classes the priest could pass something on to young people with guitars: "This is for the campfire, that is for the Mass."'[35] In another comment:

> We must acknowledge that there is such a trend as Christian popular music. Let's shepherd them to forums where their style is appropriate and where they are necessary. We must know what it is that truly lives within the walls of the church and what is better to talk about God in the bustle of the world.[36]

It is interesting, however, that while the criticism of musical aesthetics that has been discussed thus far appeared relatively early, the first opinions that endeavoured to support the lack of aesthetic quality with considered arguments appeared late:

---

unbelievably huge demand for him among audiences: he was invited by priests, and parish and youth communities. The older priests were curious about him because they had never heard such songs before, while the younger ones were happy that a person their age was expressing his faith in songs. He played in churches which had echoed with emptiness before he appeared. As a result of Jenő's music, these churches were filled to the rafters. He gave simple answers to the complex questions of life, which struck deep, and his songs were filled with emotion and could be sung easily.' Bodnár, *Lélektől*, p. 26.

[34] Jenő Bányai, p. 225.

[35] Comment: http://lista.hcbc.hu/pipermail/liturgia/2008/002105.html, accessed 22 November 2009.

[36] Comment: http://lista.hcbc.hu/pipermail/liturgia/2008/002105.html, accessed 22 November 2009.

only after the emergence of Internet forums. Besides musical aesthetics, many also criticized the lack of quality in the lyrics of Christian popular music for being 'fragmented' and containing 'forced rhymes'. Moreover, opinions based on a real analysis of the inappropriateness of its content for the Catholic liturgy were also voiced during the same period. As a commenter puts it,

> [t]he biggest problem is, however, that the content of songs accompanied by guitars does not seem to be checked or censored. As a result, believers sing or are made to sing lyrics that are suspiciously heretical. For example, one such song, 'God is the earth, God is the sky … etc.', contains lyrics which might as well be part of a pantheistic religion … . However, the biggest problem is that songbooks for guitar include recommendations for replacing the standard text of the Mass with texts that are not in compliance with the text approved and blessed by the Church. And nobody tells these – well-intentioned but – uneducated and self-promoting 'church musicians' that, for example, they shouldn't replace the Agnus Dei by playing a guitar song that begins with 'My lamb, my lamb …'.[37]

As fast as critics of Hungarian Christian popular music shared their views in public forums, defenders of the style also emerged with the same speed, both from among the clergy and laity. One of the key arguments used by defenders of popular music was the lack of regulation in the Church. Here emphasis was placed on the fact that even the Bible contains no reference based on which Christian popular music could be clearly condemned. As one contributor to an e-forum puts it,

> [e]very means can be used for missionary purposes that does not contradict scripture or the teachings of the Church. In the New Testament, Christ did not define exactly how the Eucharistic sacrifice should be made present and did not forbid popular music or prescribe Gregorian chant. As far as I know, our Church has not issued dogma against popular music. Our God is a dynamic God that keeps a universe in motion. I don't think He would object to guitar masses.[38]

The other key argument among defenders of the modern musical style has been that critics judge Christian popular music based on superficial knowledge and simply from the point of view of aesthetics. As one blogger points out, 'I don't think that guitar music can be generalized as valueless *ab ovo*. I myself find much value in it.'[39] Opinions acknowledging the existence of better, less good and bad church music for guitar exist, but they emphasize that this is not only characteristic of this style;

---

[37] Comment: http://lista.hcbc.hu/pipermail/liturgia/2008/002105.html, accessed 22 November 2009.

[38] Comment: http://igen.hu/index.php?pg=forum&topic=14, accessed 22 November 2009.

[39] Comment: http://lista.hcbc.hu/pipermail/liturgia/2008/002105.html, accessed 22 November 2009.

traditional church songs or Gregorian chant cannot be placed as the canonized and perfect musical style in opposition to low-standard Christian popular music. The same blogger asks: 'When Gregorian chant was created a long time ago, was it perfect all at once? Didn't they give it a few tries and toss out the bad apples?'[40]

The most powerful arguments were made by those who supported the function and community role of Christian popular music. They emphasized that its political and communal influence should be considered independently of the level of the aesthetic value it represented. Some stressed the view of Cardinal Casaroli, who ascribed to small communities – among them, choirs with guitars – the fact that the Church, which had grown weak by the time of socialism, did not shrink any further in the 1960s and 1970s.[41] Naturally, it was not only music and musicians that were necessary to achieve this but also recalcitrant clergy who ignored official regulations and offered them space. According to István Kamarás,

> [i]n the late 1960s and early 1970s, the re-evangelization movement – initiated by younger priests and starting with beat masses and then carried on with Jenő Sillye's mission, which was embedded in popular music and the gatherings in Nagymaros – boosted catechism in parishes. The number of young people attending catechism classes multiplied in several dozen places, which, in the majority of the places, led to the transfer of the young priest who had boosted catechism this way ... .
> On the other hand, the youth evangelization movement began or strengthened the pastoring effort among young people which had been missing or stagnating in parishes, most frequently through guitar masses, as a result of which local guitar groups developed and communities often emerged out of them.[42]

Kamarás emphasizes that guitar masses resulted not only in communication but also in communion in certain cases. Kamarás and Körmendy observe that '[h]igh art and believers had become separated, and the preference for youth

[40]   Comment: http://lista.hcbc.hu/pipermail/liturgia/2008/002105.html, Accessed 22 November 2009.

[41]   According to historian Agostino Casaroli, '[t]he Church locked away from the youth seemed weak ... . Fewer and fewer people were attending churches ... . Whole social strata, including public servants, soldiers, and teachers, disappeared from them. Except for Poland, the Church – in accordance with the hopes of the Marxists – was showing signs of dying ... . In secret, however, the "spiritual church" lived on and selected groups, ready to live underground, were organized. They often endured the severity of the law, but continually resisted and continued to spread despite the objections of their government. In such a situation, the hope of the Church – besides God's help – lay in this continually shrinking group of believers in the vanguard and in the sufferings of the bishops, priests, monks, nuns, and laypeople, who were continually persecuted by the regime even if the brutality of their methods softened with time.' Agostino Casaroli, *A türelem vértanúsága. A Szentszék és a kommunista államok. 1963–1989* [*The Martyrdom of Patience. The Holy See and Communist Countries 1963–1989*] (Szent István Társulat, 2001), pp. 83–4.

[42]   Kamarás, *Kis*, pp. 90, 94.

music, which offered an answer to alienation, has become an interest among the masses. ... There has not been such major activity in church music among young people in centuries.'[43]

In the view of many, there is clear evidence that one of the new languages of the Hungarian Catholic Church is Christian popular music. When János Tóth, parish priest of St Matthew's Church in Budapest, provided space for Imre Szilas's 'Beat Mass' in 1967, in which lyrics of traditional church songs were put to rock and roll music, it was in recognition of the evangelizing effects of the new church music. As Fr Tóth put it:

> This can be considered pioneering in nature since today's youth no longer understand the inner content of the ancient Hungarian melodies, which is brought closer to them precisely by the rhythm of the new music and made more understandable for them ... . And this inspiration could also be seen in the listeners since the way thousands of young people at the Mass participated showed an extraordinary example. This is true even for those who did not come to listen to the Mass, but were only interested in the music. And the good influence of this devotion and the Mass can also be measured in the large number of those receiving Communion.[44]

Fr Tóth's recollection is entirely in line with the theses proposed by sociologist of religion Morel, who emphasized that Christian churches in the modern age must respond to two challenges: one, the language, including the channels of communication, by which the churches convey their message; and, two,

> the structure of plausibility they may expect in contemporary society with their message, in which they no longer address the illiterate with the authority of the literate, but in which they must present a message formulated 2000 years ago to people who are semi-educated or highly educated as a result of the spread of various means of mass communication.[45]

The Main Characteristics of Music in the Post-Regime Change Era

The pluralism in values and ideologies that emerged after the regime change in 1989 also transformed Christian popular music completely. First, this musical phenomenon, now free from cultural policy, experienced a significant quantitative

---

[43] István Kamarás and Ferenc Körmendy, 'Religiózus beat? (szociográfia) II' [Religious Beat? (Sociography) II], *Új forrás*, 22/3 (1990): p. 57.

[44] István Kamarás and Ferenc Körmendy, 'Religiózus beat? (szociográfia) I' [Religious Beat? (Sociography) I], *Új forrás*, 22/2 (1990): p. 21.

[45] Gyula Morel, 'Egyház a kommunikációs társadalomban – a jelentés és a jelentőség krízise', in András Máté-Tóth and Mária Jahn (eds), *Studia Religiosa. Tanulmányok András Imre 70. születésnapjára* [Religious Studies: Papers for the 70-years-old Imre András] (Bába és Társa Kiadó, 1998), pp. 82–3.

growth. Albums by performers who were not particularly well-known were being released in large numbers, and even church choirs were publishing their own music. Moreover, because this music had reached a mass scale by the years of the regime change, a new set of tendencies and major characteristics emerged. Newer generations grew up listening to artists like Jenő Sillye; for them, rock and roll music carried neither the political nor the religious symbolic content that it did in the late 1960s and early 1970s. New popular Christian bands no longer express their value systems in symbolic opposition to the oppressive state but focus on the preservation of Hungarian culture,[46] the open confession of faith, and evangelization. In the meanwhile, the international hippie movement had also lost its rebellious nature and was replaced by newer musical trends in the mass culture, which served entertainment purposes far more than spreading social messages.

On the other hand, with the appearance of Western-style consumer culture in Hungary, Christian popular music has diversified further. Musical diversity has increased, new Christian music styles such as rap, disco and metal have emerged, and, at the same time, numerous members of the older generation that have achieved a sort of legendary status have also remained active.[47] Some of the new performers are not composing their music for liturgical use but for evangelization outside church walls under the powerful inspiration of American music, a tendency that yet again has contributed to an ambivalent response. Moreover, certain defining personalities of secular popular music also perform songs with Christian content. The dilution has also had an impact at the level of aesthetics. Christian popular music has become so complex that we can no longer speak in terms of a monolithic Christian popular music *per se*; like contemporary Christian music in the United States, it has become a 'splintered artworld'.[48]

---

[46] After the regime change, attention was turned again towards the life of the Hungarians living as minorities across Hungary's borders, which can be detected in the lyrics. See Sillye's song 'Szállj dalom, szállj, a Hargitáig szállj ...', which translates to 'Fly, song, fly, fly to the Hargitas' and refers to a mountain range in Transylvania (in present-day Romania) where Hungarians live.

[47] A chapter of my PhD dissertation deals with the possibilities of creating a typology of contemporary Christian popular music. Kinga Povedák, *Christian Popular Music in Hungary 1967–2012* (PhD diss., Univerity of Szeged, forthcoming 2013).

[48] Jay R. Howard and John M. Streck, *Apostles of Rock: The Splintered World of Contemporary Christian Music* (University Press of Kentucky, 1999). My dissertation primarily deals with popular music tied to the Catholic Church and therefore does not investigate the music of small, new Protestant churches that emerged in Hungary after the regime change. It is worth noting, however, that Christian popular music in these communities has become the exclusive music of the liturgy, one of the clear reasons for which is that small, new Protestant churches have no traditional church songs and the other is that they consider popular Christian music to be the language through which they can appeal to young people.

Debates at the Beginning of the Twenty-First Century

The period since the regime change brought nothing new in the nature of the debate although options provided by the Internet for the expression of opinion from the bottom up created a more complex forum which outlined possible ways out of the ambivalent situation. On the pages of religious weeklies and journals for young people, the criticism offered by Czigány and Dobszay is carried on today by Gábor Czakó, among others. He emphasizes that not only are there problems with the aesthetics of the music, but the essence of the entire liturgy is at stake. Czakó argues as follows:

> Western Europe tried it, and the result is tragic. All people, including the young, long for the four great divine features: beauty, goodness, truth, and love. If any of these is impaired, for example, (musical) taste deteriorates, then that which is ugly – a feature of the devil! – invades our lives, which has a negative impact on the other three features, and we can only offer the spoiled version instead of the sacred on to the seeker who happens into the church and happens among us while he, in fact, is trying to flee to us from the same thing in the life of the marketplace.[49]

In other words, it can be seen that the debates over music are far from over. This opinion is reflected in the only Hungarian monograph written about Christian popular music thus far, whose author developed Balducci's position, which is characteristically opposed to rock music. Kőrössy Soltész stresses that rock music is 'disharmonic, often painfully dissonant, unsystematic and primitive. The lyrics are usually superficial, repetitive, often lacking flow, confused, and messy.'[50] Debates on the various forums[51] dealing with the issue, however, reach beyond this and generally include the following thematic groups. First, the view that questions only the suitability of Christian popular music in the liturgy but not its existence continues to be present; here, the pastoral influence of the music on young people is recognized along with the fact that the music seems to be the most fitting for the criterion of the new language – to be able to address young people. Proponents of this view, however, are only able to accept this music outside of the church and the liturgy. As one young informant puts it:

> These are folk hymns for us. As Christian youth we can relate to this, this music has meaning for us. … The community is very important in these songs. These

---

[49]   Gábor Czakó, 'Gitárzene' [Guitar Music], 2009, www.czakogabor.hu/index. php?page=olvas&bovebben=true&id-=10&cikkid=55, accessed 26 September 2012.

[50]   Katalin Körössy Soltész, *A 'keresztény' rockzene: Érvek és ellenérvek* [*Christian Rock Music Pros and Cons*] (JÓ HÍR" Iratmisszió Alapítvány, 1998), p. 29.

[51]   These forums include Villanyhárfa Guitar Liturgy at http://www.villanyharfa.hu/, http://igen.hu/cimke/-dalsz%C3%B6veg-inkviz%C3%Adtor, accessed 22 November 2009.

songs serve as our folk hymns. This can convey a message to the younger generation and we can participate and sing these songs. This is articulated in our language.[52]

A second, new trend has surfaced among supporters, however, which not only recognizes that good and bad Christian popular music exists, but also emphasizes the necessity to examine the songs to shed light on whether their content is indeed in line with Catholic teaching and liturgical prescriptions.

At the same time, another third group of Hungarian Catholics, although small in number, has also appeared with its sights clearly set on retraditionalization. Communities that support the Tridentine Mass basically reject the liturgical renewal of Vatican II and stress the Latin Mass and Gregorian chant as the primary musical language, the one most suited to the liturgy. In this case, a return to the pre-Vatican II state is based on ideology; that is, this group refuses to accommodate to modernization, arguing that the existence of the Catholic Church is based on loyalty to traditions and not a satisfying of various trends of the day. Adherents to this view believe that the new style can only result in the dilution and loss of the original characteristic features of the Catholic Church, which may lead its secularization, that is, the erosion of its social foundation through the fading of its Catholic nature. They therefore condemn Christian music for both its content and its musical features. As one critic puts it: 'It is completely alien to me the way they bounce around the altar to the silly music. They desecrate the entire Mass this way.'[53]

Conclusion

Due to its early appearance in Hungary, Christian popular music has become a known and accepted phenomenon. Since several generations that have grown up in the last half-century have been enjoying this music, the view that this style only represents the musical language of young people can no longer be sustained. Furthermore, certain songs from previous decades now form a musical canon of sorts, while the appearance and spread of newer musical styles and of a global Pentecostal revival on a mass scale have raised religious and theological concerns. Because of opposition to this music and the resulting restrictions on its use within the Catholic Church, many of those who considered Christian popular music a new expressive musical language and means of sacred communication, have turned towards Catholic Charismatic revival or Pentecostal Charismatic revival movements that use popular music as their exclusive language.

One of the most important characteristics revealed by the Hungarian Christian music phenomenon is the constant mutual effect between the religious and

---

[52] A 20-year-old man, Szeged (2010).
[53] L.M., 30-year-old man, Szeged (2010).

the profane. The relationship between religion and mass culture is a two-way process, as can clearly be seen. It can also be observed that the appearance of religion in secular mass culture has triggered significantly smaller debates than the converse. As a result, certain questions arise: what is the extent to which the influence of this mixture, or late modern religious syncretism, reaches beyond religious music and possibly brings about changes in the whole of religiosity and in vernacular religiosity? Can it initiate an ecumenical process, or will it ultimately lead to superficiality and the weakening of institutionalized religiosity? These are questions that may perhaps only be answered decisively in the future.

Acknowledgements

This article is based on research supported by two Hungarian grants: OTKA K68325 and OTKA NK81502. All translations from the original Hungarian are Thomas Williams'.

References

Adorno, T.W. 'On the Fetish-Character in Music and the Regression of Listening', in R.D. Leppert (ed.), *Essays on Music: Theodor W. Adorno* (Berkeley: University of California Press, 2002).

Baldovin, John F., *Reforming the Liturgy* (Collegeville: Liturgical Press, 2008).

Balducci, Corrado, *Sátánizmus és rockzene* [*Satanism and Rock Music*] (Pannonhalma: Bencés-Piemme Kiadó, 1992).

Bányai, Jenő, 'Könnyűzene templomainkban? Hozzászólás az egyházi zene mai problémáihoz' [Popular Music in our Churches? Comments on the Contemporary Problems of Church Music], *Theológiai Szemle*, 12/7–8 (1969): 223–7.

Bodnár, Dániel, *Lélektől lélekig* [*From Soul to Soul*] (Budapest: Múzik Bt., 2002), in Bozsóky, Pál Gerő and László Lukács (eds), *Az elnyomatásból a szabadságba. Az egyház Magyarországon 1945–2001* [*From Oppression to Freedom: The Church in Hungary 1945–2001*] (Budapest, Vigilia Kiadó, 2005).

Casaroli, Agostino, *A türelem vértanúsága. A Szentszék és a kommunista államok. 1963–1989* [*The Martyrdom of Patience: The Holy See and Communist Countries 1963–1989*] (Budapest: Szent István Társulat, 2001).

Csomasz Tóth, Kálmán, 'Jazz az egyházban?' [Jazz in the Church?], *Református Egyház*, 21/5 (1969): 102.

Czigány, György, 'Lehet-e szent, ami rossz?' [How can it be saint if it's bad?], *Távlatok,* 3/1 (1993): 114–15.

Dobszay, László, *A magyar népének 1* [*Hungarian Folk Hymn 1*] (Veszprém: Veszprémi Egyetem, 1995).

Howard, Jay R. and Streck, John M., *Apostles of Rock: The Splintered World of Contemporary Christian Music* (Lexington: University Press of Kentucky, 1999).

Kamarás, István, *Lelkierőmű Nagymaroson* [*Spiritual Power-plant at Nagymaros*] (Budapest: VITA, 1989).

Kamarás, István, *Kis magyar religiográfia* [*A Little Hungarian Religiography*] (Pécs: Pro Pannonia, 2003).

Kamarás, István and Körmendy, Ferenc, 'Religiózus beat? (szociográfia) I' [Religious Beat? (Sociography) I], *Új forrás*, 22/2 (1990): 11–25.

Kamarás, István and Körmendy, Ferenc, 'Religiózus beat? (szociográfia) II' [Religious Beat? (Sociography) II], *Új forrás*, 22/3 (1990): 56–68.

Kőbányai, János, *Beatünnep után* [*After the Beat-festival*] (Budapest: Gondolat, 1986)

Kohli, Walter, *Rockzene és keresztyén életvitel. A XX. század legnagyobb zenei forradalma* [*Rock Music and Christian Way of Life: The Biggest Music Revolution of the 20th Century*] (Genf: Evangéliumi Kiadó, 1984).

Körössy Soltész, Katalin, *A 'keresztény' rockzene: Érvek és ellenérvek* [*Christian Rock Music: Pros and Cons*] (Budapest: 'JÓ HÍR' Iratmisszió Alapítvány, 1998).

Miller, Steve, *The Contemporary Christian Music Debate: Worldly Compromise or Agent of Renewal?* (Waynesboro: Tyndale House Publisher, 1993).

Morel, Gyula, 'Egyház a kommunikációs társadalomban – a jelentés és a jelentőség krízise', in Máté-Tóth, András and Jahn, Mária (eds), *Studia Religiosa. Tanulmányok András Imre 70. születésnapjára* [Religious Studies: Papers for the 70-years-old Imre András] (Szeged: Bába és Társa Kiadó, 1998).

Nekola, Anna Elizabeth, *Between This World and the Next: The Musical 'Worship Wars' and Evangelical Ideology in the United States, 1960–2005* (University of Wisconsin-Madison, 2009).

Povedák, Kinga, '"Did you bring new songs?" The Role of Contemporary Catholic Music in Hungary', *Acta Ethnographica Hungarica*, 56/1 (2011): 31–41.

Povedák, Kinga, 'Catholicism in Transition', in Giselle Vincett (ed.), *Christianity in the Modern World: Changes and Controversies* (Farnham, Ashgate, 2013, in press).

Povedák, Kinga, *Christian Popular Music in Hungary 1967–2012* (PhD diss., University of Szeged, forthcoming 2013).

Rajeczky, Benjámin, 'Gregorián, népének, népdal' [Gregorian, Folk Hymn, Folk Song], in Bónis, Ferenc (ed.), *Magyar Zenetörténeti Tanulmányok Szabolcsi Bence 70. születésnapjára* (Budapest: Zeneműkiadó, 1969).

Ratzinger, Joseph, *Új éneket az Úrnak!* [*Sing a New Song to the Lord!*] (Budapest: Jel Kiadó, 2007).

Romanowski, William D., 'Evangelicals and Popular Music: The Contemporary Christian Music Industry', in Bruce David Forbes and Jeffrey H. Mahan (eds), *Religion and Popular Culture in America* (Berkeley: University of California Press, 2000).

Tomka, Ferenc, *Halálra szántak, mégis élünk!* [*We were Sentenced to Death, but We are Alive!*] (Budapest: Szent István Társulat, 2005).

Török, József, *Adoremus – Az egyház liturgiájának ismerete az egyházzenét művelő fiatalok részére* [*Adoremus: About Church Liturgy to Young Church Musicians*] (Budapest: Ecclesia, 2004).

Valuch, Tibor (ed.), *Magyar társadalomtörténeti olvasókönyv 1944–től napjainkig.* [*Sources for the Social History of Hungary from 1944 to Present Days*] (Budapest: Argumentum–Osiris, 2004).

Wilson-Dickson, Andrew, *Fejezetek a kereszténység zenéjéből* [*A Brief History of the Christian Music: From Biblical Times to the Present*] (Budapest: Gemini Budapest Kiadó, 1998).

Chapter 7

'I'll Take you There': The Promise of Transformation in the Marketing of Worship Media in US Christian Music Magazines

Anna Nekola

In 1995, a handful of companies including Integrity Music, Vineyard Music Group and Maranatha! Music dominated the US popular worship music industry. Two of these companies, Vineyard and Maranatha!, could trace their roots to congregations formed in the 1970s out of the Jesus People Movement. The Jesus Movement stressed the importance of experiential and emotional Christianity and is often credited with turning the tide in contemporary evangelical worship practices by bringing popular musical sounds, especially those drawn from folk and rock, into organized corporate worship services.[1] In the mid-1990s, these record companies were marketing recordings of popular worship songs not just as tools to help church music directors and worship leaders prepare for corporate worship services but also as products for Christian consumers who could listen to these CDs to relive or even recreate the experience of worship outside of church.

This chapter examines how, from the mid-1990s to the mid-2000s, print advertisements for worship music in US Christian music magazines promised to effect a dual transformation: first, to transform any profane or secular space into a sacred 'sanctuary'; and second, to transform the listener spiritually by transporting him or her into the presence of God. Marketers have long claimed to bridge distance and provide transformative experiences to their consumers but the specifically religious experiences that these worship products promise have profound implications for contemporary US Christian religious ideology and practice. Through both verbal and visual cues, these advertisements work to reinforce the ongoing privatization of religion that has been occurring since the Reformation; they participate in the ongoing redefinition of 'worship' from a traditionally corporate to an increasingly individual act; and they position the consumption of goods and services as the key to individual spiritual autonomy. Furthermore, in their emphasis on individualized spiritual ecstasy achieved via

[1] David Di Sabatino, *The Jesus People Movement: An Annotated Bibliography and General Resource* (Greenwood Press, 1999).

technology, these marketing discourses work to normalize charismatic practice and theology within US Protestant Christianity.[2]

Selling Worship Music to Americans, 1850s–2000s

Being able to buy one's favourite worship music is not a particularly new experience for Americans. R. Laurence Moore argues that to better compete for Americans' attention, to fulfil its evangelical mandate to save souls and to assert its social and cultural authority, American Protestantism 'developed marketing strategies, ways of advertising itself, and distribution networks'.[3] Not only did religious organizations have to vie for attention with one another but they also had to compete with other forms of culture, and to do so religious leaders needed to give their messages popular appeal.

Music played a key role in the marketing and evangelizing strategies of popular evangelists, who often advertised their revivals in the entertainment section of the newspaper.[4] In the second half of the nineteenth century, preacher Dwight Moody relied on emergent capitalist business models to create widely popular urban revivals, first in England and then in the US.[5] Recognizing the emotional power of music in religious experience, Moody teamed up with singer Ira Sankey, who '[sang] the gospel' via songs by Fanny Crosby and P.P. Bliss and who placed the singing of new and old hymns on par with preaching, the central event of a revival experience. Popular demand for the music prompted Sankey to publish a series of sacred song collections that sold millions of copies and helped coin the term 'gospel song'.[6] Sankey popularized many gospel songs still sung today, such as 'Rock of Ages' and 'Jesus Loves Me', not just through his performances but by making the songs available in print versions that could circulate widely. In

---

[2]   Media and travel help circulate American worship styles and practices beyond US borders, and US styles are also influenced by music, musicians and practices from outside the world, especially in the case of contemporary commercial worship music, by worship leaders from Australia and the UK. This article focuses on media and practice in the US context because of the particular way that national ideologies of individual autonomy work to strengthen evangelical and charismatic ideas of individualized spirituality. In other words, for ideological reasons the US is a particularly fruitful site for spreading discourses of personalized belief and practice.

[3]   R. Laurence Moore, *Selling God: American Religion in the Marketplace of Culture* (Oxford University Press, 1994), pp. 91–2.

[4]   Don Cusic, *The Sound of Light: A History of Gospel Music* (Bowling Green State University Popular Press, 1990), p. 72.

[5]   Moore, *Selling God*, pp. 185–6.

[6]   Mel R. Wilhoit, 'Sankey, Ira D.,' in *Grove Music Online. Oxford Music Online*, http://0-www.oxfordmusiconline-.com.dewey2.library.denison.edu/subscriber/article/grove/music/24515, accessed 18 September 2012.

the beginning of the twentieth century, Billy Sunday's musician and song leader, Homer Rodeheaver, was the first to 'mimick' pop music styles in an effort to draw people to the faith.[7] He programmed old hymns and sought out new gospel songs that he popularized, and like Sankey, he sold print copies at the revivals. Print media helped promote gospel songs but the phonograph quickly eclipsed songbooks, and Rodeheaver's record label for gospel songs, Rainbow Records, 'began to create the Christian culture in twentieth century America, as the gospel consumer became part of a segmented market'.[8] Rodeheaver recognized that people would want to be able to sing this sacred music outside of revivals and he deliberately wrote songs that drew on popular musical styles of the day, making them easy to learn and remember so that people 'could whistle and sing [them] wherever they might be'.[9]

Many later evangelists, driven by their mandate to bring people to God and inspired by the enthusiastic responses to celebrity preachers as well as the appeal of mass and entertainment media, continued to use popular musics to draw crowds and make religion relevant to the everyday experiences of an increasingly consumer-driven society. Kevin Kee recounts that Canadian evangelist Oswald J. Smith scheduled free concerts to bring in audiences for a religious message in the 1920s, while twenty years later Charles Templeton used jazz and swing to attract teens (and classical music to appeal to their 'more refined' parents).[10] Similarly, the North American Youth for Christ (YFC) movement used 'an entertaining style and upbeat music' in the 1940s to help reach and appeal to large numbers of young people, and their first songbook *Singing Youth for Christ* drew on the music of Crosby, Sankey and Bliss. Thomas Bergler argues that the famous tunesmith and arranger Ralph Carmichael, together with YFC, helped transform American Protestants' musical taste with 'gospel pop' songs, drawing on the emotional tradition of revivalism and the popularity of American rock 'n' roll sounds to create a music that would reach youth who were ready for conversion.[11] Indeed, Carmichael to some extent 'predicted' the rise of popular worship music, arguing that, 'the music that was used at the time of a person's conversion is ordinarily the music that he'll want to stay with and worship with'.[12]

---

[7] Cusic, *The Sound of Light*, pp. 62, 75.

[8] Cusic, *The Sound of Light*, pp. 70–72, 75.

[9] Cusic, *The Sound of Light*, p. 72.

[10] Kevin Kee, 'Marketing the Gospel: Music in English Canadian Protestant Revivalism, 1884–1957', in Richard J. Mouw and Mark A. Noll (eds), *Wonderful Words of Life: American Hymns in American Protestant Theology* (William B. Eerdmans, 2004), p. 97.

[11] Thomas E. Bergler, '"I Found My Thrill": The Youth for Christ Movement and American Congregational Singing, 1940–1970', in Mouw and Noll (eds), *Wonderful Words of Life*, pp. 123, 127.

[12] Quoted in Bergler, '"I Found My Thrill"', pp. 145–6.

The popularity of folk- and rock-sounding worship music in the mid-twentieth century coincided with a charismatic 'revival' or 'renewal' that began in the 1950s and 'emerged in nearly all' American Protestant denominations as well as Roman Catholicism and Eastern Orthodoxy.[13] While the spread of charismatic belief has resulted in the establishment of new nondenominational churches and parachurch organizations, it has also had a variety of effects on mainstream denominations as churches have adopted varying degrees of charismatic belief and practice.[14] Charismatic belief encourages an emotionally expressive and experiential attitude towards worship, defining its goal as both praise of God, and personal, intimate communion between the deity and the worshipper – a 'ritual re-enactment' of the disciples' experience of the Holy Spirit at Pentecost and a 'recapturing of awe, wonder, and joy in the immediate experience of the Holy Spirit'.[15] Importantly, Simon Coleman describes the dissemination of charismatic Christianity as not just about belief but the spread of a charismatic 'habitus' inspired by a 'spiritually charged aesthetic that encompasses ritual movements, media consumption, linguistic forms and aspects of the external environment'.[16]

The Jesus People Movement, sometimes called the 'Jesus Revival', of the late 1960s and early 1970s, popularized charismatic theology and practice, especially with many young people who were looking for spiritual experiences and answers to social problems such as war and racism.[17] 'Gospel rock' records produced by those inspired by this revival became a means to evangelize as well as raise money for churches, and out of this originally independent music scene the fledgling 'Contemporary Christian Music' industry developed.[18] In the 1980s and 90s, a 'Third Wave' of charismatic practice strengthened its influence in the US, particularly via the spread of the Vineyard movement, an important producer and distributor of worship music recordings.[19] The commercial success

---

[13]   Robert Mapes Anderson, 'Pentecostal and Charismatic Christianity', in Lindsay Jones (ed.), *Encyclopedia of Religion*, 2d ed., Vol. 10 (Macmillan Reference USA, 2005), pp. 7030–31.

[14]   Robert Mapes Anderson explains that the experience of 'Spirit Baptism' is seen as a 'distinct act of grace' by Pentecostal charismatics while many Protestant and Catholic charismatics understand this experience as an extension of traditional water baptism. In addition, these groups differ on their embrace or rejection of glossolalia or the practice of speaking in tongues. Anderson, 'Pentecostal and Charismatic Christianity', p. 7030.

[15]   Anderson, 'Pentecostal and Charismatic Christianity', p. 7031.

[16]   Simon Coleman, *The Globalisation of Charismatic Christianity: Spreading the Gospel of Prosperity* (Cambridge University Press, 2000), p. 6.

[17]   Erling Jorstad, *That New-Time Religion: The Jesus Revival In America* (Augsburg Publishing House, 1972).

[18]   Di Sabatino, *The Jesus People Movement*, pp. 156–7.

[19]   Anderson, 'Pentecostal and Charismatic Christianity', p. 7031. As Anderson and Coleman note, Pentecostalism has spread beyond the US to Europe but also to Africa, Latin America and Asia, particularly through its connections with American Prosperity

of Christian popular musics, combined with the popular spread of charismatic practice and belief, have influenced both the theology of the goals of worship towards a personal and emotional experience of the divine, and the structure of corporate Christian worship away from more formal liturgies patterned on those of mainline Protestantism towards new service models focused around long episodes of uninterrupted 'free-flowing praise'.[20]

Most recently, the turn of the twenty-first century has been called a 'worship awakening' – a revival in God-centered worship and living – marked by several ongoing shifts: from traditional hymnody to rock- and pop-infused worship music, from sermons to multimedia communication, from attendance to experience, and from belief to lifestyle.[21] Robb Redman explains that the popular surge of worship products at the turn of the twenty-first century, especially worship CDs and videos, reveals contemporary Christians' overwhelming desire for worship and through it, spiritual experience and renewal. However, these products don't just reflect a desire for worship, they also work to shape and reproduce a desire for individual spiritual fulfilment and personal transcendence.

Religious Materiality and the Immanence of Sound

Reformation theology provided empowerment for a 'priesthood' of individual believers, and the rise of humanism in the eighteenth century, however ironically, strengthened Christianity's embrace of the personal and emotional, a theological move that sometimes goes unrecognized in contemporary discussions of evangelical theology. By manifesting a concern for human issues and emotions, posits Quentin Faulkner, humanism contributed to the rise of pietism, an 'intensely personal and individualistic approach to religion that emphasized human guilt and personal conversion and prized religious feeling over intellectual understanding', and had the effect of transforming God's 'transcendence' into 'immanence',

---

Gospel. Anderson, 'Pentecostal and Charismatic Christianity', p. 7031, and Coleman, *The Globalization of Charismatic Christianity.*

[20] One example of this new style of worship is called the 'Five-Phase Model', proposed by John Wimber, prominent leader within the neocharismatic Vineyard Movement. Wimber's model gives a directional contour to an uninterrupted musical section of up to forty minutes that precedes the sermon. Barry Liesch, *The New Worship: Straight Talk on Music and the Church* (Baker Book House, 1996), pp. 45–60.

[21] Robb Redman, *The Great Worship Awakening: Singing a New Song in the Postmodern Church* (Jossey-Bass, 2002), p. xii. Redman taught classes in contemporary worship at Fuller Theological Seminary from 1992–99 and also led programmes at Maranatha! Music. He currently teaches theology at Multnomah University. Robert Webber also refers to this period as a 'worship awakening.' See Robert E. Webber, *Worship is a Verb: Celebrating God's Mighty Deed of Salvation* (Hendrickson Publishers, 2004).

thus facilitating the pervasive idea of God as a close and merciful companion.[22] However, Protestants have long had an uneasy relationship with embodied religion and emotional expression, just as they have been conflicted over the role of music in communal worship practice.

Historically, some churches and groups restricted instrumentation and sang only worship music with Biblical texts, while others wrote hymns and songs in popular musical styles with newly composed texts on religious themes. For example, in the 1760s most Anglican clergy believed hymns – as music that was humanly created – were not fit for liturgy.[23] In 1762 William Riley complained that 'the Tunes they commonly use are generally too light and airy for Church-Music; and consequently have nothing in their Composure that may excite a true Spirit of Devotion',[24] and in 1768, six students at England's Oxford University were expelled for singing hymns outside of church in private houses.[25] In the American colonies, the First Great Awakening of the 1740s brought a period of revival characterized by belief in self-reflection and personal transformation.[26] The hymns of Isaac Watts and Charles Wesley played an important role in this new revivalism, and preachers like George Whitefield encouraged congregational singing as a complement to revivalism's exciting preaching style.[27] Yet some in the US objected to the hymn singing as 'crude, emotional, and anti-intellectual', or 'rowdy and unseemly', and changes to musical worship practices provoked heated theological and cultural disputes.[28]

Americans Protestants and the American polity more generally continue to struggle with perceived dichotomies of the 'sacred' and 'profane', even as national ideologies of democracy, autonomy and self-determination continue to influence religious ideologies and practices along more individualistic and emotional lines. Furthermore, Americans increasingly live their personal and collective identities through 'lifestyles' supported by products and accessories, including the emergence of a vibrant Christian material culture that helps American Christians practise their faith.[29] Christian popular music has often been discussed positively

---

[22]   Quentin Faulkner, *Wiser Than Despair: The Evolution of Ideas in the Relationship of Music and the Christian Church* (Greenwood Press, 1996), pp. 163–4.

[23]   Thomas K. McCart, *The Matter and Manner of Praise: The Controversial Evolution of Hymnody in the Church of England 1760–1820* (Scarecrow Press, 1998), p. 35.

[24]   Quoted in McCart, *The Matter and Manner of Praise*, p. 53.

[25]   McCart, *The Matter and Manner of Praise*, p. 60.

[26]   Jon Butler, 'Religion in Colonial America', in *Religion in American Life: A Short History* (Oxford University Press, 2000), p. 128.

[27]   David W. Stowe, *How Sweet the Sound: Music in the Spiritual Lives of Americans* (Harvard University Library, 2004), pp. 30–31.

[28]   Butler, 'Religion in Colonial America', p. 128; Stowe, *How Sweet the Sound*, p. 31.

[29]   Anna Nekola, 'Worldly Worship: Negotiating the Tensions of U.S. Worship Music in the Marketplace', in Suzel Reily and Jonathan Dueck (eds), *The Oxford Handbook of Music and World Christianities* (Oxford University Press, forthcoming).

as a tool for evangelism, or as a positive and clean entertainment alternative to secular popular musics, but it is important to note that, for many, individualized listening is an engaged spiritual experience that helps them maintain and even strengthen their faith. Yet, while private listening is enabled by the material culture of recordings and playback devices, the audition of music is different than the possession of religious artefacts. Music enables the listener to transcend time and space, privileging the experience of the moment; it affects us physically and mentally so that we lose track of time, but yet we also 'possess' music.[30] Here is a central paradox in the study of the material culture of listening: these devices and recordings create something very immaterial and ephemeral but yet affective and embodied: *Sound.*

Sound's ability to transport, envelop, transform and unite listeners has been both impetus and outcome of advancements in media technology, particularly the invention of the radio and, later, the Walkman and iPod, both of which made sound more intimate and personal while simultaneously enhancing the experience of connectivity. Susan Douglas explains that the radio changed Americans' relationship to sound and through it their individual and collective identities by '[disrupting] the cognitive and cultural practices of a visual culture and a literate culture' and opening up a new aural world.[31] The new technology of radio of the 1920s and 30s appeared magical, almost mystical, in its ability to envelop the listener in sound and thus allow him to enter a dream world, 'extending people's range of hearing to distances previously unimaginable'. Indeed, to 'enhance' what some described as radio's 'distinctive [affective] quality', 1930s researchers often found radio listeners listening in the dark with their eyes closed, 'their fantasies free', imagining a visual accompaniment to the sound they heard.[32] Thus personal listening technologies allowed individuals to retreat into a private, interior space, even as they were listening to a public broadcast heard simultaneously by thousands. Jason Loviglio has coined the term 'the intimate public' to describe this dual effect of isolation and connectedness in the experience of mediated sound.[33]

While listening technologies like radio enable listeners to envision themselves connected to others in the 'deep, horizontal comradeship' Benedict Anderson

---

[30]   Simon Frith, 'Towards an Aesthetic of Popular Music', in Richard Leppert and Susan McClary (eds), *Music and Society: The Politics of Composition, Performance and Reception* (Cambridge University Press, 1987), pp. 142–3.

[31]   Susan J. Douglas, *Listening In: Radio and the American Imagination* (Random House Times Books, 1999), pp. 7, 29. There is a long history after the Enlightenment of privileging the visual and connecting the gaze to the modern, what Leigh Eric Schmidt calls 'ocularcentrism', while hearing and listening have been 'othered' as 'primitive' and dangerously suspicious. Eric Leigh Schmidt, *Hearing Things: Religion, Illusion, and the American Enlightenment* (Harvard University Press, 2000), pp. 7, 16.

[32]   Douglas, *Listening In*, pp. 29–30.

[33]   Jason Loviglio, *Radio's Intimate Public: Network Broadcasting and Mass-Mediated Democracy* (University of Minnesota Press, 2005).

calls 'imagined community',[34] they can also foster a different experience of 'communion' – the immanence of the divine. Matthew Engelke provides a framework that helps bridge the gap between religious material culture and sound by arguing that 'materiality' can be understood as 'media in their wider sense as "middle grounds": something *through which* something else is communicated, presented, made known'.[35] Applying Engelke's idea to this musical case means that religious musical objects and their playback devices mediate and 'present' the divine.[36] Christian popular media communicates a discourse of the experience of divine immanence, particularly through advertisements for products meant to enrich believers' spiritual lives and guide their practices outside of corporate worship services. For instance, a 2005 advertisement from *Worship Leader* for Regal Books' 'worship series' encouraged readers to 'journey into God's presence' and 'get lost in worship' by buying and reading books about worship written by the likes of popular worship singer/songwriter Matt Redman. In the case of popular worship music, the embodied experience of listening promises not only the affective push-pull of intimacy and community, nor even simply a transformative spiritual experience, but also a very real linking of the listener with God.

Sound and the Transformation of Everyday Space and Experience

Technological developments in radio and personal stereos have continued to work to personalize listening; smaller and more affordable audio playback devices have enabled us to bring 'our' music with us in our cars or on iPods that we can carry or wear so that sound follows us from room to room, and out into the world. Douglas explains that radio has long participated in shaping our listening habits by allowing us to listen alongside other activities: 'You could do something else while listening, you didn't have to watch and you didn't have to concentrate, depending on what was on. Radio could adjust much more to physical circumstances – cooking dinner, driving to work – than any of the other media ... . This meant that radio listening also became interwoven with the ritualized routines of everyday life – reading the paper, eating meals.'[37] With the availability of personal listening technologies and popular worship musics, along with the contemporary Christian's desire for a frequent, intimate encounter with God, why wait until Sunday morning for a worship experience?

Given this long history of the intersections of music, faith and sound, it is striking that in the 1990s and 2000s a new set of tropes came to dominate print

---

[34]   Quoted in Douglas, *Listening In*, p. 23.

[35]   Matthew Engelke, 'Material Religion', in Robert A. Orsi (ed.), *The Cambridge Companion to Religious Studies* (Cambridge University Press, 2012), pp. 227–8, emphasis in the original.

[36]   Engelke, 'Material Religion', p. 213.

[37]   Douglas, *Listening In*, pp. 31–2.

marketing campaigns for popular worship music – discourses that emphasized a dual transformation of (profane) space and (autonomous) self through the power of music. Collectively, these tropes did not simply represent a shift in marketing strategy but instead both reflected and helped solidify a particular understanding of 'worship' as an increasingly individual (rather than corporate) act achieved via material products and technology.[38] Advertisements for Praise and Worship recordings in the magazine *Worship Leader* previously presented recordings as tools for congregational worship leaders; now they begin to market the recordings as also and additionally for personal use.[39] At the same time as its advertising begins to target a more general audience, *Worship Leader* reveals a similar transition towards appealing even more directly to Christian popular music listeners. For instance, reviews of worship albums continue to emphasize the utility of recordings as places to find accessible group worship music, but by 2003 the reviews reveal an awareness that worship music recordings will be used for personal listening. For example, one of the magazine's reviewers writes that Caedmon's Call *Back Home* is 'a great CD for worship leader and worshiper alike, [it] features songs that can be put to use in a contemporary worship service as well as songs that can be enjoyed by those who just enjoy uplifting praise music at home or in the car'.[40] By 2004–2005, many album reviews, especially those of the more alternative subgenre 'modern worship' don't mention corporate worship at all, often focusing instead on the music as a personal expression by its creator and the product as intended for listening and not reproduction in a group setting. It is significant that a magazine originally directed to an audience of music ministers, choir directors and other corporate worship leaders reveals the shift towards privatized religious practice, especially given that the first decade of the 2000s has been a time of anxieties across evangelical and mainstream Protestantism about declining congregations and the loss of church authority.[41]

---

[38] Conscious of the problems of a technological determinist argument, where technology is considered either dangerously homogenizing or optimistically diversifying culture, I am interested instead in the co-constitutive role of technology in shaping worship practices and theological possibilities. In particular, I'm interested instead in how the media are constructing this discourse of personal listening as a desirable and spiritually fulfilling religious practice. David Nye, 'Technology and the Production of Difference', in Carolyn de la Peña and Siva Vaidhyanathan (eds), *Rewiring the 'Nation': The Place of Technology in American Studies* (Johns Hopkins University Press, 2007), p. 44.

[39] *Worship Leader* magazine began in 1992 and in 2012 continues to publish eight issues per year. They define themselves as a 'resource for the curators of worship', including church leaders and practitioners of contemporary worship music. 'About Us', *Worship Leader*, http://worshipleader.com/about-us/ (accessed 23 November 2012).

[40] Jessica Ludwig, review of Caedmon's Call *Back Home*, *Worship Leader* (January/February 2003): p. 43.

[41] For example, see Tim Stafford, 'The Church: Why Bother?' *Christianity Today* (January 2005): pp. 42–9. For information on Americans' decline of confidence in organized religion see Lydia Saad, 'U.S. Confidence in Organized Religion at Low Point', Gallup

Early advertisements for popular worship music in *Worship Leader* were visually dense, usually centred around images of the album covers and containing lots of text. A 1995 advertisement from Vineyard Music and Praise offers solo CDs by worship leader/songwriters Brian Doerkson and Andy Park, describing the music as 'intimate praise' and 'songs you can't get out of your head', but the advertisement promotes a corresponding songbook, showing that Vineyard is still aiming the advertisement, at least to some degree, to worship leaders. In an advertisement from the same year, Integrity Music also promises that CDs featuring the 'Alleluia Worship Band' could provide 'personal praise' and 'what you want to hear, when you want to hear it', implying that the recordings could potentially be used outside of church services and worship prep. This advertisement is clearly directed to both worship leaders and a more general audience, and features testimony from two listeners. Kim Noblitt, Minister of Music at an Alabama church, states that 'songsheets let us reproduce what we heard on the album almost exactly' but the words of a female listener identified as 'M. Williams, part-time nurse and mother of two' support this music's use in an everyday context. Says Williams:

> Between the kids, the house, and errands, my day is all chopped up into little bits of time. What I like about *ALLELUIA MUSIC* is that it's a collection of songs – not a live service. That way I can fit a couple of songs in during breakfast, or while I'm carpooling, and not feel like I'm starting or stopping in the middle of something.

A year later, Vineyard still featured images of CDs and advertised songbooks in its worship music advertisements. These early advertisements for Vineyard and Integrity may appear basic and even visually cluttered when compared with those that follow in the 2000s but they mark a meaningful point in the history of Praise and Worship and, indeed, in Christian popular music more generally where worship music recordings have been designed and marketed for personal listening outside of church, and not only as tools for worship leaders.

Significantly, worship music advertisements increasingly promise not just good music but personal intimacy and the transformation of everyday spaces and routines, of personal identity and of worship practice. The most notable advertisement from the mid-1990s that advertises more than just worship music to more than a niche market of church musicians is a 1995 lavish two-page advertisement for Maranatha! Music, republished in 1996 condensed onto a single page. Unlike the previous advertisements, musical objects like CDs and songbooks are no longer the visual focus – here, one CD cover appears small and off to the side. Instead, most of the page is taken up with a dark shot of the front interior space of a luxury sedan, complete with leather seats, power windows and

Politics, http://www.gallup.com/poll/155690/confidence-organized-religion-low-point.aspx, accessed 12 July 2012.

a warmly glowing dashboard console. Huge letters read 'Welcome to the new sanctuary' while smaller type directs readers to 'make your car a place of worship with Maranatha! Music'. A still smaller grouping of powerfully evocative words promises: 'Praise. Worship. Peace. Refuge. Safety. Encouragement. Anywhere.' The message here is anything but subtle. Listeners should load worship music CDs into their stereos to transform their mundane automobiles into sacred sanctuaries, and their ordinary commutes into spirit-filled worship experiences. Maranatha's use of the car imagery is savvy, considering that one 2003 survey indicated that Americans listen to radio in the car much more than they do at home or at work, and they spend an average of fifteen hours in the car each week,[42] but, as indicated by nurse and mother 'M. Williams' in the 1995 Integrity advertisement, most Christian media companies already realized that their recordings were being listened to on the road. Worship leaders, too, were beginning to appreciate the potential use of these worship recordings for individualized use in everyday settings. Particularly revealing is how Biola University professor and congregational worship director, Barry Liesch, wrote in 1996 that he hoped weekly corporate worship would be a model for private worship so that 'when caught in a traffic jam or washing the dishes, we might be more inclined to shut off the radio and worship before the Lord alone or with a worship cassette'.[43]

Integrity Music's print advertisements in the early 2000s help reinforce this emerging discourse of a worship lifestyle where private listening to popular worship music enables one to turn ordinary everyday tasks such as doing laundry and taking the kids to soccer practice into an experience of God's presence. Unlike 1990s advertisement campaigns, images of albums and songbooks no longer dominate the ads; instead they alternately show us what we desire to escape from or to – from traffic jams to mountains, from laundry to a serene meadow. An advertisement from 2000, for instance, tells us that when we're frustrated by our commute, instead of 'bang[ing] on the steering wheel' and 'cry[ing] into our latte', we should worship and 'Yield to God' and 'slide Don Moen's "I Will Sing" into the deck and enter into the calming presence of the Living God'. Another advertisement from 2001 depicts a clothes iron and the top of a line of shirts inside a closet, saying, 'you can go about your day in your own strength believing that God is a million miles away. Or you can worship God right where you are. Slide Paul Wilbur's "Lion of Judah" into your CD player and be transported to the Holy Land.' Music, as portrayed here, can bring worship to the listener and the listener into God's presence.

Not only do these advertisements promise to transform one's everyday life into worship, they also reinforce the discourse that worship is an 'experience' that

---

[42]   Arbitron, *The National In-Car Study: Fighting for the Front Seat* (Arbitron, 2003); quoted in Alexandra A. Vagos, *A Semiological Analysis of Contemporary Christian Music (CCM) as Heard on 95.5 WFHM-FM Cleveland, Ohio 'The Fish' Radio Station (July 2001 to July 2006)* (Ph.D. diss., Kent State University, 2011), p. 63.

[43]   Liesch, *The New Worship*, p. 47.

should 'overwhelm' the listener with feeling. For instance, advertisements for worship albums by the company HeartCry published in *Worship Leader* as early as 1994 promised one could 'experience the power of God's love right where you live' through listening to their recordings. Integrity's early 2000s iWorship marketing campaign for CDs and karaoke-style worship DVDs designed for home use features large photos of natural scenes such as the sun breaking over a mountain ridge, promising that its products will provide 'a total worship experience' that is 'powerful' and 'interactive'. An advertisement for a 2001 Hillsong CD shows a single worshipper in a sunny field with arms outstretched and face turned to the sun. It promises that listening to this album can cause one to 'get overwhelmed by the presence of the living God'. Importantly, these advertisements address a singular subject, evoking not an imagined community but a dyadic and intimate connection with the deity that will inspire awe in the encounter, transforming the mundane into the sacred – turning ironing into 'worship'. Deborah Lubken notes that the Integrity's iWorship videos of Praise and Worship music overwhelmingly feature images of the natural world, including images of the sun, the sky, the ocean and broad vistas of mountains.[44] There are no people pictured in these images, allowing the viewer to imagine a one-on-one encounter between the worshipper and God.

Headphones, Earbuds and the Empowerment of Private Worship

Changing technologies, particularly the development of portable personal listening devices, continue to keep sound privatized, even when the listener inhabits public spaces. Michael Bull writes in his study of personal stereos that listeners collapse the dichotomy of public and private as their listening 'inscribe[s] "public" space with "private" meaning'. In particular, says Bull, through the use of these personal listening devices, an unpredictable urban experience becomes a technologized routine where 'the contingent nature of the everyday and the attendant awareness of risk become mediated and reduced', giving listeners a sense of safety and security as they carry a little of their own world around with them.[45] Bull notes that for some listeners, personal stereo use allows them to '[travel] back to their own narratives by visualizing situations or re-experiencing the sensation of pleasurable situations while listening', thus transporting them to imagined places.[46] And as listeners re-construct memories of pleasurable experiences, argues Bull, they become empowered.

---

[44]   Deborah Lubken, 'iPresence: Experiencing the Mediated Presence of God', paper presented at the annual meeting of the Society for the Scientific Study of Religion (Rochester, New York, 2005).

[45]   Michael Bull, 'Personal Stereos and the Aural Reconfiguration of Representational Space', in Sally R. Munt (ed.), *Technospaces: Inside the New Media* (Continuum, 2001), pp. 240, 250–51.

[46]   Bull, 'Personal Stereos', p. 251.

While Bull's study looked at generalized, secular personal stereo use, it is easy to see how his conclusions about safety and pleasure are reinforced in these advertisement campaigns for Christian music. A visual trope of listening via headphones dominates print advertising in Christian music magazines from 2002–2006, and these advertisements reinforce the powerful discourse of a specifically charismatic theology where Christianity is singularly portrayed as emotional, experiential and, above all, personal. Importantly, all these advertisements target mainstream Christian music listeners, and popular worship is often categorized less as a separate genre with different functions than as a subgenre of Christian popular music. Simon Frith claims that music is:

> the cultural form best able to cross borders – sounds carry across fences and walls and oceans, across classes, races, and nations – and to define places; in clubs, scenes, and raves, listening on headphones, radio, and in the concert hall, we are only where the music takes us.[47]

In these advertisements the rest of the world is shut out as solitary listeners close their eyes and cover or fill their ears so that their only sensory experience is their music. Although headphones can be understood more generally as an indexical sign for the audible – a semiotic code for listening – in these advertisements headphones also work to reinforce the idea that sound can both transform and transport listeners. Thus these advertisements uncannily echo Frith as they say again and again that music can take a listener from an everyday place or task into a personal experience of God's presence.

Headphone advertisements begin to appear in 1999 in *Worship Leader* magazine with an advertisement for *Wow Worship Blue*, a compilation album of popular worship songs, created by Vineyard, Maranatha! and Integrity Media. The discourse that worship recordings can create a divine 'experience' everyday is reinforced here in both image and text. Above a photo of a headphoned young man whose eyes are closed and hands clasped in a prayerful position we hear that these three record companies 'hope' that we will 'experience the Wow! of God's love – body, mind, and soul – every day' (see Figure 7.1 below).

Spring Hill Music's 2002 advertisement for Christ Church Choir's album, 'The Sweet Aroma of Praise' similarly reinforces this message. A close-up photo of a twenty-something woman's face occupies over half the page. Her eyes are closed and her mouth is pursed in a slight smile of pleasurable concentration as she holds her hands over the large headphones that cover her ears. The large text that overlays this image reads, 'No pews. No walls. No boundaries. Have church anytime with Christ Church Choir'. Next to the small album cover image, comparatively tiny text offers the CD free to the first five hundred worship leaders who write to the company. But the dominant message of this advertisement is

---

[47]   Simon Frith, 'Music and Identity', in Stuart Hall and Paul du Gay (eds), *Questions of Cultural Identity* (Sage, 1996), p. 125.

Figure 7.1   Advertisement for *WOW Worship Blue* (1999) in *Worship Leader*
               magazine

directed not to worship leaders but to listeners who want to recreate the experience
of 'live worship' anytime and anywhere.

    At the same time that images of headphoned Christian music listeners who are
experiencing God's presence appear less frequently in *Worship Leader*, beginning
in 2003 they begin to fill the pages of *CCM* magazine, a monthly magazine
focused broadly on commercial Christian popular music (including but not limited
to worship music). The most widely published print advertisement featuring a

headphoned listener comes from Walmart and ran regularly in *CCM* magazine from late 2003 to early 2007. A full-body image of a blond woman sitting in a chair in a sunny but generic waiting room fills the entire page. Her eyes are closed, her head leans back against the window, and her face is relaxed and placid. Small Walkman style headphones cover her ears and she holds a personal CD player in her lap. Above her in large type is her witness to the music's transcendent power (the only text in the advertisement besides some very small font CD titles and the Walmart logo), which reads: 'Contemporary Christian music takes me from where I am to where I want to be.' Against the window to the right of the listeners are small images of CD covers, and Walmart featured different titles, including but not limited to popular worship music, in each different run of the advertisement.

Overall, most of these advertisements encode their messages of peace, escape, spiritual ecstasy, and personal religion via the images rather than the text. For example, Integrity Music's 'Enter the Heavenlies' 2003 iWorship campaign in *CCM* features a headshot of a slightly smiling blond woman with eyes closed and headphones on against a celestial starry backdrop; Lifeway Christian bookstore's 2003 advertisement for digital music downloads shows the face of a white teenaged girl who smiles while closing her eyes and pressing her headphones closer to her ears; and Target's advertisement for Christian pop shows the white outline of a dancing woman with large headphones against its signature red backdrop.[48] Advertisements for *CCM*'s Top 100 Greatest Songs in Christian Music that ran in 2004 all feature listeners in the act of private listening via headphones, though they depict a little more gender and racial diversity: a black woman, black man, and white woman all have their eyes closed as they listen, and while a white teen girl's eyes are open it is clear from her gaze that her attention is directed inward to her own listening. SongTouch, a Christian music download site, ran a set of advertisements in *CCM* in 2005 that also depict individuals listening to Christian music via headphones: a black teen boy plays air guitar along with his music in one, while twenty-something young women (one white and one black) smile broadly and turn their eyes up towards the heavens. A 2005 Borders advertisement shows a young Asian woman holding her headphones on while she smiles inwardly, and another depicts an older white man listening to headphones while reclining on a plush couch.

In many cases, listening to music provides escape from the stresses of modern life and, in the case of a 2006 Integrity Music advertisement from *CCM*, soothing relief in the words of scripture communicated through song (see Figure 7.2 below). Verbal messages of music's transportational and transformational powers accompany a visual depiction of ecstatic individualized listening. Here a young white woman can be seen lying stretched out on the grass. Her eyes are closed, her mouth is smiling, and her right hand cradles the iPod that is playing through the earbuds in her ears. Like a testimonial, and complete with biblical references, the text reads: 'When I feel overwhelmed (Ps 61:1–2), super stressed (Ps 91:1–2, 5–7),

---

[48]   The outlined nature of the figure in this ad evokes iPod advertisements from the same year that feature a black silhouette of a listening figure against a colourful background.

Figure 7.2   Advertisement for Integrity Music in *CCM* magazine (2006)

or just having [sic] one of those anxious days (Phil 4: 6–7), the Word of God speaks to my soul and calms my mind.'

Print advertisements depicting headphoned listeners disappear completely from *Worship Leader* by 2005, as advertisements for best-seller compilations of worship music such as *WOW! Worship* also become more rare. Instead, *Worship Leader* advertisements after 2003 are more likely to be for worship resources (some of which have given up using physical discs and books at all in favour of downloads) or for solo albums by worship leaders and other Christian musicians. By 2007, headphone advertisements also become infrequent in *CCM* magazine.

Print advertisements themselves become more rare as *CCM* moves from print format to exclusively online content after 2008. The discourse of worship as experience, though, especially as it is tied to music, has continued to remain strong into the second decade of the twenty-first century. Albums such as Marvin L. Winans' 2012 *The Praise & Worship Experience* continue to promote a worship experience achieved via recordings. Interestingly, some churches now refer to corporate worship services and other music-based church events as 'worship experiences'.[49]

Through repeated promises of spiritual transformation, marketing discourses about the purpose and practice of worship work co-constitutively to both reflect and reinforce changing attitudes towards worship in the US. The enveloping intimacy of technologically reproduced sound especially as experienced via headphones breaks down distinctions between the listener and the music, allowing listeners to transform or, as Bull argues, to 'reclaim' and 'colonize' their physical environment with the sounds of their choosing, thus enhancing their pleasure even to the point of creating a personalized and individualized 'audiotopia'.[50] Yet, personal stereos also simultaneously give the listener a sense of 'we-ness' – a critical shift in how she views her own subjectivity, even as she listens alone.[51] Advertisements position these products as having the power to transform potentially solitary acts of media consumption into corporate worship with an imagined community of other Christians. Yet, most of these advertisements speak of another kind of 'we-ness'; they promise that the music will transport listeners into the holy presence of God. In the words of Simon Frith and Walmart: it 'takes us' from where we are to where we want to be.

Conclusion: Longing for a Technological Sublime

Media technologies have long promised to deliver experiences rather than goods. Radio helped its listeners transcend distance and feel connected to faraway people and places. Television became our window to the world. Personal stereos make it possible to relive a corporate worship experience without being in church. Karaoke-style worship videos seem to bring the church right into our homes.

---

[49]   Two examples include Woodlands Church, a multi-campus church organization in the Houston, Texas metro area, as well as Victory World Church in suburban Atlanta.

[50]   Michael Bull, 'IPod Culture: The Toxic Pleasure of Audiotopia', in Trevor Pinch and Karin Bijsterveld (eds), *The Oxford Handbook of Sound Studies* (Oxford University Press, 2012), pp. 528–30. While I find Bull's argument for the creation of audiotopias to be useful for understanding the transformative experience of personalized listening, I'm less convinced by his argument that this audiotopias have the potential be 'toxic' when they put a listener into an adversarial relationship with all experience outside the audiotopia.

[51]   Bull, 'Personal Stereos', p. 242.

Christian media promises to take each of us 'there' – to assist us in transcending this physical world so that we may, on our own, journey to meet the divine.

This transcendent possibility promised by Christian pop music purveyors depends on a theology of an interpersonal relationship with God as well as an emotionalism derived from charismatic practice, but in its contemporary manifestation in music marketing, it also relies on what David Nye has called the 'technological sublime'. Nye claims that Americans have repeatedly sought to experience and re-experience a transcendent sublime, an 'extraordinary break' in mundane experience that we hope will overwhelm us with emotion and feeling. This desire, he argues, animates our creation and adoption of new technologies; once sought primarily in the natural world and religious experience, this sublime has become increasingly technologized: 'Those operating within this logic embrace the reconstruction of the lifeworld by machinery, experience the dislocations and perpetual disorientations caused by this reconstruction in terms of awe and wonder, and, in their excitement, feel insulated from immediate danger.'[52]

The advertisements analysed above, particularly through their articulation of 'worship' music to a technologized and individualized listening space for Christian transcendence, brings together the technological sublime and the religious sublime. Promising both spatial and individual transformation through the act of privatized musical consumption, they thus participate in the promotion of an ecstatic, spirit-filled worship practice – yet one that, importantly, is increasingly divorced from traditional notions of worship as a corporate practice. In other words, the marketing of Christian music echoes worship leaders who urge their congregations to bring ecstatic, spirit-filled worship into everything they do, turning their ordinary everyday life into an experience of divine immanence. These advertisements teach customers to use technology and the products of the Christian music industry to practice an individualized charismatic faith where even the most ordinary tasks *should* become praise and the most ordinary commute *ought* to be a communion.

References

Anderson, Robert Mapes, 'Pentecostal and Charismatic Christianity', in Lindsay Jones (ed.), *Encyclopedia of Religion*, 2d ed. vol. 10 (Detroit: Macmillan Reference USA, 2005).

Bergler, Thomas E., '"I Found My Thrill": The Youth for Christ Movement and American Congregational Singing, 1940–1970', in Richard J. Mouw and Mark A. Noll (eds), *Wonderful Words of Life: American Hymns in American Protestant Theology* (Grand Rapids: William B. Eerdmans, 2004).

Bull, Michael, 'Personal Stereos and the Aural Reconfiguration of Representational Space', in Sally R. Munt (ed.), *Technospaces: Inside the New Media* (London: Continuum, 2001).

---

[52]   David E. Nye, *American Technological Sublime* (MIT Press, 1994), p. 282.

Bull, Michael, 'IPod Culture: The Toxic Pleasure of Audiotopia', in Trevor Pinch and Karin Bijsterveld (eds), *The Oxford Handbook of Sound Studies* (New York: Oxford University Press, 2012).

Butler, Jon, 'Religion in Colonial America', in *Religion in American Life: A Short History* (Oxford: Oxford University Press, 2000).

Coleman, Simon, *The Globalisation of Charismatic Christianity: Spreading the Gospel of Prosperity* (New York: Cambridge University Press, 2000).

Cusic, Don, *The Sound of Light: A History of Gospel Music* (Bowling Green, OH: Bowling Green University Popular Press, 1990).

Di Sabatino, David, *The Jesus People Movement: An Annotated Bibliography and General Resource* (Westport, CT: Greenwood Press, 1999).

Douglas, Susan J., *Listening In: Radio and the American Imagination* (New York: Random House Times Books, 1999).

Engelke, Matthew, 'Material Religion', in Robert A. Orsi (ed.), *The Cambridge Companion to Religious Studies* (New York: Cambridge University Press, 2012).

Faulkner, Quentin, *Wiser Than Despair: The Evolution of Ideas in the Relationship of Music and the Christian Church* (Westport, CT: Greenwood Press, 1996).

Frith, Simon, 'Towards an Aesthetic of Popular Music', in *Music and Society: The Politics of Composition, Performance and Reception* (Cambridge: Cambridge University Press, 1987).

Frith, Simon, 'Music and Identity', in Stuart Hall and Paul du Gay (eds), *Questions of Cultural Identity* (London: Sage, 1996).

Jorstad, Erling, *That New-Time Religion: The Jesus Revival In America* (Minneapolis: Augsburg Publishing House, 1972).

Kee, Kevin, 'Marketing the Gospel: Music in English Canadian Protestant Revivalism, 1884–1957', in Richard J. Mouw and Mark A. Noll (eds), *Wonderful Words of Life: American Hymns in American Protestant Theology* (Grand Rapids: William B. Eerdmans, 2004).

Liesch, Barry, *The New Worship: Straight Talk on Music and the Church* (Grand Rapids: Baker Book House, 1996).

Loviglio, Jason, *Radio's Intimate Public: Network Broadcasting and Mass-Mediated Democracy* (Minneapolis: University Of Minnesota Press, 2005).

Lubken, Deborah, 'iPresence: Experiencing the Mediated Presence of God', paper presented at the annual meeting of the Society for the Scientific Study of Religion (Rochester, New York, 2005).

Ludwig, Jessica, Review of Caedmon's Call *Back Home*, *Worship Leader* (January/February 2003): 43.

McCart, Thomas K., *The Matter and Manner of Praise: The Controversial Evolution of Hymnody in the Church of England 1760–1820* (Lanham, Md.: Scarecrow Press, 1998).

Moore, R. Laurence, *Selling God: American Religion in the Marketplace of Culture* (New York: Oxford University Press, 1994).

Nekola, Anna, 'Worldly Worship: Negotiating the Tensions of U.S. Worship Music in the Marketplace', Suzel Reily and Jonathan Dueck (eds), *The Oxford Handbook of Music and World Christianities* (New York: Oxford University Press, forthcoming).

Nye, David, *American Technological Sublime* (Cambridge, Mass: MIT Press, 1994).

Nye, David, 'Technology and the Production of Difference', in Carolyn de la Peña and Siva Vaidhyanathan (eds), *Rewiring the 'Nation': The Place of Technology in American Studies* (Baltimore: Johns Hopkins University Press, 2007).

Redman, Robb, *The Great Worship Awakening: Singing a New Song in the Postmodern Church* (San Francisco: Jossey-Bass, 2002).

Saad, Lydia, 'U.S. Confidence in Organized Religion at Low Point', Gallup Politics, http://www.gallup.com/poll/155690/confidence-organized-religion-low-point.aspx, accessed 12 July 2012.

Stafford, Tim, 'The Church: Why Bother?' *Christianity Today* (January 2005): 42–8.

Stowe, David W., *How Sweet the Sound: Music in the Spiritual Lives of Americans* (Cambridge, MA: Harvard University Library, 2004).

Vagos, Alexandra A., *A Semiological Analysis of Contemporary Christian Music (CCM) as Heard on 95.5 WFHM-FM Cleveland, Ohio 'The Fish' Radio Station (July 2001 to July 2006)* (PhD diss., Kent State University, 2011).

Webber, Robert E., *Worship is a Verb: Celebrating God's Mighty Deed of Salvation* (Peabody, MA: Hendrickson Publishers, 2004).

Wilhoit, Mel R., 'Sankey, Ira D.', *Grove Music Online. Oxford Music Online*, http://0-www.oxfordmusiconline.com.dewey2.library.denison.edu/subscriber/article/grove/music/24515, accessed 18 September 2012.

Chapter 8

(Hillsong) United Through Music: Praise and Worship Music and the Evangelical 'Imagined Community'

Gesa Hartje-Döll

In the world of Praise and Worship music,[1] songs move among churches in a steady stream of new songs springing from various songwriters' inspiration and popular favourites. Rooted in the Jesus People Movement of the 1960s and 70s, the popular music style of Praise and Worship music (hereafter, 'P&W') makes it stand apart from organ-led traditional church music.[2] Yet because it stylistically 'imitates' different popular music genres and thus adapts to changes in style and taste of contemporary culture, its 'sound' is not fixed. Originally, the music was inspired by folksongs, producing the simple but catchy 'Praise choruses' as published by Maranatha! or Vineyard from the 1970s onward. The most recent compositions in P&W, however, closely follow the sound and timbre of popular bands like Coldplay and U2. Indeed, it seems that the only common denominator for P&W is biblically inspired content.[3]

---

[1] Throughout this article, I will be using the term 'Praise and Worship music' (P&W). Other authors have opted to follow John Frame by using his term 'contemporary worship music'; see John Frame, *Contemporary Worship Music: A Biblical Defense* (P & R Publishing, 1997). The phrase 'Praise and Worship music' seems more appropriate for the theses presented in the present work, as it is the expression used by the recording industry (for example GMA Dove Award for Praise and Worship Album) and also a term used in the global context. Other designations for the music include 'Modern Worship' or 'Worship music'.

[2] For a historical overview on the development of music during the era of the Jesus People, see Andrew Mall, 'The Stars are Underground: Undergrounds, Mainstreams, and Christian Popular Music' (PhD Diss., University of Chicago, 2012); David W. Stowe, *No Sympathy for the Devil: Christian Pop Music and the Transformation of American Evangelicalism* (University of North Carolina Press, 2011); Bob Gersztyn, 'Jesus Music', in Don Cusic (ed.), *Encyclopedia of Contemporary Christian Music: Pop, Rock, and Worship* (Greenwood Press, 2010), pp. 269–77; or Larry Eskridge, *Sweet, Sweet Song of Salvation: The Jesus People Movement and American Evangelicalism, 1967–1977* (Oxford University Press, 2009).

[3] This is almost universally referred to in songwriting guidebooks. For example, see Paul Baloche, Jimmy Owens and Carol Owens, *God Songs: How to Write and Select Songs for Worship* (Leadworship.com, 2004).

From the churches founded during the Jesus People movement, the music gradually spread to churches of various backgrounds and traditions within the US. With the rise of megachurches and their so-called 'seeker sensitive' approach,[4] the music received an even bigger platform, as its popular music sound was deemed capable of attracting the 'unchurched' attendants. Today, many churches in the US use at least some P&W songs in their repertoire and the popularity of P&W is increasing.[5]

The music's success story, however, is not restricted to North America. Starting in the UK, it spread across Europe and eventually made its way to Australia. The continent is home to the globally popular worship band 'Hillsong UNITED'[6] which currently influences what songs are being sung by congregations worldwide.[7] It is through bands like 'Hillsong UNITED' that P&W has turned into a highly international music genre, a development backed up by the recording industry and the developments in media and technology.[8] A consequence of the music's internationalization is a musical repertoire that is shared among Christian churches around the world.

----

[4]   The 'seeker' aspect of the church growth movement targets those attendants that have not yet been saved in the evangelical sense of accepting Jesus Christ as their personal Saviour. By creating entertaining services that feature music, drama and dance, churches hope to attract those new to the Christian faith by making them feel comfortable in the church. For an in-depth analysis of the seeker movement see: Kimon Howland Sargeant, *Seeker Churches: Promoting Traditional Religion in a Nontraditional Way* (Rutgers University Press, 2000).

[5]   The Faith Communities Today Project (working in conjunction with Hartford Institute for Religion Research) released a report 'FACTs on Worship: 2010', http://faithcommunitiestoday.org/sites/faithcommunitiestoday.org/-files/FACTs-on-Worship.pdf (accessed November 2012) that shows that 51% of Evangelical Protestant churches often or always use electric guitar or drums in their services. This number has risen from 35 per cent in 2000. For all the Christian groups in the survey, the use of contemporary worship was 29 per cent in 2000 and 43 per cent in 2010.

[6]   Hillsong United developed out of the youth ministry at Hillsong Church close to Sydney, Australia in the 1990s, releasing their first album in 1999. Its leader is Joel Houston, son of the church's founders and senior pastors Brian and Bobbie Houston. Hillsong Church's publishing arm, Hillsong Music Australia, produces several other album lines, most notably the Hillsong LIVE series. Since 1991, HMA has sold over 12 million albums worldwide (http://www.thepowerindex.com.au/and-the-winner-is/hillsongs-power-in-determining-the-sound-of-christmas/-20111218858, accessed November 2012).

[7]   Hillsong songs routinely appear on the Top 25 reports compiled by the Christian Copyright Licensing International (CCLI) which measures the use of P&W songs through self-reporting by churches around the world and distributes royalties to the copyright holders accordingly. These reports can be accessed via the CCLI website for each region at http://www.ccli.com/Global.aspx, accessed September 2012.

[8]   Other songwriters whose songs are also sung around the globe include Americans Rick Founds and Chris Tomlin, Canadian Brian Doerksen, Matt Redman from England and Darlene Zschech from Australia. Their names appear in the majority of reports compiled by the CCLI where the songs are sorted according to their reported frequency for every participating country or region (Americas, Africa, Europe, Asia Pacific).

Praise and Worship is of course not the only shared global Christian musical repertoire. More traditional denominations like Roman Catholics or Lutherans share songs worldwide that have been transmitted to other linguistic regions via missionaries over the course of centuries (such as Martin Luther's 'Ein feste Burg ist unser Gott'). An example of a shared global repertoire originating in the twentieth century are Taizé songs. They are disseminated mainly via the pilgrims coming to the Taizé community in France, but are also available as live recordings and songbooks directly from the Order.

What sets P&W apart from the first example is its relative recentness of only several decades and the rapidity with which new songs move around the globe by means of recordings. Also, songs quickly overcome language barriers through officially provided translations.[9] And although Taizé songs and P&W songs are both a phenomenon of the second half of the twentieth century, disseminated quickly through modern technology, they differ in that Taizé songs share a single background and a consistently similar sound based on meditative melodies. In contrast, P&W comes from many different songwriters and varies significantly in style as its arrangements and sound are constantly updated, following popular music trends. This variety, then, sets P&W apart from other church music traditions that have also established a shared musical repertoire across international borders.

The shared repertoire that arises from the international dissemination of P&W songs is part of a larger phenomenon: a sense of community among believers fuelled by common media.[10] Extending around the globe, the community united by P&W songs shows traits of an 'imagined community' in the sense of Benedict Anderson.[11]

The present chapter discusses the different facets of how evangelicals use music to 'imagine community' by using 'Hillsong UNITED' as an illustration. In the first part, I detail in what way I view the community of evangelicals as 'imagined'. I then examine the recording industry's role in the development of a shared P&W musical repertoire. I conclude by analysing how this shared repertoire affords the feeling of unity necessary for the construction of an 'imagined community' of evangelicals.

The 'Imagined Community' of Evangelicals

Evangelical Christianity is deeply rooted in the history of the New World, as waves of people who found themselves on the margins of society in the Old World due to their religious beliefs sought religious freedom in the North American colonies.

---

[9]   Hillsong Music, for example, maintains its own database for Spanish, French, German, Italian, Portuguese and Greek translations free of charge (http://distribution. hillsong.com/translations, accessed September 2012).

[10]   See Simon Coleman, *The Globalisation of Charismatic Christianity: Spreading the Gospel of Prosperity* (Cambridge University Press, 2000).

[11]   Benedict Anderson, *Imagined Communities: Reflections on the Origin and Spread of Nationalism*, revised ed. (London: Verso, 1983/2006).

Removed from unwanted outside influences, they established communities based on shared religious convictions.[12] Religious freedom was officially guaranteed in the First Amendment to the United States' Constitution's Bill of Rights in 1791, although the eighteenth century had already seen various Protestant denominations prospering through religious revivals, especially the Great Awakening. The later revival movements of the nineteenth and twentieth century led by particularly charismatic Protestant ministers – also called Great Awakenings – resulted in the creation of new denominations throughout the country. Evangelicalism became 'the functional equivalent of an established church'.[13] Thus, while in Western Europe Roman Catholicism and a few forms of mainline Protestantism were (and continue to be) the most visible forms of Christian faith,[14] a variety of Protestant Christian churches could be found in North America, a plurality that continues to grow today.[15]

As a result, the evangelical Protestant churches of the US are extremely widespread and diverse. Their gathering places range from large church buildings resembling convention centres to very small home churches formed of only a few congregants meeting in private living rooms. Not surprisingly, this great variety in size is coupled with a great variety in conventions and style. The end of the twentieth century has seen the rise of what Miller calls 'new-paradigm churches'.[16] These postdenominational churches adhere to teaching 'rooted in first-century biblical

---

[12]   See Patricia U. Bonomi, *Under the Cope of Heaven: Religion, Society, and Politics in Colonial America* (Oxford University Press, 1986); and Jon Butler, *Religion in Colonial America* (Oxford University Press, 2000).

[13]   Quote attributed to Daniel Walker Howe in Darryl G. Hart, *That Old-Time Religion in Modern America: Evangelical Protestantism in the Twentieth Century* (Ivan R. Dee, 2002), p. 12.

[14]   According to the 'Evangelische Kirche in Deutschland', 62 per cent of the German population in 2009 identified as Christian, with close to 50 per cent belonging to each of the Lutheran Evangelical and the Roman Catholic Church (around 24 and 25 million people, respectively). A small number of Christians identified as Orthodox (a little more than one million), and very few (around 300,000) were in other Protestant churches (Evangelische Freikirchen) (http://www.ekd.de/statistik/mitglieder.html, accessed August 2012).

[15]   The 2012 Yearbook of American and Canadian Churches reports on 228 national church bodies, noticing 'a continuing decline in membership of virtually all mainline denominations'. At the same time, '[m]ost churches which have been increasing in membership in recent years have continued to grow', including many Pentecostal groups (http://www.ncccusa.org/news/120209yearbook2012.html, accessed August 2012).

The Association of Religion Data Archives (ARDA) released a census of US religions in 2012 (http://www.thearda.com/rcms2010/, accessed November 2012) reporting a 'modest increase in the number of evangelical Protestants, and a drop in the number of Catholics and mainline Protestants' according to the Christian Post (http://www.christianpost.com/news/religion-census-increase-in-evangelicals-mormons-muslims-decrease-in-catholics-mainline-protestants-74207/#JbGBeQkgHWLRCXtT.99, accessed November 2012).

[16]   Donald E. Miller, 'Postdenominational Christianity in the Twenty-First Century', *Annals of the American Academy of Political and Social Science*, 558 (1998): p. 197.

narratives about Jesus and the early Christian church'[17] while using 'the technology and cultural idiom of post-modern culture'.[18] In the introduction to his book *An Introduction to Pentecostalism: Global Charismatic Christianity*, Allan Anderson explores how these churches extend globally. He states that while Charismatic and Pentecostal churches around the world demonstrate 'several common features'[19] such as an emphasis on congregational participation, there 'are as many different types of Pentecostal and Charismatic churches as there are thousands of organizations'.[20] Although referring to subcategories of evangelicalism, Anderson's discussion on the difficulty of defining the terms highlights the challenge of defining 'evangelical': 'because of the great diversity within Pentecostal and Charismatic movements, it is very difficult to find some common unifying features or distinctiveness by which they might be defined'.[21] As he points out, this observation is even more relevant when looking at the global Church.

Consequently, it seems futile to speak of '*the* evangelicals' as if the different groups and churches constituting the entity were a homogenous ensemble. Although many scholars seem to largely agree on the hallmarks of evangelicalism as defined by David Bebbington,[22] the definitions of what it means to be an evangelical Christian are diverse. They can include as well as exclude denominations and movements depending on who defines the term and for what purpose.[23] Several researchers have even questioned whether the term 'evangelical' adequately describes an existing entity.[24] An article by The Institute on Religion and

[17] Miller, 'Postdenominational Christianity', p. 203.
[18] Miller, 'Postdenominational Christianity', p. 203.
[19] Allan Anderson, *An Introduction to Pentecostalism: Global Charismatic Christianity* (Cambridge University Press, 2004), p. 9.
[20] Anderson, *Introduction to Pentecostalism*, p. 9.
[21] Anderson, *Introduction to Pentecostalism*, p. 10.
[22] As listed by the National Association of Evangelicals, Bebbington's criteria for evangelicalism are 'Conversionism: the belief that lives need to be transformed through a "born-again" experience and a life long process of following Jesus'; 'Activism: the expression and demonstration of the gospel in missionary and social reform efforts'; 'Biblicism: a high regard for and obedience to the Bible as the ultimate authority'; 'Crucicentrism: a stress on the sacrifice of Jesus Christ on the cross as making possible the redemption of humanity', http://www.nae.net/church-and-faith-partners/what-is-an-evangelical, accessed November 2012. For a fuller discussion, see David W. Bebbington, *Evangelicalism in Modern Britain: A History from the 1730s to the 1980s* (London and New York: Routledge, 1989).
[23] John Daniel Lindenbaum, 'The Industry, Geography, and Social Effects of Contemporary Christian Music' (PhD diss., University of California, Berkeley, 2009), p. 4; Monique El-Faizy, *God and Country: How Evangelicals Have Become America's New Mainstream* (Bloomsbury 2006), p. 9.
[24] See Darryl G. Hart, *Deconstructing Evangelicalism: Conservative Protestantism in the Age of Billy Graham* (Baker Academic, 2004).

Democracy[25] on the National Association of Evangelicals concludes that '[i]n the end, evangelicalism seems to be more a matter of attitude. Anyone who wants the label "evangelical" can claim it.'[26] Hence, the term '*the* evangelicals' is a broad category indeed, often applied to conservative Christian groups of all kinds from both within and outside of the groups.

Perhaps one better way to describe the 'community of the faithful'[27] branded as 'evangelical' is to apply Benedict Anderson's concept of an 'imagined community'. Referring to national communities, Anderson states that no member of the nation will ever 'know most of their fellow-members, meet them, or even hear of them, yet in the minds of each lives the image of their communion'.[28] Following Anderson, Ingalls argues that the 'imagined community' of evangelicals is 'a body of people too large to meet face to face who are nevertheless united by a shared discursive framework that has been enabled by various mass media technologies'.[29] This image is furthered by the many organizations acting interdenominationally, 'a shifting set of central figures, institutions, and media outlets'.[30] Coleman extends this perspective to a global phenomenon actively pursued by the 'imagined community' of charismatics:

> These Christians are concerned to prompt the 'flow' of people, ideas and material objects across the globe, and the idea of cementing interconnections between believers united in 'Spirit' is powerfully articulated by them in sermons, oral testimonies and literature. Conferences, prayer networks and media are valued partly because they sustain a sense of participation in impermanent, free-flowing structures.[31]

[25] Located in Washington, DC, the IRD is – in its own words – 'an ecumenical alliance of US Christians working to reform their churches' social witness, in accord with biblical and historic Christian teachings, and to contribute to the renewal of democratic society at home and abroad', http://www.theird.org/page.aspx?pid=220, accessed August 2012.

[26] Alan Wisdom, 'Uncertain Future: The National Association of Evangelicals After Ted Haggard', http://www.theird.org/page.aspx?pid=513, accessed August 2012.

[27] Coleman, *The Globalisation of Charismatic Christianity*, p. 67.

[28] Anderson, *Imagined Communities*, p. 6.

[29] Monique M. Ingalls, 'Singing Heaven Down to Earth: Spiritual Journeys, Eschatological Sounds, and Community Formation in Evangelical Conference Worship', *Ethnomusicology*, 55/2 (2011): p. 263. While drawing from Benedict Anderson, Ingalls also includes in her discussion Ulf Hannerz, *Transnational Connections: Culture, People, Places* (Routledge, 1996).

[30] Monique M. Ingalls, 'Awesome in this Place: Sound, Space, and Identity in Contemporary North American Evangelical Worship' (PhD Diss., University of Pennsylvania, 2008), p. 13.

[31] Coleman, *The Globalisation of Charismatic Christianity*, p. 67.

Another aspect of Anderson's understanding of the term 'community' is that the entity is 'conceived as a deep, horizontal comradeship'[32] or 'fraternity'.[33] This description holds equally true for the 'imagined community' of evangelicals: two individuals identifying themselves as evangelical Christians can establish a connection that could be compared to sharing the same nationality. The central links establishing the 'horizontal comradeship' then are the shared belief in the Gospel and the assumed evangelical core values. When two individuals not only share the same core values but also know and like the same music, their connection finds a concrete form of expression. I would therefore claim that shared musical repertoire is a means of amplifying the 'fraternity' Anderson mentions with regard to the 'imagined community'.

One Industry to Unite them All

The Christian recording industry has played an important role in expanding the realm and the popularity of P&W within the United States and internationally. An increasing number of recordings have seen the light of day, and the popularity of those writing and singing the music has reached a dimension hitherto unknown.[34] Thereby, the catalogue of P&W songs has extended numerically. At the same time, the musical choices seem to be more condensed globally as the recurring names of songwriters on the international CCLI charts referred to in the introduction show.

It is notable that while the production of P&W was formerly focused on compilations of popular P&W songs such as Vineyard's 'Touching the Father's Heart' series or the 'Praise Series' by Maranatha! Music, today more and more artist-driven projects are to be found.[35] These cater to a much broader audience. The primary goal of the worship compilations was to spread the material among those performing the music, that is the worship leaders and music directors, but also the musicians in the worship bands or teams. Vineyard Music, for example, was started and still works as an extension of the Vineyard Church movement to facilitate the dissemination of music from within its different adhering congregations.[36] The new, artist-driven releases with complex musical arrangements and professional mixing and mastering, however, are conceived for listening as well – be it in the car, at home or anywhere else. Both the sound and the visual design aim as much at

---

[32]   Anderson, *Imagined Communities*, p. 7.

[33]   Anderson, *Imagined Communities*, p. 7.

[34]   Deborah Evans Price, 'Thank Heavens for the Music! Praise & Worship Genre Thrives', *Billboard* (24 April 2004): pp. 35–6.

[35]   Price, 'Thank Heavens for the Music!'

[36]   Vineyard Music, 'About Vineyard Music', http://www.vineyardmusic.com/vm/content/about-vineyard-music, accessed September 2012.

consumers as they are targeting music ministers.[37] The industry-driven music has thus gained a much greater presence within the realm of contemporary Christian music altogether: the *Billboard* charts for Christian music regularly feature worship bands among the top 25 albums or songs. As Price put it as early as 2004: 'the genre [P&W] has expanded beyond church pews to dominate Christian radio, has sold briskly at retail and has launched several popular series …'.[38]

Furthermore, the fact that many albums today are solo releases by bands or singers means that the recording musicians are more visible to their audiences. While previously songs were known by their title, now songs are also related to specific names and disseminated in the bands' particular version(s). This may lead to a situation where musicians are treated like pop stars by their supporters as is apparent in the footage of a DVD created by Hillsong UNITED: *The I-Heart Revolution: We're All in This Together*.[39] Several sequences show the band getting off the tour bus at a concert location, and their fans meet them with screaming and cheering as one could expect with any popular music band.

For those believers listening to P&W outside of church services, musicians who perform in concerts, lead workshops at conventions and release solo albums (compared to the former more 'anonymous' compilations) provide models with which to identify. The newer releases have equipped P&W with a more tangible identity as it has become associated with particular individuals and groups. An increased radio presence equally boosts listeners' familiarity with the music, as the recordings allow once-anonymous songs to be related to a celebrity name.

Thanks to both the modern modes of music production and distribution (both physical and virtual) and the international co-operations among record labels,[40] the increase of P&W recordings within the American and other markets has led to an expansion of the music worldwide.[41] Consequently, celebrity worship leaders (read: recording artists) face an international presence of their music and a broad

---

[37]   Deborah Evans Price, 'Praise and Worship Genre Blessed with Global Growth', *Billboard* (15 February 2003): pp. 1–3.

[38]   Price, 'Thank Heavens for the Music!', p. 35.

[39]   The feature-long documentary was released in 2010 and includes material filmed over the course of two years on the band's travels across six continents. *The I-Heart Revolution: We're All in This Together*, DVD, Hillsong United (Hillsong Music Australia, 2010).

[40]   Hillsong Music, for example, reached a distribution agreement with the EMI Christian Music Group for distribution in North and Latin America in 2010. EMI Music, 'EMI CMG and Hillsong form exclusive alliance for North America and Latin America', http://www.emimusic.com/news/2010/emi-cmg-and-hillsong-form-exclusive-alliance-for-north-america-and-latin-america/, accessed October 2012.

[41]   For a more detailed discussion on the global expansion of the music see, for example, Monique Ingalls, 'International Gospel and Christian Music', in John Shepherd and David Horn (eds), *Encyclopedia of Popular Music of the World*, Part III: Genres, Volume 6: International Genres (Continuum Press, forthcoming 2013); Pete Ward, *Selling Worship: How What We Sing Has Changed the Church* (Paternoster, 2005).

audience base. This impact is illustrated in Hillsong UNITED's documentary *We're All in This Together*, which shows the band performing to large crowds across all six continents. The worship events take place in mega churches, theatres or arenas that seat several thousand people who have sometimes travelled long distances to attend the event.[42]

By using the available resources, the recording and other music industries around P&W have thus contributed to building a large and extended platform for the music on a global scale. This engages the 'community of the faithful' by making the performers visible and creating a shared repertoire for the listeners.

The Evolving Community

That P&W contributes to the globalized 'imagined community' of evangelicals is illustrated by Hillsong UNITED and its multimedia-based social justice project *The I-Heart Revolution*. *The I-Heart Revolution* consists of three components: (1) a record compilation called *With Hearts as One*, (2) a documentary titled *We're All in this Together* and (3) an interactive website: *The I-Heart Movement* (www.i-heart. org). Information about all three is also provided via various Hillsong-associated websites as well as Facebook and other social media. *With Hearts as One* contains thirty songs recorded live during worship events held by the band over the course of two years around the world. (Not all songs included in the album were new at the time.) It debuted as #117 on the *Billboard* 200 album charts and #5 on the Billboard Christian album charts on 19 April 2008, hitting #8 on the top 50 albums of the Australian music sales charts upon its release on 23 March 2008.

The second component, the feature-length documentary *We're All in this Together*, contains footage from the same two years. It was released on DVD in November 2010.[43] In the film, the band members find themselves 'confronted and ultimately overwhelmed by the stories of remarkable individuals facing injustice and the uncomfortable paradox of being united in worship yet divided in circumstance'.[44] Footage from worship events is intertwined with passages showing the band's travels and activities on-site. There are also animated parts in the movie that retell specific moments in history when social injustice was overcome by individual effort. The film serves as the basis for a curriculum package released in 2012. This is intended for use in church groups as 'a tool to help build this culture [that is "the culture of administering justice across the earth"] into the fabric of

---

[42]   In an interview on beliefnet.com, members of the band describe the band's international stance as well as its musical developments. Chad Bonham, 'A Conversation with Hillsong United', http://blog.beliefnet.com/wholenotes/-2011/07/a-conversation-with-hillsong-united-part-1.html, accessed October 2012.

[43]   The I-Heart blog, http://www.i-heart.org/blog_entry.php?intid=637, accessed September 2012.

[44]   Hillsong Music, 'I-Heart', http://us.hillsongmusic.com/i-heart/, accessed August 2012.

their daily lives'.[45] Part three of '*The I-Heart Revolution*', *The I-Heart Movement*, consists of an interactive web platform for social justice projects.[46] Be it local causes or global undertakings, the website allows participants to post about their undertakings in order to recruit help and/or inspire others.

'Social justice' concerns, including poverty, human trafficking and clean water needs both locally and globally, have recently received increased attention among evangelicals. With worship leaders like Hillsong UNITED touring the world and witnessing various kinds of unjust environments in other countries, the global disparities between human conditions become more immediately felt. For Christian musicians, social justice commitment directs the attention away from the artists as well as from the music and the singing. As worship leader Israel Houghton explains: 'They [songs] are simply the vehicles we often use to accomplish [worship]' whereas he sees the Church's ultimate purpose in 'righting the wrongs in the earth'.[47] Regarding the multimedia '*I-Heart Revolution*' project, Hillsong UNITED's lead singer Joel Houston is quoted on the Hillsong Music website: 'it's not about "united" or even the songs ... It's about the heart cry of a generation consumed with their Maker.' The website further states that '[t]he end result is the sound of a generation across the earth singing praise and worship to our God ... The sound of the nations joining as one in the same song.'[48] The project thus actively tries to unite believers across borders and create a community based on collective action as well as faith and music.

As international projects like Hillsong UNITED's '*I Heart*' trilogy attest, the 'imagined community' of evangelicals arises across national borders. Facilitated by mass media (audio and video recordings as well as print-media, but most of all the internet-based media), it spreads a feeling of 'fraternity' among those that feel part of the community, transcending denominational boundaries as the music's listenership is not refined to particular groups within evangelicalism. In this, P&W becomes an 'important shared cultural product and practice which helps to mediate a common discourse among evangelicals and which serves as an important site for negotiating evangelical identity'.[49]

Because P&W circulates in easily available media such as radio, the Internet or CDs, individuals no longer depend on specific services, congregations, denominations or networks to access it. Fans of the genre can choose freely from the commercially available output. On the one hand, this allows listeners to be familiar

---

[45] Hillsong Music, 'I-Heart Curriculum Starter Pack', http://us.hillsongmusic.com/i-heart-curriculum-starter-pack/, accessed October 2012.

[46] The I-Heart Movement, 'Home', http://www.i-heart.org/index.php, accessed August 2012.

[47] Both quotes from: 'Wake-Up Call', interview with Israel Houghton, *Worship Leader Magazine*, http://worshipleader.com/wake-up-call/, accessed November 2012.

[48] All of the above quotes from: Hillsong Music, 'With Hearts as One', http://eu.hillsongmusic.com/the-i-heart-revolution-with-hearts-as-one-cd/, accessed August 2012.

[49] Ingalls, 'Awesome in this Place', p. 13.

with current trends even if their worship leaders in church rarely change or update the congregation's repertoire. On the other hand, worship leaders are most certainly affected by the large amount of available and promoted music either first- or second-hand. They are exposed to the current work of leading worship bands or songwriters on a regular basis when attending conventions, listening to Christian radio stations or being part of one of the networks around P&W (for example the readership of *Worship Leader* Magazine). Within their congregations, they might receive input from other members asking for or presenting specific songs. This way, a personal song repertoire evolves that is not necessarily congruent with the individual's congregation's song repertoire. It is, however, a repertoire that links the individual to others rendering the 'community of the faithful' tangible on a personal level.

Next to this, an international repertoire of P&W is forming that encompasses both the 'imagined community' of evangelicals and the music industries. There are two aspects to this repertoire: On the one hand, the great amount of newly written music regularly floods the churches with little time delay, leading to a rapid turnover in one part of the music sung in congregations around the world. The top 10 songs featured in the US CCLI reports since August 2010, for example, were almost exclusively written after the year 2000. There is a similar tendency for Australia, while the UK and African CCLI reports show a higher number of 'older' songs.[50] On the other hand, a canon is forming in P&W with songs that seem to withstand or prove adaptable to the shifting tastes of pop (Christian) culture, songs that are potent enough to speak to different generations. These songs present the other part of music sung in congregations around the world. For example, the 1993 worship ballad 'Shout to the Lord' by then Hillsong worship leader Darlene Zschech has been in the top 15 songs of worldwide CCLI reports for years, mostly featuring among the top five songs.[51]

Regarding the rapid turnover, the lack of printed repertoires that characterizes P&W encourages the music's fast rate of replacement as no hymnbooks need to be planned or purchased. Furthermore, the great availability of song and chord charts along with the recordings provided by the recording industry and the songwriters (often via the internet or on CD-ROM) makes the incorporation of new songs easy.[52] Hillsong UNITED's album *With Hearts as One*, for example, is available as a 'Music Book CD-ROM' containing lead sheets, scores and charts aiming

---

[50]   All information was collated from the CCLI reports accessible on the company's website: http://www.ccli.com/Support/LicenseCoverage/Top25Lists.aspx. The lists do not display how many churches play each of the listed songs and with what regularity.

[51]   This information also stems from the CCLI website. (http://www.ccli.com/Support/LicenseCoverage/-Top25Lists.aspx). The song *Shout to the Lord* continues to feature in the top positions in the UK and Africa while it has been replaced with newer songs in both Australia (position 10 in August 2012) and the US (position 20 in August 2012).

[52]   Resources like worshiptogether.com – a project of the EMI CMG record label providing a database as well as direct links to purchasing the material – give music directors the necessary tools to quickly use songs in church settings.

directly at 'musicians and especially those involved in their local Church'.[53] The technological possibilities can thus have a considerable impact on a church's repertoire.

Frequent changes in the active repertoire of churches imply that a passive repertoire is growing continuously: while different songs might replace those that were sung or listened to at a specific moment in the daily routine, these songs are not erased from one's memory. Rather, they remain stored, most likely linked to specific events and emotions. And it is this growing active as well as passive repertoire that unites the believers, contributing to their image of the 'imagined community' of evangelicals. A moment experienced personally during fieldwork illustrates this: the song 'Shout to the Lord' was spontaneously sung at the end of the service at the Christian music industry's yearly convention in Nashville in 2008. Several nights before, the song had been used in an *American Idol* fundraising special, replacing the opening words 'My Jesus' with 'My Shepherd'.[54] Acknowledging this, the service's worship leader pointed out that those gathered on this Sunday morning did not need to change the lyrics. The whole congregation then joined him in singing the song a cappella and by heart. It was a very uniting moment as those gathered for the service seemed to claim the song back for their community.

The other part of the P&W repertoire that contributes to the creation of the global 'imagined community' of evangelicals is a song canon that is emerging. In this canon are songs like the aforementioned 'Shout to the Lord' (Zschech, 1993), the 'classic' Praise chorus 'Lord I Lift Your Name on High' (Founds, 1989) as well as 'Come Now is the Time to Worship' (Doerksen, 1998), 'Here I am to Worship' (Hughes, 2000), 'Blessed Be Your Name' (Redman, 2002) and 'How Great is Our God' (Tomlin et al., 2004).[55] This incomplete list illustrates how the international canon consists of an international repertoire with songwriters coming from the US, the UK and Australia. The forming song canon is thus itself a display of the idea of a globalized 'imagined community' of evangelicals.

Another way that evangelicals are creating an 'imagined community' by means of a shared recording is through historicization. For example, the record label Integrity Music published the CD/DVD box *25 Songs that Changed the Way We Worship* in 2012. Although confined to the relatively young label and its artists, this release illustrates the emerging concept of P&W's historicity. Integrity Music

---

[53]   Hillsong Music, 'FAQs', http://eu.hillsongmusic.com/faqs/, accessed October 2012.

[54]   The recorded version available on iTunes the next day (apparently rising to the day's number one download) as well as next night's result show's performance, however, used the original wording (*American Idol* – 'Idol Gives Back', 9 April 2008, Results Show, 10 April 2008).

[55]   These songs were listed in all regional top 25 reports CCLI of August 2012 and previous reports. Other songs that are certainly part of the canon were not necessarily part of all top 25 reports. What is more, the CCLI licence does not cover all songs sung in churches. Nonetheless, it seems safe to assume that it provides a good impression of the status quo of songs used.

states about the song collection: 'the global impact of these songs can never be fully measured; only to say, they have changed the way we worship'.[56] This release echoes a 2012 list of '20 Most Influential Worship Albums of the Past 20 Years' published by Worship Leader Magazine that also references the international connections in P&W.[57]

The musical arrangements of the songs within the emerging canon are being updated regularly to keep up with the changing musical tastes. So it is the songs' content that speaks to those singing them. The emerging canon thereby shows how the international network enabled by the recording industry and the internet ties the evangelical churches of the world together as they share songs, mutually influencing each other's concept of Christianity as it is lived in the churches through the songs.

This last aspect stands out if thinking of the 'imagined community' of evangelicals as evolving through music. Anderson's historically informed argumentation on 'imagined communities' contains one important element for spreading ideas: the use of 'vernacular'.[58] The ubiquity of popular music sounds today seems comparable to a globalized vernacular language: many people are familiar with it and can consequently be reached through it. In using these familiar sounds, P&W adapts the method identified by Anderson for reaching a large audience. The ideas of Christianity spread through its lyrics are then formative for negotiating evangelical identity as the music 'puts the Christian faith on the tongues of the people, letting it work its way down to the soul'.[59] The fact that Hillsong UNITED recorded the songs to its live-album *With Hearts as One* in different locations all around the world witnesses to the fact that P&W has become a vernacular for the global 'imagined community' of evangelicals.

Conclusion

As the world and also the Church are becoming more globally connected, allowing the exchange of goods – especially music – and ideas in the blink of an eye with the help of the new technologies, P&W plays a crucial part in the formation of a globalized 'imagined community' of evangelicals. The recording industry's

---

[56] Integrity Music, '25 Songs That Changed The Way We Worship', http://www. integritymusic.com/index.php?-option=com_artists&task=audio&aid=113&did=662&Ite mid=72, accessed November 2012.

[57] *Worship Leader* Magazine, 'Top Twenty. 20 Most Influential Worship Albums of the Past 20 Years', http://worshipleader.com/top-20-worship-releases/, accessed November 2012.

[58] Anderson's historic perspective regards the spreading of the idea of national consciousness through print-capitalism's use of 'vernacular' instead of Latin to address a larger audience. Anderson, *Imagined Communities*, pp. 37–43.

[59] Greg Scheer, *The Art of Worship: A Musician's Guide to Leading Modern Worship* (Baker Books, 2006), p. 55.

increased output and the international co-operations among record labels have given the music an unprecedented platform within the Christian community. It has also catapulted recording worship leaders to a status of stardom that was previously unknown in the world of modern church music, as the band Hillsong UNITED illustrates. With their fan base extending around the world, its influence on the global 'imagined community' of evangelicals is emphasized through the band's touring and social justice projects like '*The I-Heart Revolution*'. Both contribute to the music's and the worship leaders' high profile among evangelicals lending the community musical models to identify by.

new
canon

The global 'imagined community' of evangelicals is further facilitated by an increasingly international musical repertoire as songs are disseminated through new media (especially the internet with websites and music downloads or streams) and musicians and their songs are present globally. As has been demonstrated, this repertoire consists both of a forming canon of established songs that keep speaking to the believers and most recent songs that are an expression of current developments and musical taste.

This chapter has outlined how P&W actively partakes in the construction of an 'imagined community' of evangelicals around the world. In the process, it has illustrated how the music presents a means of rendering the global 'imagined community' of evangelicals tangible for the individual thereby fuelling the feeling of fraternity among those constituting the 'community'. As the 'imagined community' of evangelicals finds itself united through P&W music, perhaps the music will become a platform for social justice, as the 'community' focuses not merely on self-creation but also on global social engagement for the greater good.

References

Anderson, Allan, *An Introduction to Pentecostalism: Global Charismatic Christianity* (Cambridge: Cambridge University Press, 2004).

Anderson, Benedict, *Imagined Communities: Reflections on the Origin and Spread of Nationalism*, revised ed. (London: Verso, 2006).

Baloche, Paul, Owens, Jimmy and Owens, Carol, *God Songs: How to Write and Select Songs for Worship* (Lindale: Leadworship.com, 2004).

Bebbington, David W., *Evangelicalism in Modern Britain: A History from the 1730s to the 1980s* (London and New York: Routledge, 1989).

Bonham, Chad, 'A Conversation with Hillsong United', http://blog.beliefnet.com/wholenotes/-2011/07/a-conversation-with-hillsong-united-part-1.html, accessed October 2012.

Bonomi, Patricia U., *Under the Cope of Heaven: Religion, Society, and Politics in Colonial America* (New York: Oxford University Press, 1986).

Butler, Jon, *Religion in Colonial America* (New York: Oxford University Press, 2000).

Coleman, Simon, *The Globalisation of Charismatic Christianity: Spreading the Gospel of Prosperity* (Cambridge: Cambridge University Press, 2000).

EKD-Statistik, *Christen in Deutschland 2009*, http://www.ekd.de/statistik/mitglieder.html, accessed 12 August 2012.

El-Faizy, Monique, *God and Country: How Evangelicals Have Become America's New Mainstream* (New York: Bloomsbury, 2006).

EMI Music, 'EMI CMG and Hillsong form exclusive alliance for North America and Latin America', http://www.emimusic.com/news/2010/emi-cmg-and-hillsong-form-exclusive-alliance-for-north-america-and-latin-america/, accessed 11 October 2012.

Eskridge, Larry, *Sweet, Sweet Song of Salvation: The Jesus People Movement and American Evangelicalism, 1967–1977* (New York: Oxford University Press, 2009).

Faith Communities Today, *FACTs on Worship: 2012*, http://faithcommunitiestoday.org/sites/-faithcommunitiestoday.org/files/FACTs-on-Worship.pdf, accessed 16 August 2012.

Frame, John, *Contemporary Worship Music: A Biblical Defense* (Phillipsburg: P & R Publishing, 1997).

Gersztyn, Bob, 'Jesus Music', in Don Cusic (ed.), *Encyclopedia of Contemporary Christian Music: Pop, Rock, and Worship* (Santa Barbara: Greenwood Press, 2010).

Hart, Darryl G., *Deconstructing Evangelicalism: Conservative Protestantism in the Age of Billy Graham* (Grand Rapids: Baker Academic, 2004).

Hillsong Music, 'FAQs', http://eu.hillsongmusic.com/faqs/, accessed 12 October 2012.

Hillsong Music, 'I-Heart', http://us.hillsongmusic.com/i-heart/, accessed 16 August 2012.

Hillsong Music, 'I-Heart Curriculum Starter Pack', http://us.hillsongmusic.com/i-heart-curriculum-starter-pack/, accessed 12 October 2012.

Hillsong Music, 'With Hearts as One', http://eu.hillsongmusic.com/the-i-heart-revolution-with-hearts-as-one-cd/, accessed 16 August 2012.

The I-Heart Movement, 'Home', http://www.i-heart.org/index.php, accessed 16 August 2012.

Ingalls, Monique M., 'Awesome in this Place: Sound, Space, and Identity in Contemporary North American Evangelical Worship' (PhD Diss., University of Pennsylvania, 2008).

Ingalls, Monique M., 'Singing Heaven Down to Earth: Spiritual Journeys, Eschatological Sounds, and Community Formation in Evangelical Conference Worship', *Ethnomusicology*, 55/2 (2011): 255–79.

Ingalls, Monique M., 'International Gospel and Christian Music', in John Shepherd and David Horn (eds), *Encyclopedia of Popular Music of the World*, Part III: Genres, Volume 6: International Genres (London: Continuum Press, forthcoming 2013).

Lindenbaum, John Daniel, 'The Industry, Geography, and Social Effects of Contemporary Christian Music' (PhD Diss., University of California, Berkeley, 2009).

Mall, Andrew, 'The Stars are Underground: Undergrounds, Mainstreams, and Christian Popular Music' (PhD Diss., University of Chicago, 2012).

Miller, Donald E., 'Postdenominational Christianity in the Twenty-First Century', *Annals of the American Academy of Political and Social Science* 558 (1998): 196–210.

Price, Deborah Evans, 'Praise and Worship Genre Blessed with Global Growth', *Billboard* 115/7 (15 February 2003): 1–3.

Price, Deborah Evans, 'Thank Heavens for the Music! Praise & Worship Genre Thrives', *Billboard* (24 April 2004): 35–6.

Sargeant, Kimon Howland, *Seeker Churches: Promoting Traditional Religion in a Nontraditional Way* (New Brunswick: Rutgers University Press, 2000).

Scheer, Greg, *The Art of Worship: A Musician's Guide to Leading Modern Worship* (Grand Rapids: Baker Books, 2006).

Stowe, David W., *No Sympathy for the Devil: Christian Pop Music and the Transformation of American Evangelicalism* (Chapel Hill: University of North Carolina Press, 2011).

Vineyard Music, 'About Vineyard Music', http://www.vineyardmusic.com/vm/content/about-vineyard-music, accessed 12 September 2012.

Ward, Pete, *Selling Worship: How What We Sing Has Changed the Church* (Milton Keynes: Paternoster, 2005).

Wisdom, Alan, 'Uncertain Future: The National Association of Evangelicals After Ted Haggard', *The Institute on Religion and Democracy*, 16 January 2008, http://www.theird.org/page.aspx?pid=513, accessed 16 August 2012.

PART III
Experience and Embodiment

Chapter 9

The Sensual Theology of the Eighteenth-Century Moravian Church

Sarah Eyerly

Wir und des lams seine blutgemein,	We, and the Lamb's blood-community,
wir wollen ewiglich zeugen seyn,	we intend to witness for eternity,
daß im opfer JEsu allein zu finden	that only in the sacrifice of Jesus can be found
gnade und freyheit von allen sünden,	grace and freedom from all sins,
für alle welt.	for the entire world.
JEsu gemeine ruht seliglich,	Jesus' community rests blessedly
an ihrem freunde, da lehnt sie sich,	in its friends, it reclines,
das ist ihre sache, im meer der gnaden	that is its thing, in the sea of grace,
in JESU blut schwimmen und baden,	swimming and bathing in the blood of Jesus,
ihr element.[1]	its element.

The Moravian single brothers waited anxiously inside the worship hall. A solo voice sang repeatedly 'Du weißt wohl worauf wir warten' [You know what it is we're waiting for]. Suddenly, the door opened, and their leaders entered, wearing white robes in imitation of Christ himself. 'Today, you will be embraced by the Side Hole', they exclaimed. The brothers sang together of the side wound of Christ until some of them were physically unable to rise from the floor. Later that day, they returned to their communal home to find an illuminated representation of Christ, soaked with blood, covering the entrance. A brother, dressed as the Roman soldier Longinus, appeared and violently pierced the image with a spear. Blood burst from the wound and splashed onto the brothers nearby. They washed their hands in the blood. Suddenly, an image of the side hole appeared, big enough for a man to enter, and each brother bent down and entered their home, singing 'deep inside, deep inside, yea, deep therein'.[2]

---

[1] *Herrnhuter Gesangbuch: Christliches Gesang-Buch der Evangelischen Brüder-Gemeinen von 1735*, eds. Erich Beyreuther, Gerhard Meyer and Gudrun Meyer-Hickel (G. Olms, 1981), hymn 1360, verses 13–14.

[2] This description of the Single Brothers Choir Festival at Herrnhaag on May 2, 1748, appears in the *Jüngerhausdiarium* for 1748, and UA R.4.C.III.7.b. See Paul Peucker, 'Inspired by the Flames of love': Homosexuality, Mysticism, and Moravian Brothers around 1750', *Journal of the History of Sexuality*, 15/1 (2006): pp. 30–64, especially pp. 45–9; See

Eighteenth-century archival records from the utopian communities of the Moravian church preserve countless transcriptions of communal rituals such as this record of the Single Brother's Choir Festival which took place in Herrnhaag, Germany, in 1748. For the Moravians, sensual experience of Christ's suffering was a necessary component of theological learning. And music, with its ability to elicit emotion, was particularly useful in guiding comprehension of theology 'through the heart'. Two decades before the emotionally charged poetry, art and music of the *Sturm und Drang*, and the publication of Laurence Sterne's *Sentimental Journey* (1768), Moravians charged their hymns with emotional and sensual metaphors designed to transmit Christian theology without mediation by the rational mind. Believers longed to be caressed and cradled inside Christ's body, pierced and gashed by thorns and nails, their mouths overflowing with blood. They prayed to become 'little wound bees which burrow into the side hole of Christ'.[3] They sang together very softly, sometimes prostrate upon the floor, meditating upon graphic representations of the suffering Christ. These controlled ecstatic experiences allowed their bodies to resonate and attune to God's word, and created a sense of Christian community through the shared experience of embodied theology.

One of the most powerful transmissions of Moravian theology occurred when worshippers channelled Christ's body into their own through improvised hymn singing. Improvising hymns was a religious practice, and demonstrated a commitment of body, mind and soul to the community. Improvisation silenced the singer's own thoughts and compositional impulses, so that the singer could channel Christ into their body and sing with His voice. Improvised singing also cast a powerful aural boundary around the community: those who channelled the divine voice were physically transformed – blood, sinew, bones and voice – into the crucified body of Christ, and marked with the *Lammesblut* [Lamb's blood]. The transformed 'bled through the mouth', shedding the blood of the Lamb upon their fellow worshippers through song.[4] In so doing, they connected the physical and spiritual realm into one harmonious whole. During the ecstasy of improvised singing, Christ's cleansing blood transfused the worshipper's own blood, and the vibrations of divine songs altered the very nature of their bodies, from merely human, to members of the godhead.[5] The litanies, hymns and rituals

also A.P. Hecker, *Gespräch eines Evangelisch-Lutherischen Predigers* (Buchhandlung der Berlinischen Real-Schule, 1751), pp. 47–50.

[3] This terminology is found in many Moravian hymns, including hymns 1267 and 1316 in the *Herrnhuter Gesangbuch*. See Alice Caldwell, 'Music of the Moravian "Liturgische Gesänge": From Oral to Written Tradition' (PhD diss., New York University, 1987), pp. 49–50, for a description of a doorway decorated to resemble the Side Wound.

[4] *Herrnhuter Gesangbuch*, hymn 2144.

[5] The idea of the resonating body is a metaphor with particularly eighteenth-century sensibilities. See Elisabeth Le Guin's discussion of music and sensuality in the eighteenth century in *Boccherini's Body: An Essay in Carnal Musicology* (University of California Press, 2006), p. 184.

of the Moravians emphasized the sacred in the everyday, connecting the physical bodies of worshippers with the divine body of God, in the physical form of Jesus' blood.[6] Out of the blood of Christ was born the Moravian *Blutgemeine* [blood community], a physical and communal praxis of theological learning known as 'heart religion'.[7]

The idea of 'heart religion', or comprehending theology through the senses, was not unique to the Moravians. They belonged to a long tradition of Christian mystics who believed in the bodily experience of Christ's suffering and physical contact with the divine body and blood as a transformative, almost alchemical process. In the Gospel of John, blood pours from the side wound of Christ, and Jesus himself urges his followers to drink his blood in order to find eternal life.[8] In the Middle Ages, mystics worshipped the streaming blood of Christ's Crucifixion wounds, and medieval artists drew innumerable images of Christ's wounds and blood. Seventeenth-century Italian mystic Mary Magdalene de Pazzi (1566–1607) beheld in a vision the gaping side of the wounded Christ, dripping with blood. She cried out to him, 'Make those beautiful rills to descend and bathe all hearts, all.'[9]

Like mother's milk, blood imparted life.[10] Saint Catherine of Siena (1347–80) sang to the blood of Christ, for 'only in the blood can we be sated, since the blood is intertwined and kneaded with the eternal Godhead, the *Natura infinita*, the greater than we'.[11] Even Mother Ann Lee (1736–84) of the American Shaker community, gripped by the power of the Holy Spirit, exclaimed: 'I feel the blood of Christ running through my soul and body, washing me.'[12] In ecstatic visions, saints beheld the bleeding heart of Christ through the opening of his side wound. As she died, Catherine of Siena cried: 'Blood, blood!'[13]

---

[6]   'Nearly every aspect of life in Bethlehem [a Moravian community in the United States] was incorporated into communal rituals in order to bring the secular into the sacred sphere by connecting daily life to the life and death of Jesus.' Craig D. Atwood, *Community of the Cross: Moravian Piety in Colonial Bethlehem* (Pennsylvania State University Press, 2004), p. 157.

[7]   For more information on the Moravian *Blutgemeine*, see Craig D. Atwood, 'Zinzendorf's "Litany of the Wounds"', *Lutheran Quarterly*, 11/2 (1997): pp. 189–214.

[8]   Atwood, *Community of the Cross*, p. 95.

[9]   Quoted in Atwood, *Community of the Cross*, p. 96.

[10]   Piero Camporesi, *Juice of Life: The Symbolic and Magic Significance of Blood*, trans. Robert R. Barr (Continuum, 1995), p. 70. Quoted in Atwood, *Community of the Cross*, p. 96.

[11]   Catherine of Siena, *La lettere*, ed. P. Misciattelli (Marzocco, 1939), vol. 2, pp. 72–3. Quoted in Camporesi, *Juice of Life*, p. 67.

[12]   *Testimonies of the Life, Character, Revelations and Doctrines of Our Ever Blessed Mother Ann Lee* (Hancock [MA], 1816), pp. 47–8.

[13]   Pietro Canigiani, *Dialogo della serafica vergine, et sposa di Christo S. Catherina da Siena. Diviso in quattro trattati* (G. Sarzina, 1611), pp. 631. Quoted in Camporesi, *Juice of Life*, p. 19.

Graphic Crucifixion stories assisted the faithful to transfer the suffering of Christ onto their own bodies:

> You will have seen our good Jesus, out of natural fear, tear out the hair of his head. You will have seen his arms flailing, his thighs shaking, all of those milky members chilled to ice and trembling … . A hot river of blood courses headlong from all the torn victim's body to his feet. From the flayed Lord a pure, warm lake of blood appears. And blood again from the plummeting lashes, spattering the walls all around, hanging on the rough walls in gross, thick lumps.[14]

These bloody stories facilitated contact with the sensual self:

> The ambiguity of the metaphors, and the erotic symbolism of these visionary experiences, far from canceling the sensual language of the flesh, actually reinvigorate and excite it, expressing as they do the omnipresence of bodiliness and the senses, through which even religious allegories must necessarily pass. We all possess an anatomical, physiological sieve, without which it seems that discourse cannot begin, cannot be ordered with any rationality, cannot render itself intelligible. At the origin of mystical language is a sensual alphabet, which strives, by its innermost calling, to be delivered from the sense and from the body, not by canceling them, but by sublimating them, by transferring them to God, by immersing them in a laver of 'thirsting, slaking … concupiscence'.[15]

This sublimation manifested itself in the tormented body of Christ, the resurrected body that breathes new life into its creatures. Ingestion of the body and blood, like the *aqua vitae* of legend, effected the magical transference of divine life to the believer.[16] This sensual metaphor promised hope of redemption from sin and eventual release from the bonds of a corrupted physical body, and the imparting of a new spiritual body.

For the Moravians, it was through Leviticus 17:11, 'the life of the flesh is in the blood', that a connection could be established between blood and eternal life. The blood of Christ became a figurative blood transfusion for the Moravians: the blood that flows through the heart of Christ is also the blood that presses through the veins of the sinner.[17] The sinner is resuscitated through daily immersion in the blood of Christ: 'we have indeed the great blessing that we are bathed in and swim

---

[14] Emmanuele Orchi, "La passione per il Venerdì Santo", in *Prediche quaresimali* (Venice: Giunti e Baba, 1650), pp: 409–10. Quoted in Camporesi, *Juice of Life*, pp: 55–6.

[15] Camporesi, *Juice of Life*, p. 70.

[16] The rite of Holy Communion is communal spell-casting of the highest order. It is 'the darksome, complex rite in which the inexplicable transubstantiation of wine into blood is effected by the ritual invocation'. Camporesi, *Juice of Life*, p. 59.

[17] Atwood, *Community of the Cross*, p. 100.

in Jesus' blood'.[18] Like Catherine of Siena, Moravians also cried out to 'hide in the wounds of Christ crucified, and bathe in his precious blood'.[19]

Those who bathed in and ingested the blood were transformed. They shed their former bodies and assumed new, clean ones, in preparation for the passage into eternal life: 'From the fountain of suffering, from the fountain of blood from the heart ground of the little Lamb, there is always something supernatural, that is connected with the same Creator's Spirit and grace, that brings life into all conversation and association, in the love among one another, in all life from Jesus' blood.'[20] An early spiritual leader of the Moravian church, Count Nikolaus Ludwig von Zinzendorf, asserted that the power of Christ's blood had transformed and indeed re-made the entire world, through a kind of spiritual transformative alchemy: 'His blood of reconciliation is the *proprium quarti modi* of the entire holy creature, of the entire blessed universe.'[21]

An eighteenth-century Moravian devotional painting, entitled 'Zinzendorf und der Heiland in sechs allegorischen Vorstellungen' [Zinzendorf and the Saviour in Six Allegorical Scenes],[22] portrays Zinzendorf bathing in the blood that spurts from Christ's side wound, and adoring the sweat drops of Christ's agony that fall to earth.[23] Every sense is alive for Zinzendorf: he touches, tastes, smells, hears and sees Christ, drawing salvation through physical contact. Bits of poetry surround the 'six allegorical scenes' in the painting – small love songs sung to the Saviour by Zinzendorf. The painting shows them lying down together in the grave's bed, transformed by the *mors mystica*.[24] Zinzendorf exclaims:

Ave, mein lieber Mann!	Hail, my dear man!
Ave, vor deinen Plan!	Hail, to your plan!

---

[18]   Zinzendorf, 'Gemeinreden', in *Hauptschriften* 4, vol. 2, p. 40. Quoted in Atwood, *Community of the Cross*, p. 100.

[19]   Catherine of Siena, *La lettere*, vol. 2, p. 85. Also: '[Let us] drown in the blood of Christ crucified, and bathe in his blood and become drunk with his blood.' *La lettere*, vol. 2, p. 112.

[20]   Zinzendorf, 'Gemeinreden', in *Hauptschriften*, 4/44: p. 237. Quoted in Atwood, *Community of the Cross*, pp. 100–101.

[21]   Zinzendorf, 'Wundenlitanei Homilien', in *Hauptschriften*, 3/1: p. 8. Quoted in Atwood, *Community of the Cross*, p. 101.

[22]   'Zinzendorf und der Heiland in sechs allegorischen Vorstellungen' [Zinzendorf and the Saviour in Six Allegorical Scenes]. Devotional painting (1748), artist unknown, UA Herrnhut.TS.Mp.76.12.

[23]   'Every drop of the crucified Christ's sweat was a special blessing. In this way, it functioned essentially like holy water.' Atwood, *Community of the Cross*, p. 183.

[24]   Of parallel importance to the 'blood and wounds' theology of the Moravians is the tradition of bridal mysticism which flourished in the 1740s in such communities as Herrnhut and Herrnhaag. See Paul Peucker, 'The Songs of the Sifting: Understanding the Role of Bridal Mysticism in Moravian Piety in the late 1740s', *Journal of Moravian History* 3 (Fall 2007): pp. 51–87.

Ave, für deinen Fleiss!	Hail, for your diligence!
Ave, für deinen Schweiß!	Hail, for your sweat!
Ave, fürs Todeseis!	Hail, for death's ice!
Ave, du Mond so bloss,	Hail, you mouth so bare,
Ave du Wangen nass,	Hail you cheeks so wet,
Ave du Blick so gross,	Hail you glance so great,
Dornichtes Scheidelein!	Thorn-crowned little head!
Wundes, wundes, wundes Häutelein!	Wounded, wounded, wounded little skin!
Ave, ave, ave Seitelein![25]	Hail, hail, hail little side!

Zinzendorf identifies with the Crucified Christ through the most personal means possible, his senses. Sensual contact causes Christ to live: blood courses through veins, hair stirs on arms, Jesus presses his face into the dirt of Gethsemane, in fear of his approaching torture and death, and Zinzendorf is there not just as a witness, but to experience the suffering as if it were his own body.

If believers could be crucified and buried along with Christ, they would feel his salvation 'in their hearts'. This was the central purpose of Moravian 'heart religion'. Like Orchi's *La passione per il Venerdì Santo*, Moravians crafted graphic Crucifixion narratives and paintings to elicit such sensual encounters. Many Moravian devotional paintings were designed to highlight these sensual encounters.[26] They portray Moravians touching Christ's body on the cross, and bathing in the blood that flows from his wounds. They show Moravians visiting Christ's grave, and feeling the scars of the Crucifixion with their own hands. It is this sensual contact with the body of Christ that leads them toward an understanding of the theological doctrines of Christ's death and resurrection. Rational proof is not necessary – they simply 'know'. Every part of their body, every cell, comprehends. As members of Christ's body, they experience the world through his senses. They breathe when he breathes, and die when he dies.

Moravian congregants ministered to each other, as members of that divine body, through sensual rituals designed to elicit a non-rational connection with the divine: the kiss of peace, footwashing, *Liebesmahlen* [lovefeasts], Holy Communion, communal festivals and *Singstunden* [singing meetings]. Like their art, their hymns offered arresting portraits of the Crucifixion: its smell, its texture, the feeling of blood on skin, homesickness for refuge in the side wound of Christ.[27]

---

[25]   This hymn text was composed by the spiritual leader of the Moravian church, Count Nikolaus Ludwig von Zinzendorf, in London on 16 September 1746 (*Herrnhuter Gesangbuch*, hymn 2276). The text appears in the picture just above Christ's grave.

[26]   For a good example of this genre of eighteenth-century devotional painting, see UA Herrnhut, Andachtsbilder Mappe 9. TS Mp.375.9, artist unknown. It portrays Moravian sisters visiting Christ's tomb to touch and kiss Christ's wounds.

[27]   'So leichnams-luft-anzieherlich,/so grabes-dünste witterlich,/so wunden-naß-auss prüherlich,/so seiten-heimweh-fühlerlich.' [So the corpse's-air-inhalingly,/so the grave's-

DU blut-verwundter priester deiner arche,	You bloody-wounded priest of your ark,
du GOttes-Lämmlein, unser creuz- monarche!	you God's-Lambkin, our cross-monarch.
Lamm! das geschlachtet ist aus ihrer mitten,	Lamb, that is slaughtered from their midst,
und hast am creuze vor dein volk gelitten,	and suffered on the cross in the presence of your people.
O Lamm! dein blut, das du am creuz vergossen,	Oh Lamb! Your blood that you spilled on the cross,
komm reichlich über die Gemein geflossen.	come flowing profusely over the community.
Und wenn sie sich ins heilige begiebet,	And when she enters into the holy place,
und dem vors herze kniet, der sie liebet;	and kneels before the heart of the one who loves her.
Erinnert ihn, wie er in tod gesunken,	Remind him how he sank into death,
als er den taumel-kelch für sie getrunken.	when he drank the reeling-cup for her.
Die kinder der Gemein, die kleinen seelen,	The children of the community, the little souls,
die weidest du in deinen wunden-hölen.	you graze them in your wounds-holes.
Bis daß der ganze stamm in Juda grüne,	Until the whole tribe in Judah flourishes,
gesalbt mit blut des Lammes vor dir diene.[28]	and anointed with the blood of the Lamb serves before you.

Communal song struck at the heart of worshippers with its inherent sensuality. Just as the blood of Christ transformed believers, the physical nature of singing, in communion with others, produced sensations and vibrations that cleansed the body. Like the great psaltery of Jesus' crucified body, its strings of agony vibrating to God's word, eighteenth-century Moravians sang their way toward spiritual transformation in hymns.[29] Rituals of communal hymn singing channelled the vibrations of the 'divine voice' into the body and marked it as a member of Christ's *Blutgemeine*.

Moravians hymn texts were also designed to transform, to teach morality and theology, a technique not uncommon in early eighteenth-century religious poetry.

---

fumes sniffingly,/so the wounds'-wetly-spraying-out,/so the side's-homesickness-feelingly]. Excerpt from *Herrnhuter Gesangbuch*, hymn 2278.

[28] *Herrnhuter Gesangbuch*, hymn 1700, verses 1, 7, 12–13, 15, 20 and 21.

[29] Cassiodorus speaks about the psaltery as a musical and physical metaphor. See Le Guin, *Boccherini's Body*, p. 184.

Countless religious poets and writers employ alchemical metaphors to symbolize a 'universal renewal and salvation of man and nature'.[30] In the tradition of Christian mystics Jakob Böhme and Gottfried Arnold, Moravians infused their hymnody with a sense of the universal and transformative power of music and text.[31] As a young child, Zinzendorf had internalized his grandmother's respect for the teachings of Jakob Böhme, who taught of 'universal renewal' through Christ's bodily sacrifice. Music, for Böhme, could tap into the spiritual vibrations of God's voice. Christians should sing with the 'universal vibrations', allowing their 'hearts to sing' of that which was beyond words and reason. In addition to Böhme's vibrational alchemy, the original Moravian community of Herrnhut owned alchemical manuals of French and German origin, and community members may have read of music's use as a transformative agent, along with other elements and chemical processes of change, such as the blood of Christ.[32] Many community members would have been familiar with the writings of Jan Amos Comenius, an early forefather of the Moravian church and a Rosicrucian, whose science of pedagogy advocated teaching through the senses: 'Access to the inner man is through the senses, not reasoning, and surely not the reiteration of stock phrases. Everything that is to be learned should be placed insofar as possible before the senses, and if the objects themselves are not available the master ought to obtain copies or models.'[33] This philosophy of congregational singing as 'vibrational alchemy' attracted separatists, mystics, and religious seekers to Zinzendorf's utopian communities. For instance, the Bohemian and Moravian refugees, some of the first inhabitants of the Herrnhut, Germany, settlement, were descended through Jan Amos Comenius and the Ancient Unity to the Rosicrucian movement centred around the printing

[30] Burkhard Dohm, 'Des Blutes Licht-Tinctur: Alchimistische Koncepte in Herrnhutischer Poesie', in *Künste und Natur in Diskursen der Frühen Neuzeit*, ed. Harmut Laufhütte (Harrassowitz Verlag, 2000), p. 1171. See also Burkhard Dohm, *Poetische Alchemie: Öffnung zur Sinnlichkeit in der Hohelied- und Bibeldichtung von der protestanischen Barockmystik bis zum Pietismus* (Max Niemeyer Verlag, 2000).

[31] Dohm, 'Des Blutes Licht-Tinctur,' p. 1173.

[32] Around the turn of the nineteenth century, Christlieb Suter, church archivist, destroyed potentially hundreds of controversial documents from Zinzendorf's lifetime, including Zinzendorf's personal diaries, with the permission of church authorities. However, he also made lists of the destroyed documents, called '*Kassation Liste*'. One of these lists mentions alchemical manuals, but they were viewed as controversial and destroyed. See '*Kassation Liste 2*', penned by Christlieb Suter on 9 August 1802, UA Herrnhut R.4.E.9.2. Numbers 70 and 71 on the list refer to: 'miscellanea, piècen und briefe: geistliches und weltliches, philosophisches, medizinisches und alchimistiches Allerley, aus deutschen und französichen Schriften extrahirt'. Paul Peucker's article 'In Staub und Asche: Bewertung und Kassation im Unitätsarchiv 1760-1810,' in Rudolf Mohr (ed.), *'Alles ist euer, ihr aber seid Christi', Festschrift für Dietrich Meyer* (Köln, 2000), provides an excellent discussion of the history of document purging in the Archives of the Moravian Church.

[33] Frank E. Manuel and Fritzie P. Manuel, *Utopian Thought in the Western World* (Belknap Press of Harvard University Press, 1979), p. 315.

presses of the Palatinate in the sixteenth century. These presses were some of the first to publish the alchemically-charged treatises of the Rosicrucians.[34]

Given the mystical lineage of the Moravian church, it is not surprising to find that music and blood were viewed and discussed through alchemical metaphors, even from the earliest days of the first Moravian settlement in Herrnhut. Moravian hymns abound with images designed to sensually transform without mediation by the rational mind:

O Du wunderschönes Lamm,	Oh, you fairest Lamb,
ja, du schönster unter allen!	indeed, you are the fairest of all!
mir gefallen	pleasing to me are
deine wunden groß und klein;	your wounds, large and small;
Seitenschrein	Side-shrine
mich scharmiren deiner leichen	caress me, colourful martyr signs
ihre bunte marter-zeichen.	of your corpse.
Schön bist du, mein Lämmelein!	Fair are you, my little Lamb!
Wunden-Lämmlein voller blut!	Wounded-Lambkin, full of blood!
ach! die schönheit deiner wunden	Ah! the beauty of your wounds
hat gebunden	has bound
deiner knecht und mägde herz;	the hearts of your servants;
weil dein schmerz,	because your pain,
deine dorn- und nägel-ritzen	your thorn and nail scratches
ihnen in dem herzen blitzen,	flash in their hearts,
machens herz zur gnaden-kerz.	and make the heart into a Mercy-candle.
Ihr vom Lamm erwehltes volk,	You people chosen by the Lamb,
wie erfreut man sich in Chören	how one rejoices to hear you
euch zu hören,	in choirs,
wenn sich euer mund aufthut,	when you open your mouths
merkt mans blut:	the blood is noticed:
ihr gesalbte geistes-tempel,	you anointed Spirit-temple,
andern seelen zum exempel,	an example to other souls,
euch beschwemmt die wunden-fluth.	you are inundated with the wounds-flood.
Ihr seyd unserm Lamme gleich,	You are like our Lamb,
bis auf seine sühnungs-wunden,	down to His reconciliation wounds,
beul und schrunden:	bruises and cracks:
aber weil der seiten-ritz	but because the side-tear
euer sitz;	is your seat;
kan man doch in eurem wesen	one can nevertheless in your being

---

[34]   See Frances A. Yates, *The Rosicrucian Enlightenment* (Routledge & Kegan Paul, c. 1972), especially her chapter 'Comenius and the Rosicrucian Rumour in Bohemia'.

etwas von dem Lämmlein lesen,	read something of the little Lamb,
merken seiner augen blitz.	note the gleam of his eye.
Lämmlein! sey gelobt davor,	Lambkin! be praised,
daß du uns das volk gegeben;	that you have given us the people;
laß es leben	let them live
frölich und voll seligkeit,	happily and full of bliss,
bis zur zeit,	until the time
da du mit dem blutgen schreine	that you will, with the bloody shrine
dich wirst zeigen der Gemeine	reveal yourself to the community
an dem tage der hochzeit.	on the wedding day.
Hosianna, preis und macht.[35]	Hosanna, praise and might.

The blood of the wounds (*Wundenblut*) transforms the sinner by the 'feurigen Leuchtkraft des Blutes Christi' [fiery light-craft of Christ's blood], the power of the Crucifixion which shines through every tear and rent in Christ's body:

> All day long we gaze into Jesus's wounds ... He always stays in our countenances with His wounds-tears, in the light of His nail-marks, where we customarily sit ... that remains constantly in front of our eyes, that distinguishes us from all other people, the countenance glows before our brows, it looks out of our eyes.[36]

This 'daily gaze' into Jesus's wounds assumed its most powerful form in improvised worship services called *Singstunden* [singing meetings]. In a *Singstunde*, individual hymn-verses and phrases of chorale melodies, from a memorized repertory of several thousand pre-existing hymns, were extemporaneously combined by a community member [*Liturg*], and repeated by other participants, to create a hymn-sermon [*Liederpredigt*]. This hymn-sermon elaborated upon a particular scriptural passage called the watchword [*Losung*], which was chosen by the casting of a lot. If no suitable verses could be drawn from the memorized repertory to suit the *Losung*, then the *Liturg* would improvise a new hymn. This practice was referred to as 'singing from the heart' [*aus dem Herzen gesungen*]. To truly participate in a *Singstunde*, an improviser needed to silence their own thoughts and feelings in favour of the 'divine voice'. True channelling of the divine represented transformation and sublimation of the worshipper's own body,

---

[35] *Herrnhuter Gesangbuch*, hymn 2144, verses 1–2, 4–6.
[36] 'Wir sehen den ganzen tag in die Wunden JEsu hinein ... Er bleibt uns immer im Gesicht mit seinem Wunden-Ritzen, in seiner Nägel-Maale Licht, da pflegen wir zu sitzen ... das bleibt uns beständig vor Augen, das distinguirt uns von allen andern Menschen, das Gesicht leuchtet vor unsrer Stirn, es blickt uns aus unsern Augen heraus.' Zinzendorf, *Die drey und dreyßigste Homilie*, p. 358. Quoted in Dohm, 'Des Blutes Licht-Tinctur', p. 1175.

in exchange for access to inner thoughts and feelings – God's voice.[37] Just as at Passover, the ancient Hebrews marked their houses with the blood of a sacrificial animal against the nightly terrors of the Angel of Death, Moravians, too, crossed their foreheads with sacrificial blood, the *Lammesblut*. As these verses clearly demonstrate, those so marked are visible from the outside, as singing members of their community, and from the inside, as transformed members who sing in harmony with the vibrations of the 'divine voice':

DU blut'ges Lamm, unser lieber GOTT!	You bloody Lamb, our beloved God!
würden wir gleich aller welt zu spott,	even if we were immediately ridiculed by the whole world,
soll dein zeugniß fortgehn; drum, theures Lämmlein!	your witness would continue; therefore, precious little lamb!
komm und entzünd dein verbindungs-flämlein	Come, and kindle your little bonding-flame
in deiner schaar.	in your flock.
Verblutete liebe durchgeh sie ganz,	Love, bled to death, penetrate it completely,
sie ist gewißlich doch deine pflanz,	it is most certainly your plant,
eine synagoge, die du erstritten,	a synagogue, that you fought to acquire,
drüber du in deinen ew'gen hütten	over which you in your eternal dwelling,
auch selber wachst.	yourself watch.
Laß doch dein leiden und tod und pein	Let your suffering and death and pain
ihnen beständig im herzen seyn,	be constantly in the heart,
dein balsamisch schwitzen, das sie errungen,	your balsam-like sweat, that they achieved,
als du mit weinen den sieg erzwungen,	when you wrung the victory with tears,
vertrete sie.	substitute for them.
Deins bluts verdienst an dem creuzes-stamm	Your blood's achievement on the cross-stem
das bleibt ihr text, allerliebstes Lamm!	remains their text, most beloved Lamb!
die durchgrabne hände, die matten augen,	The penetrated hands, the dull eyes,

---

[37]   Katherine Faull, 'Faith and Imagination: Nikolaus Ludwig von Zinzendorf's Anti-Enlightenment Philosophy of Self', in Faull (ed.), *Anthropology and the German Enlightenment* (Bucknell University Press, 1995), pp. 24–7; and 'Imagining and Learning: Utopian Visions in Early Moravian Communities', paper presented at Moravian College, Bethlehem, PA, 21 April 2006. Faull applies Foucault's ideas to the *Lebensläufen*, spiritual biographies penned by members of Moravian communities, however the same ideas also apply to the *Singstunden*. See Michel Foucault, in Luther H. Martin, Huck Gutman and Patrick H. Hutton (eds), *Technologies of the Self: A Seminar with Michel Foucault* (University of Massachusetts Press, 1988).

die doch die welt zu durchschauen taugen,	that are right for looking through the world,
und richter sind;	and are judges;
Das soll die ewige predigt seyn,	That is to be the eternal sermon,
dis fundament gelte ganz allein,	only this foundation is solid,
darauf soll'n die zeugen, wenn sie	they should witness to that, when it's
vollendet,	finished,
wozu er sie auf die welt gesendet,	why He sent them into the world,
Ihn sehen gehn.	watching Him go.
Und wenn die ganze gesellschaft dort,	And when the entire community,
die hier gehalten am leidens-wort,	that holds here to the suffering-word,
sich mit süssen psalmen wird lassen hören,	will let itself be heard with sweet psalms,
so wird es schallen in allen chören	then in all choirs it will resound
vons Lammes blut.[38]	the Lamb's blood.

Congregants sang together in a controlled ecstatic experience that allowed their bodies to resonate with the harmonies of the 'divine voice' and with each other. The Moravian way of singing was a reflection of their determination to live the tenets of their 'heart religion'. The anti-rationalist theology of the Moravians could only be accompanied by an artistic medium as emotional as their theology. For those inside the *Blutgemeine*, singing marked those chosen and sealed by the blood of the Lamb. As they listened to the voices of those around them, this mark was as audible as if their foreheads were literally painted with a cross of blood. In the words of one eighteenth-century hymn: 'Their mouths were filled with blood, and they sang together in joyful union with the heavenly spheres.'[39] In so doing, the core tenets of their theology were transmitted, consumed and ingested through the sensual vibrations of the singing body.

References

Primary Literature

Manuscript Sources
Jüngerhaus Diarium. UA Herrnhut JHD.

Printed Sources
Anon, *Testimonies of the Life, Character, Revelations and Doctrines of Our Ever Blessed Mother Ann Lee* (Hancock, MA: 1816).

---

[38] *Herrnhuter Gesangbuch* hymn 1699, verses 1–6.
[39] *Herrnhuter Gesangbuch*, hymn 2144.

Canigiani, Pietro, *Dialogo della serafica vergine, et sposa di Christo S. Catherina da Siena. Diviso in quattro trattati* (Venice: G. Sarzina, 1611).

Catherine of Siena. *La lettere*, ed. P. Misciattelli (Florence: Marzocco, 1939).

Hecker, A.P., *Gespräch eines Evangelisch-Lutherischen Predigers* (Berlin: Buchhandlung der Berlinischen Real-Schule, 1751).

Herrnhuter Gesangbuch: Christliches Gesang-Buch der Evangelischen Brüder-Gemeinen von 1735, ed. Erich Beyreuther, Gerhard Meyer and Gudrun Meyer-Hickel, (Hildesheim: G. Olms, 1981).

Orchi, Emmanuele, 'La passione per il Venerdì Santo', in *Prediche quaresimali* (Venice: Giunti e Baba, 1650).

Zinzendorf, Nikolaus Ludwig von, *Hauptschriften von Nikolaus Ludwig von Zinzendorf*, edited by Erich Beyreuther and Gerhard Meyer (Hildesheim: G. Olms, 1962-63).

Secondary Literature

Atwood, Craig D., 'Zinzendorf's "Litany of the Wounds"', *Lutheran Quarterly*, 11/2 (1997): 189–214.

Atwood, Craig D., *Community of the Cross: Moravian Piety in Colonial Bethlehem* (University Park, PA: Pennsylvania State University Press, 2004).

Caldwell, Alice May, 'Music of the Moravian "Liturgische Gesänge" (1791–1823): From Oral to Written Tradition' (PhD diss., New York University, 1987).

Camporesi, Piero, *Juice of Life: The Symbolic and Magic Significance of Blood*, trans. Robert R. Barr (New York: Continuum, 1995).

Dohm, Burkhard, 'Des Blutes Licht-Tinctur: Alchimistische Koncepte in Herrnhutischer Poesie', in Harmut Laufhütte (ed.), *Künste und Natur in Diskursen der Frühen Neuzeit* (Wiesbaden: Harrassowitz Verlag, 2000).

Dohm, Burkhard, *Poetische Alchemie: Öffnung zur Sinnlichkeit in der Hohelied- und Bibeldichtung von der protestanischen Barockmystik bis zum Pietismus* (Tübingen: Max Niemeyer Verlag, 2000).

Faull, Katherine, 'Faith and Imagination: Nikolaus Ludwig von Zinzendorf's Anti-Enlightenment Philosophy of Self', in Katherine Faull (ed.), *Anthropology and the German Enlightenment* (Lewisburg, PA: Bucknell University Press, 1995).

Foucault, Michel, in Luther H. Martin, Huck Gutman and Patrick H. Hutton (eds), *Technologies of the Self: A Seminar with Michel Foucault* (Amherst, MA: University of Massachusetts Press, 1988).

Le Guin, Elisabeth, *Boccherini's Body: An Essay in Carnal Musicology* (Berkeley: University of California Press, 2006).

Manuel, Frank E. and Manuel, Fritzie P., *Utopian Thought in the Western World* (Cambridge, MA: Belknap Press of Harvard University Press, 1979).

Peucker, Paul, 'In Staub und Asche: Bewertung und Kassation im Unitätsarchiv 1760–1810', in Rudolf Mohr (ed.), *'Alles ist euer, ihr aber seid Christi': Festschrift für Dietrich Meyer* (Köln, 2000).

Peucker, Paul, '"Inspired by the Flames of love": Homosexuality, Mysticism, and
    Moravian Brothers around 1750', *Journal of the History of Sexuality*, 15/1
    (2006): 30–64.
Peucker, Paul, 'The Songs of the Sifting: Understanding the Role of Bridal
    Mysticism in Moravian Piety in the late 1740s', *Journal of Moravian History*,
    3 (Fall 2007): 51–87.
Yates, Frances A., *The Rosicrucian Enlightenment* (London and Boston: Routledge
    & Kegan Paul, c. 1972 (reprint 1974)).

Chapter 10

Worship, Transcendence and Danger: Reflections on Seigfried Kracauer's 'The Hotel Lobby'

Martin D. Stringer

For some time now I have been struggling with what it was about the development of worship in Catholic, Anglican and other mainline churches in the West in the last quarter of the twentieth century that led a significant number of commentators to say that congregational worship in these churches had lost so much of its 'mystery'. To some extent this is a debate specifically within the field of Liturgical Studies but many of those who complained about the loss of mystery were not themselves part of the mainstream of liturgical scholars who had been so instrumental in creating the new liturgies in the first place. David Martin, for example, a sociologist of religion in the UK, and others who opposed the move away from the 1662 prayer book in the Church of England put this down to the loss of Elizabethan language and perhaps also to the loss of a deep ingrained familiarity.[1] Opponents of the move from Latin to English in the Catholic Mass, both in Europe and North America, pointed to aspects of doctrine, the sense of history and the removal of ceremonial, but essentially they were arguing that it was the 'mystery' that had been lost without being too clear where that mystery was situated. David Torevell, for example, also writing from a sociological perspective with a Catholic background, developed a more sophisticated argument but generally came to the same kinds of conclusions.[2] There are similar, but less clearly articulated, comments from the Methodist tradition and the Reformed churches. All these critiques focused primarily on text and ritual, that which was set out in the prayer books, as though it was the revision of the liturgical text, and particularly the updating of the English, that led to the decline in 'mystery'. A few have pointed to performance, specifically Kieran Flanagan, another sociologist coming from a British Catholic perspective, who argued that something changed in the way liturgy was presented, perhaps even a change in attitude on the part of

---

[1] David Martin, *The Breaking of the Image: A Sociology of Christian Theory and Practice* (Blackwell, 1980).

[2] David Torevell, *Losing the Sacred: Ritual, Modernity and Liturgical Reform* (T & T Clark, 2000).

the celebrant and the congregation, although it is difficult here to distinguish the chicken and the egg and to point to specific causes.[3]

Moving slightly wider in our view of Christian worship the so called 'worship wars' in the evangelical and free churches could be seen to point to a similar development, a move away from older, more familiar and possibly more 'sacred' music towards the use of modern instruments, pop-based formats and the intrusion of the decidedly 'profane' into Christian worship. Other papers in this book pick up aspects of this specific debate more fully and that is not really the issue that I want to focus on in this chapter. Like Martin, Torevelle and Flanagan I come from a social sciences background, more specifically from anthropology which is my home discipline. However, I feel uneasy with the criticisms levelled at the liturgical texts and performances of my sociological colleagues. My background is Anglican, I am currently a Catholic and I have been involved in liturgical study as well as anthropology working closely at times with many of those in the UK who drew up the new liturgical texts and helping churches from a range of traditions to apply them to their worship. For some reason, however, I feel strongly that many of these new liturgies did not work in practice. Whether something was 'lost' I am not so sure, as I do not recall personally what came before, but something is certainly 'missing'. Part of this is related to language, much of it to performance, but I do want to suggest that part of the change that has taken place across the 'liturgical churches' in the West in the last half of the twentieth century has something to do with music and the assumptions behind the use and reception of music within the liturgy. In order to explore this more fully, however, I want to step back to the first half of the twentieth century, to Weimar Germany and an interesting little essay by a German sociologist who was asking very interesting questions about the hotel lobby.[4]

The Hotel Lobby

Seigfried Kracauer (1889–1926) wrote 'The Hotel Lobby' as part of his work on *The Mass Ornament: Weimar Essays* in 1922–25 and first published in 1927. Like other scholars of the time Kracauer was interested in what we would today call 'popular culture' although this was more generally referred to at the time as relating to the 'masses', whether that was 'mass ornament' or 'mass observation'. There is a clear link to the kind of work that Walter Benjamin was also doing with reference to the Paris arcades,[5] and like Benjamin Kracauer aimed to combine detailed observation with high theory. In 'The Hotel Lobby', Kracauer's starting

---

[3]   Kieran Flanagan, *Sociology and Liturgy: Re-presentations of the Holy* (Macmillan, 1991); see also Torevell, *Losing the Sacred*.

[4]   Siegfried Kracauer, 'The Hotel Lobby', in Malcolm Miles, Tim Hall and Iain Borden (eds), *The City Cultures Reader*, 2nd ed. (Routledge, 2004), pp. 33–9.

[5]   Walter Benjamin, *The Arcades Project* (Harvard University Press, 2002).

point is actually the detective novel, an archetypal element of popular fiction. It is because the lobby was seen to be the principle setting for many of the detective novels of the time that Kracauer moved from the content of the novels themselves to their setting. What attracted me to this paper, however, was the way in which Kracauer compares the setting of the lobby to that of the house of God, or the congregation, on the assumption that all his readers would know and understand what the congregation was, even if they were unfamiliar with the lobby. This could not be done in contemporary essays (although it could perhaps be done in reverse, which is what, to some extent this paper aims to achieve) and provides an interesting insight into what Kracauer, and others at the time, thought of the congregation in its pre-liturgical-revision state.

The difference between the hotel lobby and the congregation, as outlined by Kracauer, is rooted in the difference between transcendence and alienation. In order to elucidate this Kracauer draws on the work of Kant on aesthetics:

> Kant ... believed there was a seamless transition from the transcendental to the performed subject-object world. The fact that he does not completely give up on the total person even in the aesthetic realm is confirmed by his definition of the 'sublime' which takes the ethical into account and thereby attempts to reassemble the remaining pieces of the fractured whole.[6]

It is Kant's concept of the 'sublime' that sits beneath Kracauer's analysis and in particular the way, for Kant, the sublime combines both an aesthetic sense of the beautiful and an ethical sense of the good.[7] That which is beautiful must also be good and, by implication, there is also a link between the ugly, or perhaps in Kracauer's world the plain or the vulgar, and the bad, or again that which is simply lacking in values. The hotel lobby, with its uniform blandness, including the non-descript background music, is archetypal of the vulgar, that which is lacking in moral value. The reason, for this, according to Kracauer, is that the décor and soundscape of the lobby does not refer beyond itself, it does not look to the transcendental, it does not aspire to the sublime:

> Just as the lobby is the space that does not refer beyond itself, the aesthetic condition corresponding to it constitutes itself as its own limit ... the aesthetic that has become an end in itself pulls up its own roots; it obscures the higher level toward which it should refer and signifies only its own emptiness ... .[8]

Both the hotel lobby and the house of God respond to the aesthetic sense that articulates its legitimate demands in them. But whereas in the latter the beautiful

---

[6]   Kracauer, 'The Hotel Lobby', p. 35.

[7]   Immanuel Kant, *Critique of the Power of Judgement* (Cambridge University Press, 2000).

[8]   Kracauer, 'The Hotel Lobby', p. 35.

employs a language with which it also testifies against itself, in the former it is involved in its muteness, incapable of finding the other.[9]

This leads Kracauer to take a further step. He not only sees the lobby as lacking in aesthetic or moral worth, he actually suggests that in some senses it a space of moral degeneration. In part this is a product of the aesthetic itself, but it is also linked, very interestingly, with the activities that are presumed to happen within the space, activities that are given particular prominence within the contemporary detective novel. To this extent the comparison between the lobby and the congregation becomes much starker and is clearly placed in the realm of ultimate moral value:

> In tasteful lounge chairs a civilization intent on rationalization comes to an end, whereas the decorations of the church pews are born from the tension that accords them a revelatory meaning. As a result, the chorales that are the expression of the divine service turn into medleys whose strains encourage pure triviality, and devotion congeals into erotic desire that roams about without an object.[10]

In order to emphasize this moral distance between the two spaces, their aesthetic forms and the soundscapes that inhabit them, Kracauer identifies one element where the two spaces are actually identical, this is the way in which each space creates a radical equality among the people who inhabit it. Within the congregation all people are equal before God. In the lobby anybody can walk in off the street and, if they can afford the price of a room at the establishment, they can legitimately sit within the lobby. All people within the lobby are equal. Of course, in reality such equality, in both spaces, is aspirational and the differences of class and monetary worth can be easily identified both in the appearance of the people and in the way others respond to them. However, for Kracauer this radical equality, and its link to the 'other', is essential in drawing his final conclusion:

> The *equality* of those who pray is likewise reflected in distorted form in the hotel lobby. When a congregation forms, the differences between people disappear because these beings all have one and the same destiny … In the hotel lobby, equality is not based on a relation to God but on a relation to the nothing.[11]

The lobby therefore de-values the human in both senses. It makes them appear worthless in themselves, of no more value than the false, theatrical and vulgar space that they inhabit. On the other hand it also de-values them in the sense that it sucks the moral values from them because of the nature of the space. While we might not agree with the logic of Kracauer's argument, rooted as it is in Kantian

---

[9]   Kracauer, 'The Hotel Lobby', p. 36.
[10] Kracauer, 'The Hotel Lobby', p. 36.
[11] Kracauer, 'The Hotel Lobby', p. 36, emphasis in the original.

aesthetics, the final conclusion is one that many commentators might agree with. The hotel lobby (and while the aesthetic has changed since the 1930s many of the pertinent features identified by Kracauer have not) is a depersonalizing space. It works through the imposition of a fiction, a façade, a stage set, and yet allows the individual to step out of their moral community and, for a short space of time, to park the values of their everyday lives. What is more, it is clear that the music that is pumped continuously into this space, in its 'pure triviality' continues to 'congeal into erotic desire without an object'. Kracauer, I would suggest, has put his finger onto something very important.

Other De-Valuing Spaces

Scholarship has moved on from Kracauer, with the work of Benjamin and others having a more lasting impact on studies of popular culture. However, more recent sociological studies of shopping malls, theme parks and airports have developed a number of themes raised by Kracauer without any direct reference to, or it appears knowledge of, his work (despite the fact that Kracauer does have a paper on the shopping arcade within his book). There are two areas of study that have been particularly developed and which come together to reinforce Kracauer's central conclusion about the de-valuing of the human person within specific spaces. The first focuses more specifically on theme parks and what Umberto Eco has defined as 'hyper-reality'.[12] This picks up the fabricated falseness that Kracauer identified in the hotel lobby, and shows how this has become normative, primarily for spaces of entertainment, but also for many neighbourhoods based on heritage sites of one kind or another.[13] The other direction develops more architecturally and focuses much more specifically on the design and use of the shopping mall. It is here, I would suggest, where Kracauer's ideas of the triviality of music have been developed most clearly.[14]

Shopping malls are an American invention, although they are now a global phenomenon.[15] The literature talks of a site set apart, a carefully designed space designed specifically for the purpose of shopping, of which the music is an essential element. There are certain elements that are important for the design of

---

[12]   Umberto Eco, *Faith in Fakes: Travels in Hyperreality* (Minerva, 1995).

[13]   Michael Sorkin, 'See You in Disneyland', in Michael Sorkin (ed.), *Variations on a Theme Park: The New American City and the End of Public Space* (Hill and Wang, 1992), pp. 205–32.

[14]   Jonathan Sterne, 'Sounds like the Mall of America: Programmed Music and the Architechtonics of Commercial Space', *Ethnomusicology*, 14/1 (1997): pp 22–50.

[15]   Margaret Crawford, 'The World in a Shopping Mall', in Michael Sorkin (ed.), *Variations on a Theme Park: The New American City and the End of Public Space* (Hill and Wang, 1992), pp. 80–110; James Farrell, *One Nation Under Gods: Malls and the Seduction of American Shopping* (Smithsonian Books, 2003).

any shopping centre. It should take shoppers away from the real world and focus their attention specifically on the act of shopping. It should be clean, unencumbered with unnecessary elements, and perhaps be hyper real in its design, referencing some other time or place. It is also a space that is secure; all the pain and troubles of the world are excluded. It is safe!

The music is clearly a part of the overall environment. Sterne describes it as part of the architecture.[16] It is designed to encourage people to move on, to shop and to spend money. There is a science devoted to it. Specifics of pace, tone, rhythm and even pitch can each combine in different spaces to encourage different activities, whether to move people on quickly to the next store, or to encourage them to stop and linger and to engage with specific products. Background music in the modern shopping mall is never entirely 'background'; it is designed with a purpose and is part of the overall experience of the mall. It can even be used to zone the spaces, keeping classes and even generations apart. It is also specifically designed not to be listened to, not to create groups or audiences that may stop and listen to the track. It is designed to isolate. It points to consumerism and not to the transcendent in any way.[17] To this extent the music is deliberately being used to create the kind of trivial erotic desire that Kracauer talks of. However, within the shopping mall, that desire does have an object, the product to be bought rather than other human persons – what we could call, to misuse Marx's oft-quoted concept, 'commodity fetishism'.

Like the lobby, we could argue that music – and other environmental elements of the shopping mall – 'de-values' the human. It is worth asking of the shopping mall the questions that Kracauer asks of the hotel lobby. There are many people who would probably agree that 'falseness', 'triviality', even 'vulgarity' typify the music in many shopping malls. In doing this they would be applying a set of value judgements that are implicit in Kracauer's analysis but are less easily supported today. Sterne's point about the lack of sonic identity of such music, rather than 'triviality' or 'vulgarity', might bring us closer to the point that matters.[18] This is not music that visitors to the centre are expected to identify with in a deep emotional fashion.

We might also take Kracauer's analysis of equality and the relation between the human and the other and apply it to this space of commerce. There are differences between shopping malls in terms of class and the assumed wealth of the clientele, but within each space there is also something of a radical equality, as there is within the hotel lobby. This is not, however, an equality in the face of the other. It is, as with the lobby, and in Kracauer's words, an equality based on 'a relation to the nothing'. For Kracauer if equality is not based on the other then it must be based on nothing, he offers no alternatives. It might be possible to look for another basis

[16] Sterne, 'Sounds like the Mall of America', p. 27.
[17] But see the discussion in Ira Zepp, *The New Religious Image of Urban America: The Shopping Mall as Ceremonial Centre* (University Press of Colorado, 1986).
[18] Sterne, 'Sounds like the Mall of America'.

for such equality, in relation to the commodity or money for example. However, that misses Kracauer's point. For Kracauer it is the united focus on the other that creates a particular bond among the members of the congregation that is lacking in the lobby, where people move through but each focuses on their own concerns so making the creation of moral bonds between them impossible. This is what he means by 'a relation to the nothing' and this is also present, I would suggest, within the shopping mall as it is in airports, public plazas and many other places where crowds simply pass through.

What is missing within the shopping mall, however, when compared to Kracauer's analysis of the lobby, is the sense of moral degeneration that Kracauer brings in with reference to the detective novel. Apart from commercial exploitation there is rarely anything morally dubious going on within the shopping mall, in fact part of the design of the space is specifically engineered to prevent morally dubious activity taking place. It is this that gives the space its identity as being 'safe'. There are those, of course, who would see the whole capitalist enterprise as morally suspect and would therefore transfer this suspicion to the shopping mall, in much the same way as Kracauer does with the detective novels and the hotel lobby. The question, however, depends on our position in relation to the wider consumerist society and I will come back to this below. This does not mean, therefore, that the shopping mall is an a-moral space or that it is not de-valuing in its own way.

Kavanagh

Bringing the various elements of this discussion together we could argue that the contemporary congregation has become, in some senses, a hotel lobby, or even a shopping mall, or that it has gained something from these kinds of environment, and that this is the reason why the worship of mainline churches have lost their mystery. Bryan Spinks talks about the 'Worship Mall' in the title of a recent book, but he is referring to something very different in his use of this image.[19] For Spinks it is the variety of options available in the stores that is drawn from the image, and the way in which individuals can select from what is on offer what suits them in particular, either buying into a 'lifestyle' as presented by one particular brand or by picking and choosing among many different possibilities. He was not specifically concerned with the public space of the mall, the spaces between the stores, that is the real equivalent of Kracauer's lobby.

Questions around the commercialization of worship have also been raised by Pete Ward among others.[20] However, once again Ward focuses on the increasing variety of options available and questions around who is producing, and profiting

---

[19] Bryan Spinks, *The Worship Mall: Contemporary Responses to Contemporary Culture* (SPCK, 2010), p. xxiii.

[20] Peter Ward, *Selling Worship: How What We Sing has Changed the Church* (Paternoster Press, 2005).

from, what is being sung in churches. While he does show a relationship between the songs produced for worship within particular evangelical traditions and popular music, and talks about 'selling out to the culture',[21] he does not really ask what impact this has on the space of worship itself or the sense of mystery that might be created or lost.

Towards the end of my *Sociological History of Christian Worship*, I commented that one of the great dangers of worship in the contemporary church is that it is becoming too comfortable.[22] The preponderance of comfortable seating, carpets on the floor, careful lighting and in many cases soft background music, creates an atmosphere within many congregations that Kracauer would probably recognize as related to the 'hotel lobby'; one which is certainly very similar in choices of furnishings, colours and sounds to many contemporary hotel lobbies around the world.

Aidan Kavanagh, writing in the 1980s, talks about the contemporary American Catholic Mass as an urban dinner party.[23] Kavanagh contrasts this scene to the butcher's slab in the centre of the city where the lamb is sacrificed and the blood allowed to flow. There is something of the consumerism of 'pre-packaged, organic Welsh hill farmed, spring lamb' about the contemporary Mass: a lack of transcendence, but also a lack of danger. What is lacking, according to Kavanagh is the danger that is always felt in the presence of the transcendent. From Adam and Eve being banished from the garden of Eden, through Moses and the burning bush, the Israelites recoiling in horror at the vision of the Lord on the mountain when Moses descended with the tablets of the law, through the visions of Isaiah and Ezekiel and the mount of transfiguration, there has always been something dangerous about encounters with God. Who can look on the face of the Lord and live?

There is also, according to Kavanagh, something very real, very earthy. Whether it is the creation of humanity from mud, the tilling of the soil and pain of childbirth, the journeys through the desert, the sexuality of the song of songs, or the horror of lamentation, the other is with us in our joy and our pain, down there in the mud and the blood and the gore. It is the act of looking into the eyes of the lamb as it is slaughtered, an experience that our pre-packaged world has removed from so many of us, that puts us in touch with this transcendence, and an act that is recalled, according to Kavanagh, and celebrated each time we celebrate the Lord's supper.

I remember an elderly priest telling me of his experience of the Moss Side riots in Manchester in the 1980s. The row of shops on the main highway faced the backs of a large housing estate. The rioters came, as if from nowhere, running down the street lobbing bricks and fire bombs into the shop fronts before disappearing almost as quickly as they had arrived. There followed an eerie silence for some minutes as the only sound, and the only light, came from the burning shops on the

[21]   Ward, *Selling Worship*, pp. 179–81.

[22]   Martin Stringer, *A Sociological History of Christian Worship* (Cambridge University Press, 2005), p. 239.

[23]   Aidan Kavanagh, *On Liturgical Theology* (Pueblo Publishing Company, 1984).

main street. Then slowly, as the old priest put it, 'like maggots emerging from a piece of rotten meat', the people from the council estate crept across the grass from their homes to the shops and began to loot. As the priest walked down the street amidst the flames and the looting he noticed a large bird fly towards him out of the dark. He ducked to let it past and noted that it was a parrot released from one of the pet shops on the strip. As he looked on at the scene of devastation and looting the only word that the priest could think of was 'freedom'.

Kracauer does not relate danger to the transcendent. This is partly because he is drawing on a Kantian understanding of the 'sublime' where beauty and goodness are one and danger, if such a term were to be used, is probably to be found at the opposite pole of the continuum. In fact, for Kracauer, danger, with its links to the detective novel and even to the erotic, is more likely to be a feature of the hotel lobby than the house of God. This, however, is to miss the point. The danger of the lobby is *illusory*, a fiction, something that is created to add a certain edge to the context itself. Ultimately it is there simply to reinforce the sense of security and 'safeness' that such a space demands. As with the shopping mall, what is of central importance to the managers of the space of the lobby is the safety of the individuals who use it, and so the removal of anything that might cause real, as opposed to fictional, danger. Recognizing the difference between the superficial, created and controlled 'danger' of a stage set lobby and the real uncertainties of the inner-city butcher's shop is an important step.

The question, however, is whether we need to, or can, make the leap from the Kantian transcendence of beauty and goodness to the kind of transcendence that Kavanagh identifies in the slitting of the throat of the lamb, or that the elderly priest noted in the 'freedom' of the riot. When the sociological critics of the liturgical reforms of the latter half of the twentieth century say that 'the transcendent', or 'mystery', has been removed from Christian worship, they may all agree that the result is the comfortable, safe hotel lobby or suburban lounge of contemporary congregational spaces. What they may differ over, however, is the kind of transcendent that they believe has been lost. If the only transcendence that was present in the liturgical worship of mainstream Western churches in the first half of the twentieth century, with its roots in the Salzburg of Mozart or the English Cathedral choral traditions, is the Kantian transcendence of truth and beauty, a transcendence that is reserved for the middle classes and which could not stand against the horrors of the First World War and the Holocaust, then perhaps both the critics and the revisers are missing something much more important: the dangerous transcendence of the butcher's shop and the inner city riots.

Examples and Counter-Examples of Transcendent Liturgies

This paper began as a personal quest to answer a question that concerned me about the so-called 'loss' of mystery, or the transcendent in late twentieth-century mainline liturgical worship. I shared the sense of a loss, or rather an 'absence', but disagreed with other sociological critics as to where that lack existed. What I have explored so far in this paper is a possible approach that sets that lack within the context of Kracauer's critique of the hotel lobby and Kavanagh's critique of the suburban dinner party Mass. Being an anthropologist I would want to test these theoretical critiques through ethnographic fieldwork. A detailed analysis of any one specific congregation, however, will not add greatly to my understanding as it would be difficult to find any example that was 'typical' or 'representative'. What I have chosen to do in the final section of this paper, therefore, acknowledging the personal nature of my question, is to develop a limited form of autoethnography, reflecting on a series of experiences where I have both felt some level of transcendence in worship and experiences where this is missing. I will then test these against the critiques of Kracauer and Kavanagh to see if there are any specific conclusions that can be drawn. In undertaking this autoethnography I will be paying particular attention to the role of music within the worship and in my own experience of that worship.

The Roman Catholic church that sits just opposite my house in Kidderminster, a small ex-industrial town in north Worcestershire, UK, is a thriving family orientated parish. They have a steady stream of ordinands (which is very unusual for a Catholic community in the UK) and the congregation is encouraged to take a full and active role in the life of the church. The music for the main Sunday Mass is like that of so many other Catholic churches that I have attended up and down England. There is a competent organist and a small choir that supports the singing, but the music itself is merely background, without any real sonic identity. It would never stop you in your tracks and force you to listen. Hymns are sung without much enthusiasm and organ music is played before and after the service, at times when people are very unlikely to listen to it. There are clearly other parts of the Mass, most notably the sermon, that do occasionally make me sit up and think, and there is a very friendly atmosphere among the congregation with a good range of social and extra-liturgical activities, something that we might call 'fellowship'. However, overall, this kind of worship is typical of what Kavanagh is referring to when he talks about the suburban dinner party.

Moving out of the English Catholic experience does not provide anything much more stimulating. I have attended a number of Methodist, Baptist, evangelical Anglican and Assemblies of God churches throughout England either through my work or because of family connections. Many of these churches began their worship with a series of hymns and choruses, and my overwhelming impression is that the opening 'worship time' in many of these churches could be described as background, almost 'wallpaper' music as the community gathers. It establishes a comfortable, secure, space, setting the worship apart from the danger and horrors of the world. Many follow a fixed pattern of tone and pace that brings the individual into the right place to respond to the Word and the Spirit.[24] There is something here that always reminds me of the shopping mall and the desire for a 'safe space',

---

[24]   Mark Evans, *Open Up the Doors: Music in the Modern Church* (Equinox, 2006).

created in part by the careful manipulation of the soundscape. 'Worship time', and the music that drives it, provides a boundary between the space of the world, whether explicitly defined as dangerous or not, and the safety and comfort of the worship itself. The décor, with carpets and comfortable chairs, soft furnishings and pastel colours, only adds to the secure nature of the space and the sense of keeping the real, dangerous world outside.

My own current experience of worship is with the Birmingham Oratory, a Catholic congregation in the centre of Birmingham, UK. Here I have been attending the main Sunday Solemn High Mass according to the 'extraordinary form of the Roman Rite'. This is a phrase used by Pope Benedict XVI to describe the liturgy of the 1962 Roman Missal, commonly referred to as the 'Tridentine Mass'. The liturgy is entirely in Latin. The ritual is pre-Vatican II and the setting, the vestments, the ornaments above and around the altar (candles, reliquaries, etc.), and the architectural space is of one piece, extravagant and yet also understated, partly I will admit because of the volume of the space. What would seem very fussy in another environment is expansive and restrained, something to which the slow measured pace of the rite does a great deal to reinforce. The music is provided by a semi-professional choir and while many Sundays and feast days draw on Palestrina, Haydn, Mozart and similar composers they do on occasion spread their wings and include more challenging and contemporary settings. I respond particularly to this worship because it provides the space in which to be with God in an intimate and personal way without the rite itself impinging too much into my own private devotion. What this rite acknowledges, unlike many of the recent liturgical revisions, is that different things can be taking place within the liturgy at the same time. So the choir can be singing, the celebrant and others at the altar engaged in ritual activity and the congregation focused on their own devotions. Each element is not dependent on the others but all come together to form a coherent whole.

As a liturgy the Solemn High Mass would be described by many in the congregation as pointing to 'the transcendent'. This would be a form of 'the transcendent' that Kracauer would recognize, the Kantian 'sublime' that links beauty with truth. It is certainly not a lobby or a shopping mall, but it is isolating, it is individualizing, it is me and my God, a kind of radical equality in individuality. There is nothing inherently dangerous about it, although to suddenly be launched into a Messiaen organ piece as the altar party left the sanctuary after Mass on the feast of the Ascension both shocked me and took my breath away, it was far from 'comfortable' at that particular moment.

Thinking of other worship where the space, environment and especially the music, played a similar role, rooted in the Kantian sense of the sublime but with an edge of danger in the margins, then I am taken back to the Moravian church on the US Virgin Island of St Thomas in the Caribbean. I was visiting my student on the island and we went to worship at the church on the Sunday morning. The space was simple, a plain white rectangle with the benches for the clergy and pulpit along one of the longer walls. Even as we arrived the church was full and crowds were gathering outside the building itself. I was shown to a seat near the front and immediately I realized that I stood out because of my colour. It was not that I was white within a black congregation (that is not an unusual experience for me); rather, it was that I had chosen to wear a green shirt, yellow tie and brown trousers and everybody else in the church appeared to be dressed in black, or at least dark blue, and white. The uniformity of the crowd hit me immediately, and shortly following that, as the service began, the strength and rich four part harmonies of the congregational singing. This was *communitas* as Victor Turner describes it, the gathering up into one of the collective and the loss of individuality, and once more a sense of radical equality.[25] There was a sense of transcendence certainly, a transcendence of power, beauty and truth, but again no direct sense of danger, at least not on that morning, except for my own rather unfortunate choice of dress.

Finally, I want to mention two acts of worship where the transcendence did include a sense of danger, a sense of uncertainty, a sense of reality breaking through. The first was my experience of worshipping with a leper colony in Tanzania.[26] It was an Anglican service in the Catholic tradition, and the Mass was made up of plainchant from the elderly British priest, the congregation singing from the English Hymnal accompanied by drums and other percussive instruments for the hymns, and local settings with drums and voice and response patterns based on local melodies adapted from vernacular singing in the Rufiji area for the Kyries, Gloria, Credo and Sanctus. It was the juxtaposition of styles (which still came together to form a coherent whole), the community, the suffering and the joy that made this both a 'transcendent' and a 'dangerous' experience for me as a visitor from the UK. For many of the regular members of the congregation, however, this was simply the weekly fare and may not have had that edge of danger and uncertainty that was so apparent to the visitor.

The other example is my experience at an independent Christian fellowship in Deal, Kent. This was a 'therapeutic community' where people were aware of their failings and were working through these as a community and as individuals. This was not a place of miracle cures, but it was a place of fellowship and of mutual love. Again I was visiting a student and the evening before the service I was asked to preach the following morning. The community met in a local hall and the worship began with an open meeting, no chairs, no structure, and the powerful use of a jazz band providing accompaniment to the singing. The band – saxophone, drums, guitar and bass – provided their own melodies to songs written within the congregation or improvised on more familiar tunes as the congregation engaged in free prayer, glossalalia or simply moved around the space praising and thanking God. The open worship only finished when the congregation was called to find a chair from the side of the room and to sit and listen to the notices, the reading I had chosen and my sermon. This is the only truly unstructured worship I have experienced, and that in itself was both transcendent and dangerous, before

---

[25]   Victor Turner, *The Ritual Process: Structure and Anti-Structure* (Penguin, 1969).

[26]   I have referred to this before in Stringer, *Sociological History*, pp. 222–3.

we added the openness and obvious pain of many in the congregation and the need to find something suitable to preach to the congregation that morning.

Conclusion

These examples are, as I have said, autoethnographical, but there is perhaps something in them that might refer back to the discussion of Kracauer, the shopping mall and Kavanagh's butcher's slab. If I begin with the music then there is a clear distinction between the almost background, banal, easy listening music of the first two forms and the claimed transcendence of the second two. Whether we see the sublime in a choir singing Palestrina or in the overfull congregation singing Moravian hymnody in four part harmonies, both are a long way from half-hearted hymnody or the medley of choruses that I have experienced in so many British mainline churches. In some senses this distinction forms the basis for many of the critiques of contemporary worship, with the underlying assumption that we are simply distinguishing between low and high culture, the vulgarity of the hotel lobby or the downmarket shopping centre against the exclusivity and elitism of the opera house or the classical concert. That, however, is not the real point.

Interestingly the level of fellowship, if by that we mean easy friendship and support among the congregation, a person to person focus or an emphasis on the horizontal in worship, is often stronger in the first kind of church than it is in the second, even if the human-other relationship is sometimes less clear to identify. The easy listening, familiar and participatory music of the first two contexts is ideal for the comfortable communal nature of the worship. It *is* the suburban dinner party, the Sunday roast at the local gastro-pub with all the family, and as such probably has a place. The kind of music, and the surrounding architecture, of the Oratory does not inspire fellowship. It does not encourage people to meet and to chat in an easy informal fashion. And even the Moravian service, with the very strong sense of community, or fellowship, even of communitas, still demands that everybody wear their Sunday best in terms of both dress and manners.

So what of the final two cases? The fact that both existed in the context of illness and healing is significant. The congregations lived with suffering, they understood from their own lives the pain of sacrifice and humiliation. What is interesting, however, is the musical response. This is not 'high culture' or 'low culture', it is the music of the suffering and downtrodden, the music of slaves, or the colonial other, brought into the context of Christian worship. If I were to reflect more carefully on what set the dangerous worship apart then I would have to suggest that rhythm was more important in both cases than melody, harmony or even singability. It was the energy of the music that lent it a certain dangerous quality, almost improvisational, certainly adapted to mood and circumstances. This was not, however, 'difficult' music, the modernist response to the tragedies of the first half of the twentieth century as seen in the Messiaen organ work. It is not music that shocks, that demands that we pay attention, that forces itself on our consciousness. Rather, this music draws us in, fills us with its rhythms, and carries us along into the heart of the pain and suffering, as well as the joy, that it so clearly expresses. It is communal, even horizontal, in many ways, but it also looks beyond itself towards the other, has an element of the transcendent, but the transcendence of the earth, of the mud from which we all emerged, the city to which we all aspire, rather than the transcendence of the sublime.

Perhaps there is no obvious answer to my initial question, and I am not advocating that we all begin to worship through jazz, or African rhythms, or even through rock or rap, although each of these might have their place. We do, however, need to learn from the lobby and the shopping mall the dangers of creating the separated commercialized 'safe spaces' and the need to revisit that butcher's shop, ransacked by the rioters, and flowing in blood, at the heart of all our cities. We must learn what songs to sing in that space. We must learn to reclaim 'value', the values by which we live our lives within the context of that bloody sacrifice, but also the value of the human person which so much of modern society, the hotel lobby included, is trying to deny.

References

Benjamin, Walter, *The Arcades Project* (Cambridge: Harvard University Press, 2002).

Eco, Umberto, *Faith in Fakes: Travels in Hyperreality* (London: Minerva 1995).

Crawford, Margaret, 'The World in a Shopping Mall', in Michael Sorkin (ed.), *Variations on a Theme Park, The New American City and the End of Public Space* (New York: Hill and Wang, 1992).

Evans, Mark, *Open Up the Doors: Music in the Modern Church* (Sheffield: Equinox, 2006).

Farrell, James, *One Nation Under Gods: Malls and the Seduction of American Shopping* (Washington: Smithsonian Books, 2003).

Flanagan, Kieran, *Sociology and Liturgy: Re-presentations of the Holy* (London: Macmillan, 1991).

Kant, Immanuel, *Critique of the Power of Judgement* (Cambridge: Cambridge University Press, 2000).

Kavanagh, Aidan, *On Liturgical Theology* (New York: Pueblo Publishing Company, 1984).

Kracauer, Siegfried, 'The Hotel Lobby', in Malcolm Miles, Tim Hall and Iain Borden (eds), *The City Cultures Reader*, 2nd ed. (London: Routledge, 2004).

Martin, David, *The Breaking of the Image: A Sociology of Christian Theory and Practice* (Oxford: Blackwell, 1980).

Sorkin, Michael, 'See You in Disneyland', in Michael Sorkin (ed.), *Variations on a Theme Park: The New American City and the End of Public Space* (New York: Hill and Wang, 1992).

Spinks, Bryan, *The Worship Mall: Contemporary Responses to Contemporary Culture* (London: SPCK, 2010).

Sterne, Jonathan, 'Sounds like the Mall of America: Programmed Music and the Architechtonics of Commercial Space', *Ethnomusicology*, 14/1 (1997): 22–50.

Stringer, Martin, *A Sociological History of Christian Worship* (Cambridge: Cambridge University Press, 2005).

Torevell, David, *Losing the Sacred: Ritual, Modernity and Liturgical Reform* (Edinburgh: T & T Clark, 2000).

Turner, Victor, *The Ritual Process: Structure and Anti-Structure* (Harmondsworth: Penguin Books, 1969).

Ward, Peter, *Selling Worship: How What We Sing has Changed the Church* (Bletchley: Paternoster Press, 2005).

Zepp, Ira, *The New Religious Image of Urban America: The Shopping Mall as Ceremonial Centre* (Niwot: University Press of Colorado, 1986).

Chapter 11

'Really Worshipping', not 'Just Singing'

Gordon Adnams

During the last decades of the twentieth century, Christian congregational music in much of the Western world and beyond underwent significant changes. In the Canadian context (where this research was conducted), the two most prominent worship styles that emerged are inadequately referred to as 'traditional' and 'contemporary' and feature very different sung material and approaches to singing. The music of 'contemporary' worship consists of songs characterized by simple, popular styles of text, music and instrumentation. These 'Praise and Worship' choruses are accompanied by guitars, keyboard and drums and often completely replace traditional chorale-style hymns and revivalist songs accompanied by organ and piano. Hymnbooks are left in the rack in favour of the digital projection of song texts onto screens, and in many cases, choirs disappear giving way to self-sufficient, amplified, small vocal ensembles fronting the band.

Congregational singing at 'contemporary' Christian worship gatherings is often referred to as 'worship' even though other significant religious actions such as prayer, scripture reading and preaching may be prominently present. Despite this conflation of singing and worship, it would be problematic to make assumptions about the inner state of any singer.

In an attempt to understand the singing experience itself and to uncover its deeper significance in Christian worship, I conducted research[1] in a church in a western Canadian city that offered two distinct types of congregational song: a group of two or three choruses accompanied by a guitar-based ensemble and two or three songs taken from the hymnal, accompanied by the organ and piano. The hymns and choruses were always equally represented i.e. if two choruses were sung, two hymns were also sung. I chose this setting because some years before my research activity, the congregation engaged in the discussion of whether or not to offer two different worship services – traditional and contemporary – and decided for this 'blended' style. Another attractive aspect was that the church had no particular ethnic roots or a majority generational component. It was comprised of a roughly equal representation of all age groups, primarily white, well-educated middle class families, with a few more recent adherents of Asian and African descent.

---

[1] Gordon Adnams, 'The Experience of Congregational Singing: An Ethno-Phenomenological Approach' (PhD diss., University of Alberta, 2008), http://www.worshipsinging.ca.

Central to my research was asking congregational singers, 'What is happening inside you as you sing?' One of the most interesting themes to emerge was a contrast of experiences interviewees called 'just singing' and 'really worshipping'. The former was expressed as a negative state while the latter seemed to be the major goal for those who preferred contemporary choruses to traditional hymns.

In this chapter, 'just singing' and 'really worshipping' are explored through the lens of hermeneutic phenomenology as espoused by Max van Manen. Phenomenology attempts to give a 'direct description of our experience as it is'[2] and engages with the pre-reflective human world, the primary experience and the significances of it. It is therefore an effective framework for approaching the anecdotes given by research participants; lived experience descriptions form the core of the data required for this type of investigation. According to van Manen:

> A good description that constitutes the essence of something is construed so that
> the structure of a lived experience is revealed to us in such a fashion that we are
> now able to grasp the nature and significance of this experience in a hitherto
> unseen way.[3]

Based on passages selected from about twenty interview transcripts, what follows are phenomenological reflections on 'just singing' and particularly 'really worshipping'. The chapter then addresses some theological implications of 'really worshipping', providing a framework for Christian church leaders and musicians to more deeply consider the experience of congregational singing from a theological perspective.

Just Singing

The negative concept of just singing can be described in general terms in the words of Helen,[4] a middle-aged teacher:

> There are far too many times in church when I'm just singing. I'm just going
> through the motions without any significant thought about what I'm singing.
> I'm there in body but not necessarily in mind. I know the song and I can sing
> the words, and my mind may be somewhere else. I could even be thinking about
> something completely unrelated to church.

---

[2]   Maurice Merleau-Ponty, *The Phenomenology of Perception* (Routledge & Kegan Paul, 1962), p. vii.

[3]   Max van Manen, *Researching Lived Experience: Human Science for an Action Sensitive Pedagogy*, 2nd ed. (The Althouse Press, 1997), p. 39.

[4]   All the names of interviewees have been changed to assure anonymity.

Can we account for this divided or shallow attention to singing – just singing – that may be the experience of some singers? There doesn't seem to be a fresh momentum of thought being stimulated and enabled by the effortlessness of singing a known song. Fresh thoughts may appear to be in the foreground of the experience of some singers but they are not necessarily thoughts in any way related to the singing. It would seem that the quality of the re-singing of a song is contingent upon the degree and nature of attention given to in the moment re-living-through the song. This is the singer's challenge.

Based on the interviews, I propose a typology of experiences within 'just singing': un-minded singing, meaningless words and dispassionate singing.

'Un-Minded' Singing

> I was singing a familiar hymn and at some point during the second verse, I 'checked out', I didn't realize it until we got to the end of the verse and then I sort of woke up to the fact that for the past few moments, I had been completely unaware of what I was singing or even that I was singing! (Janet, a young professional)

This singer apparently began to sing purposely, paying attention to what she was doing and then, at some point, her awareness was somehow redirected. Although or because the song is familiar, consciousness of it fades and singing the song becomes untended or neglected. Thinking about something else, attention is on another place or subject. Singing on autopilot is an apt metaphor: all systems are operational as prearranged and are programmed into the controlling mechanism – the autopilot – therefore there is no need for superintendence. The pilot is now free to attend to other things. In that moment the mind has wandered, as if it has places to go; there are more interesting or important things with which to occupy itself. Singing has somehow slipped away from mindfulness and is replaced by another stream of thought.

When singers return from the mental excursion away from singing, there is recognition of temporary amnesia; for a time, the singers were unaware of how their body was engaged. However, while unaware of the act of singing, there is a memory of the appealing thoughts experienced. Is this like snoring and dreaming? When we are asleep we don't hear the sounds our bodies are making, but we are enjoying what is going on in our minds. But these singers are not asleep and their thoughts are not dreams. These are people in a church, with other singers, reading words from a page or screen, making sounds. Is it like daydreaming? Any sense of 'being there' seems directed not by attention to space or time or body but only by attentiveness to thought. The mind is indeed active, but separated from any other consciousness. Singing in this state is not mindless; however, the singers are not minding their singing. Thinking about singing is apparently not necessary to its replication; it has become by rote – 'mechanical or habitual repetition'.[5] Like

---

[5]   *The Oxford English Reference Dictionary*, 2nd ed.

machines that have no thoughts, we can respond to a command and our singing is set in motion to proceed un-mindedly.

'Meaningless' Words

> Sometimes, I must admit, I just sing the words. I'm just going through the motions, without really being deep in thought about the whole song. Other times I find myself sometimes so caught up in the music or trying to harmonize or read the actual parts of the music [the melody or harmony] that I lose the sense of what the words are saying. (Vince, a university student)

In this mode of (dis)engagement, there seems to be an awareness of the sounds of singing, of what is being sung, but not a significance of it, especially the words. It is possible that the narrative and emotive meaning of the words recedes into the background or becomes dissolved into some other kind of experience of meaningfulness that has less to do with the words than with the more elemental significance of the singing experience itself. Perhaps when the hymnic quality of the text becomes more musical, then the 'message' or the meaning content of the hymn or chorus loses its prominence.

> I really get 'into' singing when I concentrate on God, but it's always a struggle for me at church. If I'm not careful, all of a sudden I'm singing not for worship, but because of the beat of the drum, the music. I get caught off guard and get really stimulated by the music. I get this high, this feeling of euphoria and excitement and I start to perspire. This happens at every church service. I can feel the beat in me. I try to control myself, even the clapping of my hands. I try not to get into this because I can get carried away with the music not thinking about God. (Tim, a young father)

Interaction with the creation of music itself or the execution of the music by accompanists can have a powerful effect. The physicality of music – the pulse, the movement – can evoke a bodily response that is so prominent that it overshadows all engagement with the text. The irresistible nature of this musical drive has resonance with the beat of a primal mechanism that sustains human life – a pulsing heart. This is much more than the unconscious tapping of the foot or hand to the beat of a song; it can become an invasion, a synchronized occupation of the body.

This contest between words about or directed towards God and the power of music has ancient roots. The fourth century philosopher and Christian church leader Augustine of Hippo, as a listener to sacred song, was similarly troubled: 'When ... it happens that the singing has a more powerful effect on me than the sense of what is sung, I confess my sin and my need of repentance, and then I would rather not hear any singer.'[6]

------

[6]   Augustine, *The Confessions*, trans. Maria Boulding (Vintage Books, 1997), p. 230.

Music by itself draws attention to itself as sound without any articulated reference that words bring.[7] We experience music alone and its 'more powerful effect' in ways that transcend accurate description, as we quickly discover when we try, often in vain, to describe our feelingful responses to pure music: that is, music without words.

But song is not music alone; song is the inseparable experience of music and word and in this marriage, many things happen to words when they are sung. Rock critic and author Greil Marcus posits that 'words in songs are sounds we can feel before they are statements to understand'.[8] Simon Frith, in his discussion of words in popular song says that '… it is the sound of the voice, not the words sung, which suggests what a singer *really* means'.[9] So, in a strange way, words may turn wordless in song; they may lose their propositional linguistic significance. When we speak a sentence propositionally we may state, claim, argue, ask or explain something; or we may urge, admonish or persuade someone to do something. But in song, these intentionalities may change. The words may become largely expressive and thus let go of their narrative or descriptive role.

> Singing enables us to step back from the word's immediacy as communication and to make it an aesthetic object; it allows us to contemplate and to celebrate the word rather than simply hear or speak it. It does not simply convey the word but places it in the context of 'something for which there are no words'.[10]

Singing a song gives us an aesthetic and artistic location, a place for us as singers to engage in musical creation. It is true that the words of a song grant us a known vocabulary, a link to our life-world, a familiar utterance within the more mysterious and less definable musical realm. In this musical experience of vocal music, words sung sometimes seem to take flight, as if being carried on the melody. They are now sculpted and directed by the music, released from their everyday semantics. Singers give breath to this non-semantic freshness of sung words and in so doing are able to articulate some sense of meaning that is other than the word.

'Dispassionate' Singing

> There are many times, probably most of the time, when I am just singing: enjoying the fact that I am singing, glad to be in church – all that positive stuff –

---

[7]   A concept proposed by Don Ihde in *Listening and Voice: A Phenomenology of Sound* (Ohio University Press, 1976).

[8]   Quoted in Simon Frith, *Sound Effects: Youth, Leisure and the Politics of Rock 'N' Roll* (Pantheon Books, 1981), p. 14.

[9]   Simon Frith, 'Why Do Songs Have Words?' in A. White (ed.), *Lost in Music; Culture, Style and Musical Event* (Routledge, 1987), p. 204, emphasis in the original.

[10]   Richard Viladesau, *Theology and the Arts: Encountering God through Music, Art and Rhetoric* (Paulist Press, 2000), p. 48.

but feeling nothing but this generic enjoyment. I could be singing about anything; it may as well not be a religious song because the rich, spiritual meanings of the texts are just not resonating with me. In my head, I believe the words I'm singing but I don't feel them in the way that tells me I am singing something special or connected to my spiritual life. (Betty, an older businesswoman)

It is also possible to sing being fully cognizant of some significance of the tune and text and yet not have an adequate feeling of the song. Can we uncover this sense of barrenness by exploring what is not there? How are we to understand the feeling that a song sometimes does not resonate? It would seem that for a song to resonate and produce a certain feeling, it must somehow be felt to have a deep inward trajectory in addition to the sense of singing out.

The Latin root of resonate is *resonatia* which means echo[11] – a repetition of sound by reflection.[12] According to the expectations of some singers, a song that 'resonates' is penetrating them, somehow addressing them and they are co-responding with and to the address. Singers want something of their being to sound back in an imitative reply to what is being sung, desiring a parallel sounding of the sound, a sympathetic vibration to be sensed profoundly within them. It is feeling that the song is beyond merely knowing; it is in some way possessed by them and they are possessed by the totality of the song.

In the light of the opposite, can we now more fully understand this dispassionate singing described by Betty? It appears that the song does not adequately penetrate her or sing to her in the desired way. She senses that in the occasion of singing, she is responding differently than that which is called for in and by the song; Betty is not sung by the song. Dispassionate singers are sounding, but not resounding from an adequate depth; but it is a safe and comfortable shallowness. Perhaps it is like having a polite conversation with friends about ordinary things – pleasant but not passionate. Do we not live most of our lives on this level? Perhaps there is an expectation that congregational singers will enter each song with the kind of vulnerability that allows the song to shape the singers, and their singing. A dispassionate singer apparently does not adequately experience this or allow this to happen.

Really Worshipping

The following are excerpts from descriptive anecdotes given by 'really worshipping' congregational singers in response to the question: 'What is happening inside you as you sing?' After the general exploration, I offer a typology within really worshipping: feeling the words, familiar words, repetition and my song given to God.

---

[11]   *The Concise Oxford Dictionary of English Etymology* (1996).
[12]   *The Oxford English Reference Dictionary.*

> When I'm worshipping, I'm paying attention mostly to the words that I'm singing and the sound of the song itself. I usually close my eyes; it's a way for me to kind of tune out the people and the distractions that are going on around me. And I find that when I've got my eyes closed, I can focus much more on the words and just get to that stage of worship a lot more quickly. Basically, worship is when you get to the point when you're communicating with God rather than just singing for singing. There's a pretty fuzzy line there. But I think it's very possible to sing a lot of worship songs and never really worship. Part of knowing you've really worshipped is the feeling of being emotionally invested in what you are singing. And sometimes it's more cerebral than that; just kind of realizing that what you're singing is applying to yourself and to the way that you feel about God. So, a good worship experience for me is when I feel like I've connected with God and when I'm not just singing the songs, but I'm singing the song for a reason. (Ruth, a young adult)

Ruth clearly contrasts 'really worshipping' with 'just singing'. It appears that just singing is not merely a type of (dis)engagement with song, but apparently missing a major point or purpose of singing in the worship service. The singer, while just singing, is not experiencing on a satisfactory level what has been interpreted as connecting with God. According to the interviewees, the recipe for just singing seems to include: not being vulnerable to music or being too vulnerable to the power of music, no relating to the text and not being able to sense that the song is really saying what I feel. Just singing is a lost opportunity for a central dimension of what has been presented and understood as the experience of worship.

The dictionary definition of worship is homage or reverence paid to a deity, especially in a formal service and in its archaic roots, it meant worthiness, merit; recognition given or due; honour and respect.[13] In the enactment under study, worship appears to be a serious endeavour in which personal devotion is proclaimed, and in this act of proclamation, it is invested with individual significance. When worship is sung, it becomes more than a song: it is a confession of a truth, a gathering of as much of self as can be expressed in sincerity and proclaimed in public to God with a sense of privacy appropriate to personal communion. And this conception of worship seems to be contingent, depending on whether or not the song and the act of singing it generates and reflects 'how I feel' about God.

Feeling the Words

Sarah, a university student said:

> There are days I'm very joyful and there are days when I'm a lot more mellow. It's just like you can read the words and they're just words or you can kind of start to feel the words. It's hard to explain what you're feeling then. If you were

---

[13]   *The Oxford English Reference Dictionary.*

to just say the words – I mean you probably could just say them and eventually you would feel like you were worshipping. But when you're singing them, you are allowed to pour so much more emotion into them. At least, for me that's the way I express myself emotionally.

Really worshipping singers seem to experience something feelingful and rich that is centred on and given form primarily by the sung word. This is a mutual investment as words are allowed to trigger a response from the singer, who then pours something of self back into the words as they are sung: sung words give impetus to feelings; feelings are given to sung words.

> There are often times when I feel that this [song] is really saying what I feel. So I guess that's worship isn't it? It's an identification, it's a relating to what is being sung, and I think that can happen even when somebody else is singing and I really, really get into … [no words here] … I guess music is the ultimate worship experience in that I can really relate to what is being spoken [sic], and that can take me into a worship experience. (Emily, a grandmother)

Simon Frith posits that 'to sing words is to elevate them in some way, to make them special, to give them a new form of intensity. This is obvious in the use of singing to mark off religious expression from the everyday use of words.'[14] To feel words, sung or spoken, they have to be drawn near, brought within reach, grasped and admitted inside our various boundaries. When words are held at a distance, they are more likely kept outside, looked at, merely read and sung dispassionately or un-mindedly, not as easily gathered into deep significance. This is just singing in its various manifestations. But when we are able to more fully engage with song and singing, the presentation of words is altered. In melody, word-sounds can be smooth or jagged, lie flat, move up or down or both, and they can change in duration and repeat in ways that would seem ridiculous if spoken. In a myriad of manners, song guarantees the delivery of its lyrics in a diversity of shapes, colours and contours. Transformed, they issue a clear invitation for sensitized singers to come near, to explore, expand and elucidate each syllable, every vowel and consonant. As a result singers can delight in expressive exploration of words' nooks and crannies – feeling them. Singers who are really worshipping are purposefully singing, deliberately mining every word to discover a greater realization of its potential for feelingfulness.

Maurice Merleau-Ponty, the French phenomenologist, says:

> If we consider only the conceptual and delimiting meaning of words, it is true that the verbal form … appears arbitrary. But it would no longer appear so if we took into account the emotional content of the word, which we have called … its 'gestural' sense, which is all-important in poetry, for example. It

---

[14]   Simon Frith, *Performing Rites* (Harvard University Press, 1996), p. 172.

would then be found that the words, vowels and phonemes are so many ways of 'singing' the world, and that their function is to represent things not, as the naïve onomatopoeic theory had it, by reason of an objective resemblance, but because they extract, and literally express, their emotional essence.[15]

But even as the emotional essence of every word is being explored, song constrains the singer within the confines of its larger structural boundaries: phrases and sentences, verses and refrains. These limit meanings and bind the song to the singer, not as a restrictive event but as a recognizable episode about something that may be full of latent journeys into self and of whatever the song sings about. Every song in its totality can then become a portal to a somewhat more definable world of thoughts and sentiments.

Familiar Words

Cathy contrasted her experience of hymn texts with those of choruses:

> With hymns it is much more about the words. There's a lot of powerful stuff packed in the hymns. I really enjoy singing them and un-compacting them and really seeing what the words mean. And with choruses, it's much more of an emotional reaction.

However, Norman said that he has to 'figure out' the hymns:

> [When a chorus is repeated] I can continue to sing it and continue to be a part of the song and continue thinking instead of just reading some words on a page that I'm not familiar with and trying to figure out the hymns and the harmonies.

It seems that some worshippers highly value words that speak quickly to them and through them, not demanding explanation or analysis. This is in contrast to a thick vocabulary which, when presented in a melody, becomes time-bound and frustrates some singers as the text is inadequately apprehended and comprehended: it is too much, too fast.

As Ben reported, 'With a hymn ... you've constantly got new things that you're singing about. Sometimes it's more difficult to get past listening to the words and music for itself, to get to the point when you're actually using them as communication.'

When words in song are perceived to be immediately accessible, hospitable and familiar they can be welcomed as native tongue. In that moment of encounter, sentiments may be more easily aroused by all of what the song is and says, for within many worshippers lie named, recognized feelings that await animation by the singing of song. However, song can also outline un-nameable feelings;

---

[15]   Maurice Merleau-Ponty, *The Phenomenology of Perception*, p. 217.

possibly it is in this capacity that the music has more power than the word. In both instances, what is sung with feeling may now effortlessly resonate with the substance of one's life and the song becomes my song given.

Repetition

Norman, a young man just beginning his career in a new city, told of his experience with the common practice of singing choruses many times over in the worship service:

> When Dad used to come to the church I went to in Vancouver, he didn't like the repetition of the choruses at all. When we got to the second or third time through, he had the attitude, 'We've sung this already.' The point was done for him, while I was still in that feeling-out-the-song stage; maybe still thinking about things that were going on at work, thinking about the words themselves – not worshipping yet – and so I don't mind repeating as much.

Reiteration draws attention. For some singers, repeating the whole or part of a song creates unnecessary or unwelcome interest. For example, if, after the first pass, the words are found to be too familiar, trite and shallow, or even immediately satisfying in their eloquence, a second incantation may be a pointless exercise.
     Norman continued:

> ... when it comes to singing worship songs, just singing them through once, I don't always have a chance to really meditate on the words. I find I can sing with much more feeling if I have a chance to kind of meditate on the words and really think about what they mean to me while I'm singing them. But I like it when a song repeats a few times. Part of that is because I really don't have a significant amount of musical talent, and when I can participate in a song more and continue to sing, I enjoy that.

Ruth, another young adult told of the significance to her of singing a chorus more than once:

> [With the choruses] there's a lot of repetition and the first couple of times through ... it takes a while to kind of switch from being aware of your surroundings to being aware of communion with God ... So the first few times, I'm listening to people around me and listening to myself sing, then after I've had the repetition, I can tune that out and focus on actual worship. I think the repetition of the words play into my focus on worship.

For some singers, repetition presents an opportunity for further discovery. It draws out a song, offering more time for participants to be in the song. As well, the song can now draw out from each singer new import, extra insight and added awareness. Some worshippers need this time for words to evolve; for ideas to become expressions of self, for voiced feelings about God to be personally felt and then authentically sung to God in and as worship. Actual worship apparently is achieved when the worshipper is able to possess, feel and offer the sung words wholeheartedly to God as a personal communication.

My Song Given to God

Ruth explained that, 'By the end [of the song] I'm able to take the words and use those as my own, whereas at the beginning I'm just singing something that is in front of me.' While singing, a transaction of importance seems to change some singers' relationship with the song. Paul Ricoeur, in analysing readers' responses to story, describes what he calls appropriation:

> [A]ppropriation is the process by which the revelation of new modes of being ... gives the subject new capacities for knowing himself. If the reference of a text is the projection of a world, then it is not ... the reader who projects himself. The reader is rather broadened in his capacity to project himself by receiving a new mode of being from the text itself.[16]

Although the contemporary worship song is not usually in narrative form, it does project a world of concepts and worshipful sentiment about and towards a Deity and calls the singer to a state of agreement and feelingfulness, a place where one can really worship relying on a sensitive awareness of one's enlarged, in-the-moment mode of being.

It is clear that singing and song provide both the means and the matter for worship. Perhaps an effective worship song can be likened to a church window of stained glass, a casement of multi-shaded expression through which the Divine is sought, adored, celebrated, petitioned. It may contain the substance of worship: the scene, the characters, the gestures, the intentions. Sometimes it may be conceptually vague, abstract, while in its form it furnishes rich layered implications.

A stained glass window has many shapes, textures and hues that are subtly dependent on light seen through and brought toward. Its effectiveness depends on from where we see or our point of view – like knowledge and experience that filters and tints meanings. We are able to worship by virtue of our position and our response. When standing before such a luminous scene, we can bathe in its light; our own bodies bear and absorb its colours, and we may see ourselves as partakers of and participants in the representation. As the transformed and transforming light is splayed upon us, we may be changed for the moment, or perhaps forever. And so it is when singing-in-song-in-worship.

---

[16]   Paul Ricoeur, 'Appropriation', in Mario Valdes (ed.), *A Ricoeur Reader: Reflection and Imagination* (University of Toronto Press, 1991), p. 97.

Some worshippers need to feel secluded, alone with God in the crowd. As one interviewee reported: 'I usually close my eyes; it's a way for me to kind of tune out the people and the distractions that are going on around me.' Kate, a middle-aged nurse similarly said:

> I quite often close my eyes, presuming I know the words and the music, because I can block out what's around me. I really don't care who's there. And I sing as if I don't care who's there, because I'm not singing for you or them; I'm really singing for the Lord.

There is irony here. Eyes are closed to shut out all of the other singers who are necessary for the occasion of singing in a worship service. But at some point in time, they apparently become a distraction for a really worshipping member whose goal appears to be a private, inner awareness of communicating to God the personalized feelings named in the communally sung words.

How are we to understand the sense of being alone with God while singing with others? Part of the feelingful response to a song is a product of singing in a group. We have all experienced the effect of communal emotion – we laugh more heartily at a TV comedy when we are watching together with friends than when we are by ourselves. Likewise, the point of the laugh track provided by the producers of the programme is to offer the illusion of not being alone in our amusement. Somehow, a group can supply additional inspiration upon which we draw for richer participation in an event. Inspiration is defined as 'a supposed force or influence on poets, artists, musicians, etc., stimulating creative activity, exalted thoughts etc.'[17] But we know that this extends far beyond the so-called creative community named. For anyone to really worship, it is evident that the content of the songs sung must be inspiring: able to stimulate exalted thoughts and feelings. As well, the intent of the singer should be to ascribe honour to God: worship. With these in place, even though singers seem to want to ignore other singers, the context of this activity remains communal and thus influential.

But the intentional awareness of the worshipper has been shifted. Like a zoom lens, the focal point excludes all but the subject; everything else is on the periphery, present in the reality outside the lens, but unseen within its bounds. Self and sentiment 'about' seem to be all that is of consequence: *my* words, how *I* feel. The wonder of *us* before God, the multi-voiced local community that has been called into being seems to be merely a setting that allows the individual to begin the journey towards communing with God privately. Many singers achieve a state of feeling something that is interpreted as an individual connection with God, a sense of personally communicating, of singing alone to Deity. The link becomes perceptible once the singer has entered this mode of being called 'really worshipping' that appears to depend on the worshippers' abilities to respond to the evocative power of a song – words and music. As feelings are felt and expressed,

---

[17]   *The Oxford English Reference Dictionary.*

they are turned towards God, each worshipper believing God to be listening, hearing not just my song but also the depth of personal significance I have given to the song and my investment of my sentiment. Emotional arousal seems to be the gauge by which each worshipper measures his or her sincerity.

Singing and worship seem to be phenomena that are intertwined. For each singer, one challenge appears as a need to know, in some manner, that in the moment of singing, what is inside is the same as what is outside; that what is sung is what is felt to be real and expressed authentically in and as worship. In this sense, each congregational singer is in his or her own reality, alone in the crowd but nonetheless necessary to the union that is the communal voice.

Theological Implications

These descriptions given by congregational singers offer clues to theological themes embedded in the experience of really worshipping. I have organized these themes in three sections: the nature of truth, the nature of faith in worship and the nature of the singing congregation.

The Nature of Sung Truth – To 'Resonate'

The term 'resonate' is much used in common parlance to describe some sort of personal identification with another person, a circumstance, an idea or an event. In contemporary culture, this feeling called resonance is often an arbiter of a kind of truth. For one who is really worshipping, a song becomes 'personal truth' – a sense that the song resonates with me, that what it is saying (text) and how it is said (music) is true for me, for this moment in my life and that I can sing it as my words, my song. The possibility of insincere or inauthentic singing drives worshippers, especially the younger cohort, to desire the feelings of resonance and personal authenticity in worship. Passionate worship is the goal as opposed to dutiful worship. However, for resonance to occur, self becomes the immovable against which the song bounces and evokes this particular kind of feeling. Theological truth of the text and the relative worthiness of the music are not prime necessities for resonance, although they may be part of the equation. That the words and music resonate is the prime condition for personal truth – authenticity. And so the self becomes the arbiter of what is true. One could say that if a song resonates, it rings with personal truth and can therefore be offered and experienced as real worship.

The view that really worshipping is inseparable from singing a certain kind of song, one that I like and therefore resonates with me in a specific way, is predicted on self-referential judgement – autonomy.

The Nature of Faith in Worship – To 'Feel'

In Christian worship, one sings to the unseen and so the communicative process of worship singing is usually understood as being through faith. 'Faith is the substance of things hoped for, the evidence of things unseen' (Heb.11: 1, KJV). Harold Best comments on this important Christian concept to say: 'Faith does not bring substance and evidence to something; faith is itself substance and evidence even in the absence of the very things for which faith hopes.'[18] But those desiring to really worship want to get to the place where they feel near to God and feel they are communicating with a Deity that has no physical presence and therefore offers no voiced or embodied response to their adoration. Perhaps it is because of this absence and silence that achieving a feelingful response in and to worship singing and song has become so important. And not only because it is deemed authentic worship but also because these feelings may be recognized as a response that encompasses a 'reply' from God who therefore must be near. And if this is so, then these generated feelings may supply substance and grant assurance that the singing worshipper is in communion with God and has been heard, understood and accepted.

The Nature of the Singing Congregation – 'For Me'

Really worshipping with all of its dimensions is best achieved in and because of the large group meeting; the affect of everyone singing, the leadership of a band (or organ) in a room are all necessary and contribute to the achievement of personally expressive worship. The crowd of singers and the leaders are a necessary ingredient for participation but they need to be backgrounded for personal worship to occur – to be aware of only God and self. In this desire for isolation, the social context, the affiliation with fellow worshippers has become instrumental to individual aspirations and at the same time essential to authentic worship or really worshipping.

Some Concluding Observations

From the witnesses who have spoken of their experiences as congregational singers, we know that singing is not merely the production of songs by vocalists. Singing involves the singer in multi-layered interactions with and around music and word, content and context, attention and intent. Such interactions may produce in each singer actions and reactions that are subtle, interior, deeply felt, or perhaps felt minimally, evoking little response other than producing sound. And all of

---

[18]   Harold Best, *Unceasing Worship: Biblical Perspectives on Worship and the Arts* (InterVarsity Press, 2003), p. 29.

these experiences of singing are melded into notions of worship and interpreted in the light of personal authenticity.

Really worshipping is an experience that is important, positive and pleasurable for the individual singer, but also narrow, exclusive and very contingent. As such, it is more sought than found. However, leaders of congregational singing in the contemporary worship tradition are often under great pressure to generate the environment that will foster really worshipping.

When disputes over congregational singing surface in the context of a local church, the pursuit of really worshipping is often overlooked as a point of contention or merely regarded as individuality. However, it is a subtle and underestimated influence that has implications for all the gathered singers. Really worshipping positions congregational singing and song as crucial components in the creation of an intensely individual, private, interior worshipful state and in so doing instrumentalizes the congregation and truncates the communal aspect of singing and its potential. In addition, as individuals pursue really worshipping, the possibility for authentically singing the song of 'the other' – a song that does not resonate with me but is cherished by a fellow worshipper – becomes problematic, if not impossible.

To better reflect the experience of congregational singers, Christian worshippers need to disentangle singing and worship in the way they think and speak and at the same time adjust their expectations of congregational singing. I join with other voices – authors such as Marva Dawn, Donald Hustad and Harold Best[19] – in advocating for a clearer differentiation between worship, broadly defined as a Godward orientation of life (communal, public, personal, individual, private) and acts of worship as actions (communal, public, personal, individual, private) that stem from a worship orientation.[20] This distinction between worship and singing positions congregational singing as only one of many possible acts of worship and may serve to take the pressure off the achievement of really worshipping. Congregational singers can then be free to reframe all congregational singing, including 'just singing', as simultaneously personal and communal offerings of variable, multi-dimensional intensity. And this broader view also opens the possibility for singers to grow beyond personal stylistic preferences used for 'really worshipping' to a more inclusive communal repertoire, which welcomes the songs of the other.

---

[19]   Any works by these authors present a wide definition of worship that is not primarily music-based.

[20]   Acts of worship may or may not generate feelings identified as worshipful, but are never-the-less actions driven by a desire to honour God. This is the subject of another discussion.

References

Adnams, Gordon, 'The Experience of Congregational Singing: An Ethno-Phenomenological Approach' (PhD diss., University of Alberta, 2008).

Augustine, *The Confessions*, trans. Maria Boulding (New York: Vintage Books, 1997).

Best, Harold, *Unceasing Worship: Biblical Perspectives on Worship and the Arts* (Downers Grove, IL: InterVarsity Press, 2003).

Frith, Simon, *Sound Effects: Youth, Leisure and the Politics of Rock 'N' Roll* (New York: Pantheon Books, 1981).

Frith, Simon, 'Why Do Songs Have Words?' in A. White (ed.), *Lost in Music: Culture, Style and Musial Event* (London: Routledge, 1987).

Frith, Simon, *Performing Rites* (Cambridge, MA: Harvard University Press, 1996).

Ihde, Don, *Listening and Voice: A Phenomenology of Sound* (Athens, OH: Ohio University Press, 1976).

Merleau-Ponty, Maurice, *The Phenomenology of Perception* (London: Routledge & Kegan Paul, 1962).

van Manen, Max, *Researching Lived Experience: Human Science for an Action Sensitive Pedagogy*, 2nd ed. (London, ON: The Althouse Press, 1997).

Ricoeur, Paul, 'Appropriation', in Mario Valdes (ed.), *A Ricoeur Reader: Reflection and Imagination* (Toronto: University of Toronto Press, 1991).

Viladesau, Richard, *Theology and the Arts: Encountering God through Music, Art and Rhetoric* (New York: Paulist Press, 2000).

Chapter 12

Moving Between Musical Worlds: Worship Music, Significance and Ethics in the Lives of Contemporary Worshippers

Mark Porter

The latter decades of the twentieth century saw the increasing adoption of forms of popular music in congregational worship (known collectively as 'contemporary worship music' or simply 'worship music'), initially within the American and British church, but increasingly on a broader international scale. Within the discourses of contemporary worship music[1] it is often assumed that music is, in many senses, a fundamentally neutral medium.[2] Differences in musical taste are on the one hand frequently set aside as matters of personal preference of little relevance to the spiritual task at hand during congregational worship. On the other hand, they are engaged in a purely pragmatic manner in order to connect with particular demographics that are assumed to be attached to a certain style.[3] Whilst these discourses have served an important function in the growth of the contemporary worship music scene, providing a defence for the admission of certain styles of music into worship and teaching worshippers to set aside self-centred concerns when gathering together, they have also served to hold back the discussion of important aspects of musical practice, meaning and experience, relegating them to the realm of private feeling or simple preference and restraining

---

[1] That is, the public discourses present and employed within the context of the Church by leadership, musicians, and congregation members where contemporary worship music has become established practice, as well as those employed in its support where there still remains an element of contestation. See Anna E. Nekola, 'Between This World and the Next: The Musical "Worship Wars" and Evangelical Ideology in the United States 1960–2005' (PhD diss., University of Wisconsin-Madison, 2009). For how this collective/official discourse often differs from that of ordinary individuals, see Martin D. Stringer, *On the Perception of Worship: The Ethnography of Worship in Four Christian Congregations in Manchester* (University of Birmingham Press, 1999), p. 69.

[2] Monique M. Ingalls, 'Awesome in This Place: Sound, Space, and Identity in Contemporary North American Evangelical Worship' (PhD diss., University of Pennsylvania, 2008); Nekola, 'Between This World and the Next'.

[3] Gerardo Marti, *Worship Across the Racial Divide: Religious Music and the Multiracial Congregation* (Oxford University Press, 2012).

their contestation and entry into discourse – a move which raises important ethical as well as political questions.

Monique Ingalls suggests that opening up the discourse to include a broader range of concerns 'involve[s] rejection (or at least a heavy reworking) of contemporary Christian music's founding ideology that style is a neutral vehicle for the Christian message',[4] a position that might render doing so a somewhat problematic exercise. The prospect of reworking the ideology, however, seems less problematic than a complete rejection. Whilst the ideology is common within contemporary worship music it is not one that is necessarily essential to its on-going life. The presentation of musical style as neutral came about largely as a reaction against those who would dismiss popular styles of music as bad or inappropriate for Christian usage – the initial ascription of neutrality to musics arose as a plea not to be rejected out of hand.[5] The wider Church has since come to a level of acceptance of a range of musics which renders such discourse less necessary than it once was, and provides space for a move beyond the founding ideology. Moreover, a framework which seeks to open up discussion of a range of concerns surrounding the significance of a variety of aspects of different musics is one in which worship music's initial bid for acceptance could have been evaluated in a less polemical manner. A conversation that allows each voice to the table and surrounds and engages it with a range of others is one that has the potential to deepen and broaden rather than undermine the purposes that gave birth to the contemporary worship movement.

Ascriptions of neutrality have also, over the course of time, acquired other significance. The fear of distraction from the spiritual aspect of worship is a recurring theme within talk about worship music.[6] Christians worry that talking about music and potentially ascribing power to it in a setting where direct encounter with God is expected risks ascribing power to an aspect of the experience that should not become powerful and potentially confuses the source of encounter. Talk about music, in other words, is talk that has the potential to detract from 'proper spirituality' rather than open up important aspects of spiritual experience, mediation and negotiation. Such concerns again seem to stem from a particular conception of what music-talk might be expected to look like – if musical style is neutral and primarily a matter of personal preference then talk about music will have significance only on a relatively meaningless level and thus will inevitably be a distraction from the true purposes of worship. I want to suggest that in examining experiences in which music already takes on a range of meanings and significance we find that rather than distract from the core concerns of worship we enter more deeply into them.

---

[4] Ingalls, 'Awesome in This Place', p. 248.

[5] Ingalls, 'Awesome in This Place', p. 110; Nekola, 'Between This World and the Next', p. 261.

[6] Gordon Adnams, 'The Experience of Congregational Singing: An Ethno-Phenomenological Approach' (PhD diss., University of Alberta, Spring 2008), p. 115; Marti, *Worship Across the Racial Divide*, p. 88.

In my research interviews, undertaken in the early months of 2012 as part of my doctoral research, I asked approximately 40 members of St Aldates church in Oxford firstly to talk to me about their musical lives and experiences, and then to talk specifically about their experiences of music in worship. We then went on to discuss any interesting points of contact or divergence between the two narratives they offered. This came out of an interest in how people negotiate the movement between different musical worlds and the varying ways in which this negotiation can take place.[7] In focusing initially on experiences of music outside of worship I deliberately geared the discussion in such a way as to attempt to cut through the normal patterns of worship-music discourse (in which music is often marginal to discussion) and to open up a space for taking concerns centred specifically around music seriously.[8] The research serves to open up the question of the relationship between a worshipper's individual musical life and their experience within the worshipping community of the church. Through discussion of musical experience the interviews opened up a broad range of issues touching on themes such as community, value, meaning, boundaries, diversity, ethics, mission, character and divine encounter, many bound up closely with questions of musical style. Through the interviews it can be very quickly seen that questions of musical style within the church, even one in which a relatively stable pattern has been reached, are far from neutral, indeed they embody, enact and negotiate a range of key theological, ethical and ecclesiological questions in ways that reach beyond those typically acknowledged in the community discourse.[9] Such conversations serve to reinforce the importance of taking music-talk seriously within the church community and within theological discussion of music and provide a wide range of starting points for discussion.

The range of issues that arise serves to highlight the complex negotiations that take place around the musical life of a worshipping community and, as such, they avoid pointing to any particular model of what the musical practices of the church should look like. They suggest, instead, the importance of opening up an

---

[7] Timothy Rice, 'Time, Place, and Metaphor in Musical Experience and Ethnography', *Ethnomusicology*, 47/2 (2003): pp. 151–79; Tia DeNora, *Music in Everyday Life* (Cambridge University Press, 2000); Tia DeNora, *After Adorno: Rethinking Music Sociology* (Cambridge University Press, 2003); Nancy Tatom Ammerman, *Studying Congregations: A New Handbook* (Abingdon Press, 1998). Antoine Hennion, 'Pragmatics of Taste', in Mark Jacobs and Nancy Hanrahan (eds), *The Blackwell Companion to the Sociology of Culture* (Wiley-Blackwell, 2005); Harris M. Berger, *Metal, Rock, and Jazz: Perception and the Phenomenology of Musical Experience* (University Press of New England [for] Wesleyan University Press, 1999); Harris M. Berger, *Stance: Ideas About Emotion, Style, and Meaning for the Study of Expressive Culture* (Wesleyan University Press, 2009).

[8] Antoine Hennion, 'Music Lovers: Taste as Performance', *Theory, Culture & Society*, 18/5 (2001): p. 5.

[9] Stringer, *On the Perception of Worship*; Mathew Guest, '"Friendship, Fellowship and Acceptance": The Public Discourse of a Thriving Evangelical Congregation', in Mathew Guest, Karin Tusting and Linda Woodhead (eds), *Congregational Studies in the UK: Christianity in a Post-Christian Context* (Ashgate, 2004).

on-going conversation within the church community that allows its worshipping life to be enriched by the diverse range of perspectives on music present within it. The communal discourse of the church needs the ability to handle the range of experiences and perspectives of its members. Such discussion would move worship music away from being seen as a neutral canvas towards a performative space rich with meaning. In allowing dissenting voices to be heard it would bring them into dialogue with a range of other perspectives, into an open forum of negotiation and transformation.[10] In realizing that musical style is not simply a matter of private taste a valuable space is opened up, where values and issues can be raised in ways that enable genuinely meaningful dialogue that breaks beyond the bounds of the self.

Dialogues: Talking About Music at St Aldates Church

St Aldates, the church I have attended since 2002 and the location of my fieldwork, is a large Anglican church in the centre of Oxford, UK. The church operates within the charismatic evangelical tradition and would often identify more closely with other churches within this stream than it would with the Anglican Church as a whole.[11] The church building seats between 500 and 600 people and, whilst its origins date back to Saxon times, it has been remodelled and extended over the years. Its most recent reordering occurred around the turn of the millennium, with the seating orientation being turned sidewards in order to provide a state-of-the-art auditorium style environment rather than the more traditional east-facing interior that had previously been in existence. There are three regular Sunday services, at 10:30am, 6pm and 8:15pm, each following a similar pattern centred around an initial 'worship set' lasting between twenty and thirty minutes and a sermon lasting five to ten minutes longer. The church has a large team of musicians[12] and periods of sung worship are led either by one of the paid staff or another leader with band backing. The style of music fits well within the genre of contemporary worship music, which tends to adhere closely to the style of soft rock. During the set the congregation attempt to engage in worship through singing and are encouraged to enter into an experience in which they approach God through the musical medium of worship.

Whilst the church has a particular reputation for hosting a large student community, there is nevertheless a range of people at the church who are there for a variety of different reasons and who bring with them a variety of different musical lives and backgrounds. Music forms a large part of the service not only in terms

---

[10]   Hennion, 'Pragmatics of Taste', p. 132.

[11]   See James H.S. Steven, *Worship in the Spirit: Charismatic Worship in the Church of England* (Paternoster Press, 2002).

[12]   Between 30 and 40 play regularly on Sundays with many others contributing to the music at other events and groups which take place during the week.

of time but in terms of significance. In serving as a medium for encounter with God it forms what can be an intensely emotional space in which many different experiences, struggles and deep aspects of spirituality are brought together and interact. The presence of a fairly defined style of music within this significant and diversely inhabited space makes the relationship of the music with the rest of the worshippers' musical lives, identities and tastes highly significant and interesting.

Timothy Rommen suggests that personal relationships with musical style can perform significant ethical functions within the life of the church. He coins the term 'ethics of style' as a framework within which to examine the relationship between individual and community, discourses of value and meaning, and the significance of identification or dis-identification with style as a place of ethical significance. He highlights how an identification or dis-identification with the musical style of a church can change a worshipper's relationship to the church community in a theologically significant manner.[13] The relationship a worshipper forms with the musical worship of the church carries a much broader spiritual and communal, and therefore ethical, weight. In a similar manner, Nanette Nielsen and Marcel Cobussen highlight the space between the personal and the collective as one of the key places in which music takes on ethical significance,[14] as the process and interaction at the heart of music-making allow music to be 'an art form that can be world-disclosive, formative of subjectivity, and contributive to intersubjective relations'.[15] The fieldwork interviews that I conducted investigate some of these areas within the life of St Aldates church, examining some of the ways in which worshippers negotiate musical style within their own lives and the life of the community. Many, but not all, of my interviewees are musicians, and, reflecting the congregational makeup, many of them are in their 20s or 30s. I selected the majority of interviewees because I was aware they had musical tastes that are both significant to them and that diverge from the kind of music used on a Sunday. These tend to be the people where issues of musical style and significance are most intense and also those who are best able to articulate their feelings about such things. My hope is that a framework built up from these might be applicable to larger portions of the worshipping community, but I don't want to assume that an easy generalization is possible or to suggest that my sample provides an unbiased representation of the congregation.

I have organized the experiences of worshippers into three broad categories of experience according to the different relationships formed between areas of their musical lives.[16] The first common thread running through the interviews

---

[13] Timothy Rommen, *'Mek Some Noise': Gospel Music and the Ethics of Style in Trinidad* (University of California Press, 2007).

[14] Marcel Cobussen and Nanette Nielsen, *Music and Ethics* (Ashgate, 2012), p. 90.

[15] Cobussen and Nielsen, *Music and Ethics*, p. 4.

[16] For a similar approach within a sociological study, see Rachel Kraus, 'They Danced in the Bible: Identity Integration Among Christian Women Who Belly Dance', *Sociology of Religion*, 71/4 (2010): pp. 457–82.

demonstrates the ways in which the malleability of different experiences allows commonalities to be formed between different musical worlds. Second, other interviews show the ways in which separate musical worlds can co-exist; third, others highlight situations where the transfer of values between different musical worlds can potentially become problematic or in which there is some need for worshippers to suppress particular aspects of experience in order to positively evaluate an activity. Each of these categories is intentionally broad so as to encompass a range of different experiences; within each of them ethical, spiritual, experiential, social and musical questions arise in a number of ways, swirling together in a way that illumines the significance of musical style for the way in which worshippers negotiate the world around them and the role of musical worship within it.

Bridging Worlds Through Common Modes of Being in Music

At least one of the rationales behind the emergence of contemporary worship music in the 1960s was the need to use musical styles that people related to in daily life.[17] This function, however, can potentially be called into question by the diversity of church membership, opening up a much wider range of experiences and understandings of the relationship. Despite potentially very large differences in musical culture some interview participants found and/or formed significant bridges between worship music and other parts of their musical lives, allowing the possibility for significant inter-contextual meaning to arise through the interplay of significance between settings. For some this links closely to questions of self-conception and personal identity, but whilst this is foregrounded in some experiences it is more frequently a question of wider relationships and ways of being in the world that, whilst involving the self, do not necessarily place it as the central issue at stake.

An example of the bridging of musical worlds can be seen in my interview with Graham, who is a member of the congregation and who plays French horn in the worship band. He is also a member, and was chair, of the Oxford Symphony Orchestra. When asked about the nature of his enjoyment when initially encountering worship music, Graham responded:

> I enjoy playing and, I guess, performing as a horn player, and know I can make a fairly reasonable noise. But that's never been the primary purpose for me in terms of worship, or in terms of orchestral playing. You want to play your own stuff well, but you're contributing to part of an overall impact …The same is true orchestrally as was true in a worship context: that you were able to bring different impact through the sound and the quality of what you were able to

---

[17]   Ingalls, 'Awesome in This Place', p. 57; Nekola, 'Between This World and the Next', p. 170.

bring in. And that was then both making for a fuller, richer music, and then hopefully helping people to be able to worship.[18]

For Graham, orchestral playing and participation in worship become common musical worlds through the idea of coming together to 'create an impact'. Later in the interview, Graham forms further connections between worlds through the similar ways in which he evaluates the different musical experiences. He highlights the importance of an orchestra being in tune with each other both literally and metaphorically in order to come together as a cohesive force and create a positive experience. Within the world of the Sunday service he highlights the need for the musical worship to be in tune with the congregation and with God. Graham expresses the two worlds in some of the same terms, with the quality of relationships found within an orchestra also being part of the key to a good quality of worship on a Sunday. He conceives of worship music according to some of the criteria found within an orchestral setting, whilst thinking about orchestral music in terms of criteria that are not necessarily distinctive purely to itself but can carry across between differing musical worlds. Graham does not employ conceptual categories that frequently serve to distinguish these two musical realms but instead is able to evaluate both musical experiences using a common set of terms. Graham's ability to connect with the music of the church community is not reliant upon its connection with personal stylistic preferences, but neither is his other musical experience laid aside when entering the church building, his conception of musical good allows him to form positive relationships in a largely unproblematic manner.

Charlotte, another member of the congregation, does not self-identify as a musician; nevertheless, she participates in amateur music-making outside the church. Charlotte's chief context for engaging with music is musical theatre. For her there seem to be two key elements that bridge the two worlds: the idea of having a 'good sing', and the public expression of emotion that is enabled by the stage:

Although it's not a style of music that I really listen to in any other bit of my life, I do still enjoy the music at Aldates. And I think one of the things for music that I'm participating in – be that in church, or singing in G&S [Gilbert and Sullivan] or something, it is nice for there to be something that lets you have *a good sing*. Particularly, I always think it's quite interesting about worship music that on stage you have lots of people pouring out their emotions and sort of singing love songs or 'O woe is me' type songs [features typical of much musical theatre]. And because that's happening in a stagey context it's inevitably going to be slightly artificial, and it seems to me that worship music is one of the few points I can think of where people in the course of their everyday life will use music as a way of expressing their own emotions and their own feelings.[19]

---

[18] Interview with the author, 11 February 2012.
[19] Interview with the author, 25 February 2012.

For Charlotte there is a common set of values that bridges the two worlds and helps her to move between them. There is more than this, however, because Charlotte isn't simply finding qualities within the music which allow her to say 'this is what I appreciate about it': rather, she frames her experience of the music according to these categories and thus, to a certain degree, reconceives the Sunday worship in terms of qualities experienced primarily within musical theatre, transforming it into something different as she experiences it in those terms.

Some of the elements that come to the foreground of her experience are already present within the public discourse of the church – emotion, singing and the enabling role of the worship team are all regular topics of discourse. Their emphasis in Charlotte's experience, however, is very different. The stage element is one that is not generally emphasized in the church for fear that the worship might be thought of in terms of a performance;[20] the visibility of musicians on the stage will certainly be discussed, but it is generally not thought of as a separate kind of space in the way that it seems to be for Charlotte. The visibility of musicians is thought of as enabling congregational worship as they lead and set an example. In contrast, Charlotte's experience draws attention to the artificial nature of the stage context as she highlights the way in which it enables a different mode of experience from everyday life. This theatrical conception of the stage moves away from ideas of authenticity inherent within rock and worship music.[21] Likewise the element of emotional singing is one that is important within the life of the charismatic church, however it would generally be an element that is thought of on a secondary level as something that has to take place in response to the work of God rather than something that can be a primary transformative element within a service.[22] Worship would not generally be thought of either in terms of joining in with a 'good hearty sing' – the importance of singing passionately from the heart is certainly a key element of discourse, but to emphasize hearty singing in such a way that its secondary role to the activity of worship is not made clear is something which strikes against the regular patterns of discourse.[23]

For worshippers who routinely find spiritual meaning in other areas of musical activity the interrelation between musical worlds is one that can be rooted in much broader views of God's work and presence in the world and which will therefore carry with it immediate theological weight. St Aldates member and artist Tim's experience of music is illustrative of the way in which this can occur, rooting itself in a way of being in the world which connects to his artistic sensibility and informs

---

[20]   Ingalls, 'Awesome in This Place'.

[21]   Elizabeth L. Wollman, 'Much Too Loud and Not Loud Enough: Issues Involving the Reception of Staged Rock Musicals', in C. Washburne and M. Derno (eds), *Bad Music: The Music We Love to Hate* (Routledge, 2004); Jay R. Howard and John M. Streck, *Apostles of Rock: The Splintered World of Contemporary Christian Music* (University Press of Kentucky, 1999), p. 173.

[22]   Ingalls, 'Awesome in This Place', p. 90.

[23]   Adnams, 'The Experience of Congregational Singing'.

his conception of worship on a Sunday so as to place it in close relation to his on-going experience of God in the world:

> Intimacy I think is key, really ... I listen to all music for that purpose of bringing me back to something – ultimately God – because listening to music bring[s] me back to myself and what I know and what I'm about ... it's soul stuff. I love listening to music which connects to my soul, but that's what music does, isn't it?[24]

For Tim, the spirituality of worship music ceases to be its defining characteristic over and against other forms of music, the different musics instead becoming part of a continuum of spiritual experience. He may have particular expectations of spiritual experience within Christian worship services, however they are not completely unique expectations. This connection means that worship music is not the sole provider of spiritual meaning in music but must instead share this role with the other musics and art-forms of daily life.

Anna Nekola draws attention to the tension between the authority of the church to define what constitutes worship and the autonomy of the individual to do so that has been present in much of the history of protestant worship[25] whilst Timothy Rice highlights the way in which musical meaning is often impossible to control due to the diverse range of ways in which music can take on a variety of meanings.[26] The life of a large congregation in which regular members are often able to inhabit a space at arm's-length from authority can allow these tensions to exist without becoming particularly problematic, indeed, they can lead to productive and positive ways of inhabiting the space of worship. However, in becoming a feature of community structures, they nevertheless impact the nature of relationships between individuals, community and leadership, the manner in which they build a shared congregational life together and the nature of their identification with each other. They thus carry a great deal of ethical significance within the dynamics of the church community.

Communal and Private, Spiritual and Secular

One rationale for the use of popular music in church is the desire to break down the distinction between the sacred and the secular that an elevated or distinctive church style can serve to reinforce.[27] In contrast to the previous section, this section shows how certain dynamics at work in the lives of congregation members can nevertheless allow this musical world to be a distinct realm within their musical lives.

---

[24] Interview with the author, 9 March 2012.

[25] Nekola, 'Between This World and the Next', p. 225.

[26] Timothy Rice, 'Reflections on Music and Meaning: Metaphor, Signification and Control in the Bulgarian Case', *British Journal of Ethnomusicology*, 10/1 (2001): p. 34.

[27] Ingalls, 'Awesome in This Place'.

Tom, an English graduate and former intern at the church, tends to listen to music that he describes as 'indie', 'literate', 'witty', 'alternative', 'melancholy' and fairly introspective. He specifically contrasts this with the atmosphere at a stadium gig; giant musical collectives are something he would generally avoid. However, expressive charismatic worship in a Sunday service seems to be unproblematic for him. When I commented on the similarities between the Sunday setting and some of the qualities he avoids in the larger stadium atmosphere, Tom responded:

> I'm quite an introvert, and I tend to process things quite inwardly. [But] I love the joy of being able to come together in a stadium setting – [correcting himself] well, I say in a stadium, in a *church* setting – and declare [shared purposes] with others, knowing that this is something I've thought through deeply in my own time [...] I think the music I listen to personally helps me process and helps me work out what I'm actually thinking, or shapes my thoughts. And then the music I respond to in church, I appreciate that, because it's got a congregational dynamic. It is a response; it is designed to be with a range of different people all coming together to affirm one common faith.[28]

For Tom, there are two counterbalancing poles to this musical life. On one pole is the introspective way in which he processes things and deals with life, not just musically but intellectually and emotionally. On the other pole is the confident expression of faith within community. For Tom, neither the reflective music he listens to in private nor the expressive worship music in church is completely adequate on its own; instead, he finds that they each fulfil a role in relation to the other, together completing the pattern which helps him to navigate life as a believer.

Nemi, a singer on the worship team, outlines a similar divergence between the public and private aspects of her musical life. For Nemi, music is something that takes on a large degree of emotional significance in relation to different people, events and situations. Her own tastes in music take her a little away from the church style to music that is often more 'messy' and 'unpredictable'; however, the church music is still able to become important to her due to its potential emotional significance and attachments. For Nemi, the music doesn't migrate out of this worship setting, either in terms of listening or of significance; in fact, she even goes so far as to say that listening to some of this music elsewhere would be weird.

> Maybe it's not my style of music, and other than the church and what God is doing in Aldates it doesn't have any other significance to me personally. With [traditional] hymns on the other hand, I've been singing hymns with my family since I was younger, so it, I can travel, I can remember things but with the church and Aldates it's just Aldates.[29]

---

28   Interview with the author, 15 February 2012.
29   Interview with the author, 12 March 2012.

This musical boundary carries a parallel in the personal realm; Nemi forms and enjoys significant friendships, even with members of the congregation, outside of the services rather than finding a place for them in the church. For both Nemi and Tom, the divergence in musical style is something laden with deeper significance for the way in which they negotiate the world and conceive of the church community. The corporate spiritual life of the church is something distinct from the experiences of daily life in specific and meaningful ways. Whilst their experiences within the church services may conform quite closely to church expectations, musical features and style carry with them additional significance in relationship to other parts of their lives. This relationship is something of particular ethical and spiritual significance in a context where the living out of faith is a primary concern[30] – there is a deep connection between questions of musical style and significance and personal, social and theological relationships and attitudes.

At the Edges: Value Transfer, Judgements, Discontent

The third category that I trace through the interviews encompasses a broad range of experiences in which musical value judgements formed outside of church either become problematic for worshippers or need to be consciously suppressed in order to maintain a positive experience of Sunday worship. Liz, a dancer and clubber with particular interests in heavier rock, has a broadly positive experience of the worship music of the church but, nevertheless, in certain contexts is able to express negative value judgements of the music:

> [My] first year at university I gave up non-Christian music for Lent [...] it nearly killed me [...] because I love music and I had almost no music. And actually I don't like worship CDs [...] it's often a bit ... wet round the edges. There's not much punch or bite to it ... To me it feels quite generic and quite samey and often quite predictable, and it's not the sort of ... There are bands who are like that in the secular world, and I don't listen to them ... because I don't like that, because it just feels boring.[31]

The experience of Stephen, a rapper and medic, illustrates the kind of inner struggle that can occur when the balance shifts so that the negative experience of the music is foregrounded to a much greater degree whilst the worshipper is still seeking to engage with the other purposes that the music is aiming to facilitate.

> I don't enjoy it [worship music] at all; I find it very cheesy. The jazz part of me finds the chords incredibly boring and the melodies incredibly boring. The hip hop part of me finds the lyrics dreadful and generally empty [...] I feel that God has helped me to get past a lot of my own silly judgments in these ways and

---

30   Ingalls, 'Awesome in This Place'.
31   Interview with the author, 3 February 2012.

actually to say, well, these [worship songs] are still truth, and this is still ... and you know, singing truth is a wonderful thing. I love the church and I love joining in with my brothers and sisters to praise God, and so I've kind of found joy in that, but in the music itself, it's a battle.[32]

These two quotations illustrate a much wider range of feelings and judgements that worshippers bring to the worship music within the church. On occasion this can lead to a deep struggle with the musical aspect of congregational activity, but often it sits on a much more ambiguous level where value-judgements only occasionally raise their heads because worshippers put then to the back of their mind in favour of other purposes. The judgements will sometimes be framed as purely musical in nature but often they connect to broader modes of being in the world. Stephen later discussed how the judgements about lyrics that come from his hip hop background connect with attitudes towards the way in which good theology should be expressed alongside music that does justice to the darker sides of human existence. Liz went on to highlight how even positive value judgements are something that can be problematic, as they can lead to a distraction from what she sees as the principal purpose of worship.

One further quotation from Ben, a musician who feels stylistically constrained by the imposition of a uniform pop-rock style, serves to highlight the close connection between musical value judgements and deeper questions of spirituality:

When I play music properly in any setting, it's about the connection between your soul and the other band and whoever's there, and just expressing yourself truly honestly [...] I totally let go when I'm playing, and that could be in a church setting or a contemporary music pub scene. The difference is that I actually felt for a long time that the church was a better connection, [that it] was a more true and honest connection to worship, whereas now I'm finding at the moment it isn't necessarily, but that's more of the style and the system.[33]

The close relationship which Ben feels between musical experience and the soul leads him to feel the imposition of stylistic constraint that emerges from a system of authority within the church (alluded to towards the end of quotation) as a constraint of the soul, with music-making in a pub setting becoming a more authentic location of worship than the church itself.

Discussion/Analysis

As these last few interviews have demonstrated, within the framework of the church, church members sometimes suspend (although often only partially) their

---

Interview with the author, 10 April 2012.
[33] Interview with the author, 6 March 2012.

musical value judgements because they understand music to serve other purposes within the worshipping life of the church. The question of what to do with value judgements in a context in which they're not a regular part of public discourse is something that can create tension for those who find them to be part of their experience and is the area in which ethical dilemmas are most-readily present both for worshippers and for the leaders shaping the church's musical life and values. Worship team leaders emphasized in interview how they would encourage worshippers to set aside problems encountered in relation to musical style in favour of a direct engagement with God that can happen regardless of musical context. Beliefs about the nature of music shift discourse away from musical valuations and instead frame music simply as a tool for worship. If worshippers regularly experience tension between the music they value and the music the church sings, they may learn to regularly suppress key aspects of their experience (or they may eventually move to a different church as a way of escaping these tensions). This habituation is likely to have consequences for the way in which these worshippers learn to relate church and world, spiritual and material. Some of these consequences may be positive, fostering self-discipline, selflessness in community, a move away from consumerist attitudes to music and the development of attitudes that allow them to relate to the divine in a broad range of situations. Other consequences are likely to be negative, where they are forced to hold back key elements of their experience and activity from dialogue with the church community; they are restrained from valuing important aspects of experience and Sunday worship is prevented from being a place of fully open and honest coming before God as community.

A parallel in public life serves to highlight the importance and potential of opening up space for dialogue. Rowan Williams in his reflections on secularist attitudes to the role of religion in the public square uses language that connects this manner of neutralizing aesthetic judgements and negotiation of religious difference. Williams suggests that 'by defining ideological and religious difference as if they were simply issues about individual preference, almost of private "style", [secularist] discourse effectively denies the seriousness of difference itself'.[34] He maintains that such a situation is undesirable in society and that instead, in order to create a healthy liberal democracy, there is the need for public negotiation of difference in an environment where different voices can be heard and taken seriously without the assumption that in doing so the product would be inevitable animosity, conflict or disloyalty to the larger community. Indeed, he argues that the situation operates almost the opposite way around and that in providing a space for these differences to be taken seriously there is the potential for a more powerful level of social identification to take place. The history of the worship wars has served to embed similar anxieties within the consciousness of those involved in the contemporary worship music scene, a memory of community divisions rooted in musical loyalties being close at hand whenever issues of musical difference

---

[34]   Rowan Williams, *Faith in the Public Square* (Bloomsbury Continuum, 2012), p. 25.

are raised. The constraint of meaningful discussion surrounding music, however, can serve to impoverish aspects of the life of the worshipping community just as it can serve to weaken societal bonds. The problems the church is quick to see in the privatization of religious meaning can serve as a spur to self-examination and reflection around the areas of its common life where it might be complicit in similar problems.

Lutheran scholar and musician Lorraine Smith Brugh proposes a framework that she entitles 'responsive contextualization' as a basis for examining and shaping the liturgy of worship. As worshippers bring their own horizons of experience to the truths of worship 'Every dramatic action, every piece of music, every preached word is received in a local context, where it completes its meaning. [...] the truth of art must intersect with the particularity of each new context in order to have meaning.'[35] She emphasizes the importance of identifying and bringing into conscious awareness meaning as it is expressed in the community due to the way in which worship expresses the values of a community and those things that it finds meaningful and valuable in all of life. In examining the range of experiences present at St Aldates we have seen how such processes of meaning-making are already at work within the church community in a range of ways both productive and problematic. Brugh observes that existing liturgical meaning often goes unnoticed or unrecognized in the community, and she argues that churches need a process that 'reflects to the community who it believes itself to be under God and with God'.[36] This seems to be particularly true in the case of contemporary worship music where key elements of discourse serve not just to deflect attention away from such meaning but to deny its relevance or very presence. In some situations such a process of examination may well lead to a reconfiguration of worship practices; in others it may instead lead to an enrichment of existing practices as church members develop a clearer understanding of the rich variety of meanings and experiences which they currently encounter in a largely one-sided fashion. In acknowledging and engaging with a broad range of experience, meaning and significance relating to music, participatory energy can be unleashed and a road to deeper individual and communal flourishing opened up; and in opening up space for mutual dialogue about music-making, churches can reduce the potential for reinforcing and cementing fixed positions and resulting experiences of alienation.[37]

---

[35] Lorraine Smith Brugh, 'Responsive Contextualization: A Liturgical Theology for Multicultural Congregational Worship' (PhD diss., Northwestern University, June 1998), p. 39.

[36] Smith Brugh, 'Responsive Contextualization', p. 161.

[37] Williams, Faith in the Public Square, p. 102.

References

Adnams, Gordon, 'The Experience of Congregational Singing: An Ethno-Phenomenological Approach' (PhD diss., University of Alberta, 2008).

Ammerman, Nancy Tatom, *Studying Congregations: A New Handbook* (Nashville: Abingdon Press, 1998).

Berger, Harris M., *Metal, Rock, and Jazz: Perception and the Phenomenology of Musical Experience* (Hanover, NH: University Press of New England [for] Wesleyan University Press, 1999).

Berger, Harris M., *Stance: Ideas About Emotion, Style, and Meaning for the Study of Expressive Culture* (Middletown, Conn.: Wesleyan University Press, 2009).

Cobussen, Marcel and Nielsen, Nanette, *Music and Ethics* (Farnham: Ashgate, 2012).

DeNora, Tia, *Music in Everyday Life* (Cambridge: Cambridge University Press, 2000).

DeNora, Tia, *After Adorno: Rethinking Music Sociology* (Cambridge: Cambridge University Press, 2003).

Guest, Mathew, '"Friendship, Fellowship and Acceptance": The Public Discourse of a Thriving Evangelical Congregation', in Mathew Guest, Karin Tusting and Linda Woodhead (eds), *Congregational Studies in the UK: Christianity in a Post-Christian Context* (Aldershot: Ashgate, 2004).

Hennion, Antoine, 'Music Lovers: Taste as Performance', *Theory, Culture & Society* 18/5 (2001): 1–22.

Hennion, Antoine, 'Pragmatics of Taste', in Mark Jacobs and Nancy Hanrahan (ed.), *The Blackwell Companion to the Sociology of Culture* (Oxford: Wiley-Blackwell, 2005).

Howard, Jay R., and Streck, John M. *Apostles of Rock: The Splintered World of Contemporary Christian Music* (Lexington: University Press of Kentucky, 1999).

Ingalls, Monique M., 'Awesome in This Place: Sound, Space, and Identity in Contemporary North American Evangelical Worship' (PhD. diss., University of Pennsylvania, 2008).

Kraus, Rachel, 'They Danced in the Bible: Identity Integration Among Christian Women Who Belly Dance', *Sociology of Religion* 71/4 (2010): 457–82.

Marti, Gerardo, *Worship Across the Racial Divide: Religious Music and the Multiracial Congregation* (Oxford: Oxford University Press, 2012).

Nekola, Anna E., 'Between This World and the Next: The Musical "Worship Wars" and Evangelical Ideology in the United States 1960–2005' (PhD diss., University of Wisconsin-Madison, 2009).

Rice, Timothy, 'Reflections on Music and Meaning: Metaphor, Signification and Control in the Bulgarian Case', *British Journal of Ethnomusicology*, 10/1 (2001): 19–38.

Rice, Timothy, 'Time, Place, and Metaphor in Musical Experience and Ethnography', *Ethnomusicology*, 47/2 (2003): 151–79.

Rommen, Timothy, *'Mek Some Noise': Gospel Music and the Ethics of Style in Trinidad* (Berkeley: University of California Press, 2007).

Smith Brugh, Lorraine, 'Responsive Contextualization: A Liturgical Theology for Multicultural Congregational Worship' (PhD Diss., Northwestern University, June 1998).

Steven, James H.S., *Worship in the Spirit: Charismatic Worship in the Church of England* (Milton Keynes: Paternoster Press, 2002).

Stringer, Martin D., *On the Perception of Worship: The Ethnography of Worship in Four Christian Congregations in Manchester* (Birmingham: University of Birmingham Press, 1999).

Williams, Rowan, *Faith in the Public Square* (London: Bloomsbury Continuum, 2012).

Wollman, Elizabeth L., 'Much Too Loud and Not Loud Enough: Issues Involving the Reception of Staged Rock Musicals', in C. Washburne and M. Derno (eds), *Bad Music: The Music We Love to Hate* (New York: Routledge, 2004).

Afterword
Theology and Music in Conversation

Martyn Percy

How does faith *feel*? The question, I think, is surprising in its simplicity, and rich in complexity. For some, the answer will be deeply personal. The feeling of faith is known through a personal encounter: 'Blessed assurance, Jesus is mine', as the old gospel hymn puts it. For others, it is the sense of smell – incense, polish, flowers, and so forth – the redolence of tradition and renewal, in which the olfactory imagination combines with liturgical rhythm. For others still, what is felt is set aside from what can be known – through taste or touch, or through apparently rational confessional statements.

The theology that ultimately shapes and informs faith is both implicit and explicit. The explicit is, perhaps, obvious: the creeds, the articles and the tradition. But as this volume has shown, we can gain considerably richer understandings of faith traditions when we attend to the implicit – the apparently 'background' material of music, for example – that not only supports the tradition, but also actually contributes to its shape and eventual reception. 'Amazing Grace', sung to an old hymn tune, is deeply reassuring. Sung to the tune of 'The House of the Rising Sun', it gains a new place and relevance in a believer's composition of faith. For music moves us; it is not merely an accompaniment to faith, but rather, an actual expression of it.

This volume, of course, has intentionally sought out conversations about faith, feeling, reception and performance. The field of theology and religious studies has been thoroughly exposed to conversations with social sciences such as anthropology and sociology; and more recently, with psychology and cosmology. But conversations about faith and theology with musicology[1] are still relatively new, and to some extent nascent. There are perhaps good reasons for this, since few scholars want to trespass on the soul and sentience of believers. How does faith feel, exactly? It is not, perhaps, for the academic assessor to venture into such territory. Yet this volume has sought to take some tentative steps in this direction, and address the implicit aspects of faith that rarely receive critical attention.

A focus on implicit theology seeks to pay attention to the normally neglected and often over-looked dimensions of ecclesial life that are constitutive for belief

---

[1]   By 'musicology', I refer to the interdisciplinary study of music, whether from the perspective of historical musicology, ethnomusicology or music analysis, rather than to any of these sub-disciplines in particular.

and practice. The realization of a relationship between the gentle framing of faith and belief through structures and practices allows us ponder the significance of many things we might take for granted, and their theological weight. The type of music a congregation chooses, how it moves (or doesn't!) to that music, dress codes, manners, the moderation of the collective emotional temperature – all have a bearing on the emerging vision of God within each congregation and denomination. It is not that one causes the other. The emerging task for implicit theology is not to distinguish between God and the world, but rather to realize that in the apparently innocuous and innocent beliefs and practices, there are in fact 'texts' that demand interpretation. This is because the shape of the church is partly brought about by the subliminal as much as by the liminal; and by the implicit as much as by the explicit.

These trajectories have been traced perhaps more clearly through the gospel music of Black churches. Three recent books – Robert Darden's *People Get Ready!: A New History of Black Gospel Music*, Henry Mitchell's *Black Church Beginnings: The Long-Hidden Realities of the First Years*, and Mark Sturge's *Look What the Lord Has Done!: An Exploration of Black Christian Faith in Britain*[2] – are instructive in this respect. Strictly speaking, of course, all theology is ultimately rooted in people's stories and experiences. The transformation of people's lives, through their encounters with Christ, marks the first stage of gestation in a long process that leads from narratives and ritual through to reflection, and eventually to a formed ecclesial community. For theologians and ecclesiologists, the recognition of this trajectory has increasingly meant paying more attention to the origins and formative context of Christian communities.

Liberation theology, for example – although easily accessible through a plethora of weighty tomes – cannot really be understood without reference to the original conditions of oppression that gave birth to the movement. (And perhaps to similar, contemporary first-hand accounts of oppression.) Likewise, no-one can pretend to understand feminist theology without reference to the original stories of marginalization and renewal that first nourished it into being.

Of course, all theology is contextual. The favoured faux-Platonic reasoning that has dominated so much of Western theology is as much a product of its context and authors (white, male, Euro-centric, etc.) as that which is produced by any other group. It is perhaps against this background that Black theology has not only begun to discover the power of is own voice, but also come increasingly to the fore in universities and theological colleges. And of course the flowering of Black theology – led by scholars such as James Cone in the US – challenges many

---

    [2]   Henry Mitchell, *Black Church Beginnings: The Long-Hidden Realities of the First Years* (William B. Eerdmans Publishing Co., 2004); Robert Darden, *People Get Ready!: A New History of Black Gospel Music* (Continuum International Publishing Group Ltd., 2005); Mark Sturge, *Look What the Lord Has Done!: An Exploration of Black Christian Faith in Britain* (Scripture Union Publishing, 2005).

preconceptions about and calls attention to the material shaping of theological and ecclesiological endeavour.

Robert Darden, a Professor of English at Baylor University, has produced a remarkable study of Black gospel music. Like jazz (arguably one of the few distinctive art forms to emerge from modern America), Black gospel music is a synergy of musical genres – Negro spirituals, minstrel music, blues and so forth – that preach and teach harmony (and ultimate unity) through both text and tempo. Bringing together joy and sorrow, despair and hope, Black gospel music liberates through its willingness to express the experience of oppression as much as it also points towards a more utopian future. Darden's study, although primarily historical, is exemplary for attempting to capture something of how theology and ecclesiology is communicated through the cadence and rhythm of the music, not simply the creedal formulae that might be expressed in the song.

Mitchell's *Black Church Beginnings*, rather like Darden's study, is essentially an intimate history that discloses the struggles of African Americans as they sought to establish a distinctive spiritual community within the harsh realities of the slave colonies. Mitchell, a former professor at the Interdenominational Center in Atlanta, Georgia, traces the growth of independent Black churches from the mid-1700s to the end of the nineteenth century. This, as Mitchell shows, is a history of struggle, that meanders its way through issues of class, denominationalism, theological formation, ecclesial schism, together with significant cultural clashes brought about through the emergence of major cities and urban conurbations in the nineteenth century. The particular strength of Mitchell's work is the close attention paid to nineteenth-century developments (therefore beginning and ending his account before the Azusa Street revival), including fine chapters on social activism, the emergence of denominational structure, and the development of theological schools.

With the exception of the work of Robert Beckford[3] and perhaps one or two others, Black theology and its perspectives on ecclesiology have been much slower to materialize in Britain. But thankfully this is now beginning to change, and Mark Sturge's book provides a welcome home-grown perspective, exploring the explosive growth of Black Christian churches in Britain. Sturge, a former General Director of the African and Caribbean Evangelical Alliance (ACEA), provides a sympathetic account of the origin and development of African and Caribbean churches, and also takes the opportunity to address the problems and opportunities that currently face congregations. His use of biblical reflection, coupled to a sharp analysis of theologies and doctrines in Black majority churches, combine to make this an engaging and perceptive monograph. Although it is the most confessional and empathetic of the three volumes, readers will nonetheless gain considerable insight from the account that Sturge offers.

For all studying the burgeoning economy of denominations – whether in the US, or in Britain – these three books offer insights on the emerging history of

---

[3]   Robert Beckford, *Jesus Dub: Faith, Culture and Social Change* (Routledge, 2006).

Black churches. In so doing, they raise intriguing questions about the delicate relationship (in ecclesiology) between music and faith; as well as between the local, cultural or ethnic organization, and meta-constructions of catholicity. If a tension remains between these apparent antinomies (which is almost certainly the case), then it is surely for the older historic denominations to reconsider their ingrained cultural aloofness, and the extent to which one kind of theology, church polity or Christian praxis has been steadily privileged over another. It is precisely this dynamic that the presence of Black theology and churches engages with, and increasingly challenges. In many ways, the mature fruit of deep discourse and mutual exchange is still awaited. We can only reap what we sow.

Ultimately, no church or theology is ever culture free. The task for the churches, therefore, is to try to comprehend the catholic in the contextual, and to be open to and learn from the multifarious expressions of the church that will vary from time to time and place to place. Darden, Mitchell and Sturge offer us three intriguing portraits of Black churches, theology and spirituality. In so doing, they challenge all complacencies, beckoning dialogue and hospitality.

So what, finally, of the shaping of faith communities, churches and congregations in relation to music? This volume has been a serious attempt at relating musicology to a variety of Christian faith traditions, and offers some serious insights into the kinds of academic conversations we, as authors, believe need to take place within the realms of theology and ecclesiology. Much more could be said, of course. Naturally, there is no doubt that faith communities, churches and congregations do look to formal theological propositions, creeds, articles of faith and the like to order their inner life, establish their identity and maintain their distinctiveness in the world. Yet it is also true that music, moods and manners, informal beliefs and learned (and therefore valued) behaviour, apparently innocuous and innocent practices and patterns of polity, performance, dance and dramaturgy, together with aesthetics and applied theological thinking, are no less constitutive for the shaping of the church. Attention to the role and vitality of the implicit is therefore vital if one wishes to comprehend the depth, density, identity and shaping of faith communities.

That said, it does not follow that all differences are rooted in proclivity or context. All that can be said here is that such factors, whilst significant, and worthy of theological evaluation, are not necessarily determinative. Although variable ecclesial accents (e.g., Baptist, Anglican, Methodist, etc.) sometimes accentuate differences, ecclesial communities cannot evade their intrinsic and extrinsic unity. Equally, they cannot escape developing and diversifying into something of the vision that Paul may have glimpsed for the early Christian church. Twice in his letter to the Colossians, he uses the word 'knit' – first of 'hearts knit together', and then of 'the whole body knit together' (Col 2: 2 and 19). 'Knitting' is a compelling and suggestive concept. It mirrors the density and complexity of the cultures and contexts that ecclesial communities find themselves immersed in; and it invites us to pay just as much attention to the implicit as the explicit. And it also suggests that somehow, different strands of theology, music, practice – the variety of notes, sounds, threads, materials and colours that make up the whole of the church – can be woven together to make something richer and stronger. This is a mystical vision, of course: one where faith and life interweave as the church worships and works together, continually believing and practising to become the body of Christ in the world.

In summary, there may be something to be said for faith communities, churches and congregations attending to conversation as a 'mode' of existence. By not only performing music – but also tuning in to what musicology can teach churches – the Christian witness may become more self-aware, helpfully self-critical, and ideally more outwardly-orientated. Here, we are simply very close to emphasizing those great Benedictine virtues of hospitality, service and listening. Each of these is vital to the flourishing of the community of learning and the individual in formation. Being open to God, paying attention to others and deep listening – these are the profound spiritual exercises that allow individuals and communities to attend to the cadence, timbre and rhythm of what they are about.

So how can musicology ultimately help us to better understand the dynamics that take place within faith communities, churches and congregations? Mere 'musical description', will never be able to do justice to the depth and richness of the multifarious processes that take place in churches and congregations. The language we need – to capture in the identity and journey of faith communities – often comes to fruition by being framed in paradox; of the heart and the soul, for example. And this is where the analogical imagination can be helpful. Thus, one aspect of what takes place in the formation of faith communities is that participants often learn to find themselves in what one writer describes as 'God's orchestra'. John Pritchard puts it like this:

> Christian leaders are like conductors of God's local orchestra. Our task is multi-layered. We have to interpret the music of the gospel to bring out all its richness and textures and glorious melodies. We have ourselves to be students of the music, always learning, and sharing, with the orchestra what both we and they have learned about this beautiful music. We have to help members of the orchestra to hear each other, and to be aware of each other as they play their 'instrument' or use their gift. Without that sensitivity to each other both an orchestra and a church descend into a cacophony of conflicting noises .... [4]

To continue with this analogy, and to apply it more directly to faith communities, three key observations seem to be particularly pertinent. First, whatever part one plays in the orchestra, institutions and individuals try to pay attention to the bass-line, and to not get overly distracted by the counter-melodies The bass line is all about patience, depth and pace. It may also contain the givens of theological discourse. It is about developing sustainable rhythms for the entire symphony –

---

[4] John Prichard, *The Life and Work of a Priest* (SPCK Publishing, 2007), pp. 109ff.

not just the short movements in which one part of the orchestra might mainly feature.

Second, teachers, pastors and priests often have the task of coaching and conducting. There may be some new scores to teach as well; and the performance of these helps to form the necessary skills in theological and pastoral discernment for faith communities. In turn, this enables individuals and churches to develop intuitions in relation to knowledge; to become reflexive, yet also sure-footed. Thus, congregations carry the responsibility for developing the natural and given talents, rather than simply replacing them with new instructions. Education is both input and drawing out: conversation to enable spiritual, pastoral and intellectual flourishing.

Third, just as scripture is symphonic in character – many different sounds making a single, complex but beautiful melody – so it is with God's church, and the institutions that ultimately form the ministers for the communities in which they serve. The task of the teacher and mentor is, then, not just to help students or disciples understand and critique the scores they read and perform, but also to try and help each person play beautifully and function faithfully – and all within the context of the diversity of the many different sounds and notes that God gives each church and each person to make.

The study of music, then, can help us decode the rhythms and movements of faith communities. Musicology can aid us in the comprehension of not just what the creed says, but how it sounds. Musicology can show us that the medium may just be as important as the message. Accompaniment is a strangely under-rated spiritual virtue. In travelling alongside and supporting individuals and faith communities – whether as guides, spiritual mentors or pastors – we often easily understand the value of those individuals who walk with us. Yet as this volume has shown, music is truly one of the great accompaniers in religion and spirituality. It lifts plain text; it succours souls; it raises the spirits. To somehow miss or ignore the place of music in religious life is to overlook a whole dimension to how worship works, and how faith is fully formed. Musicology can help us to take note.

References

Beckford, Robert, *Jesus Dub: Faith, Culture and Social Change* (London: Routledge, 2006).

Darden, Robert, *People Get Ready!: A New History of Black Gospel Music* (Continuum International Publishing Group Ltd., 2005).

Mitchell, Henry, *Black Church Beginnings: The Long-Hidden Realities of the First Years* (Grand Rapids: William B. Eerdmans Publishing Co., 2004).

Pritchard, John, *The Life and Work of a Priest* (SPCK Publishing, 2007).

Sturge, Mark, *Look What the Lord Has Done!: An Exploration of Black Christian Faith in Britain* (Scripture Union Publishing, 2005).

Index

185 - conflation of worship & song lore)
137ff - repertoire

141 - dimensions of a single local identity
142 - Benedict Anderson, Imagined Community
150 - new canon

Printed in Great Britain
by Amazon